ELDER CARE IN CRISIS

HEALTH, SOCIETY, AND INEQUALITY SERIES
General Editor: Jennifer A. Reich

Elder Care in Crisis: How the Social Safety Net Fails Families
Emily K. Abel

Elder Care in Crisis

How the Social Safety Net Fails Families

Emily K. Abel

NEW YORK UNIVERSITY PRESS

New York

NEW YORK UNIVERSITY PRESS
New York
www.nyupress.org

© 2022 by New York University
All rights reserved

References to Internet websites (URLs) were accurate at the time of writing. Neither the author nor New York University Press is responsible for URLs that may have expired or changed since the manuscript was prepared.

Please contact the Library of Congress for Cataloging-in-Publication data.
ISBN: 9781479815388 (hardback)
ISBN: 9781479815395 (paperback)
ISBN: 9781479815432 (library ebook)
ISBN: 9781479815418 (consumer ebook)

New York University Press books are printed on acid-free paper, and their binding materials are chosen for strength and durability. We strive to use environmentally responsible suppliers and materials to the greatest extent possible in publishing our books.

Manufactured in the United States of America

10 9 8 7 6 5 4 3 2 1

Also available as an ebook

CAREPORT

A caregiver needs authority all the more
in moments like helping her husband catch
a plane (seemingly on his own). At an airport door
she's transformed into commander-on-watch
rolling him onward like luggage-to-load
(this does cross her mind). Once she's assured
all charge of him is hers (her stance and mode
a lieutenant's), she'll maneuver him aboard,
she'll direct him right through security,
order him straightaway toward the plane!
But guards stop her short: no ticket / i.d.
Surely she'll settle for a view: (him walking alone).
Then she's bent double, innards clubbed. Who knew
she cared so carnally to see him through?

—Mary Felstiner

CONTENTS

Introduction: New Perspectives on Caregiving   1

1. Reformulating Stress and Burden   9

2. Challenging the Medical Model of Dementia   27

3. Looking to the Past: What the Nineteenth Century
   Can Tell Us   49

4. The Elder Care Crisis: The Tyranny of the
   Family-Responsibility Ethic   64

5. "That Was No Respite for Me!": Using Services at Home
   and in the Community   81

6. "They Can't Possibly Love Him as I Do": The Anguish
   of Institutional Placement   101

7. "Oh No, Don't Feel Guilty": Advising Others and
   Fighting Back   117

8. "No One Is Coming out of This Unscathed": The Nursing
   Home Tragedy in the Pandemic   129

9. "This Being Homebound Is So Hard": Confronting
   Hospital Regulations, Sheltering in Place, and
   Interacting with Workers   151

   Conclusion: How the Pandemic Exposed and Exacerbated
   the Crisis in Care   167

   Acknowledgments   177

   Notes   179

   Index   213

   About the Author   223

Introduction

New Perspectives on Caregiving

After the COVID-19 pandemic struck early in 2020 and examples of both care and callousness began to be blazoned across the media, I decided to circle back to a topic I last examined thirty years ago—family care for elderly people.* As the population continues to age, the topic becomes increasingly critical. I quickly discovered that much remains the same. Today, as in 1990, family members deliver the great bulk of long-term care services their elderly relatives receive. Caregiving work also remains unevenly divided between the genders. Men provide more assistance than they previously did, but caregiving responsibilities continue to fall primarily on women. And, although the work often imposes serious physical, emotional, social, and financial problems, the government still leaves family caregivers largely on their own.

But I also found that a number of striking changes have occurred in the past three decades. One is that the subject has gained new visibility. According to PubMed, the government's database for journal articles on medicine and the health sciences, the number of publications on family caregiving for the older population increased from 93 in 1990 to 313 in 2000, 637 in 2010, and 1,478 in 2020. By the end of that year, a total of 16,043 publications had appeared. A high proportion focused on the stresses of caregiving and the health problems that ensued. Public interest also mushroomed. A steady stream of resources, including workshops, books, articles, and audio and video products, were produced

---

* I define family as anyone the care recipient designates as such. Family caregivers are often called "informal caregivers" to distinguish them from paid or formal ones.

for family caregivers. Once a term used only by researchers, "caregiver" increasingly has become a label people apply to themselves, suggesting that they no longer consider their endeavor simply a natural extension of their family role.[1]

Moreover, the broader topic of care captured the attention of scholars in a wide variety of disciplines. When sociologist Margaret K. Nelson and I began to collect essays for our 1990 volume, *Circles of Care: Work and Identity in Women's Lives*, we could look only to Britain and Scandinavian countries for models.[2] Since then, US academic writing about care and caregiving has exploded in such fields as history, philosophy, political science, economics, sociology, anthropology, social work, and nursing. Feminist philosophers, for example, argue that theories of justice must direct more attention to vulnerability and dependency, two conditions that are part of all human life and generate a need for care.[3] Economists propose methods for calculating the value of care and including it in measures of the economic well-being of nations along with goods and services.[4] Policy scholars analyze the impact of neoliberalism on the social provision of care in Europe and the United States.[5] Sociologists explore the gendered division of care and the possibilities for change.[6] Anthropologists examine care as a practice that involves attention to individual needs rather than the application of general rules.[7] Insights from those various disciplines have helped to broaden the gerontology literature.

A growing number of scholars also have investigated the relationship between waged and unwaged caregivers. Sociologist Evelyn Nakano Glenn reminds us that "the often untenable strains to which family caregivers are subject and the parlous situation of paid caregivers are closely intertwined and need to be examined together."[8] Thirty years ago, however, it was difficult to find information about direct care workers (personal care assistants, home health aides, and nursing assistants). Recent studies demonstrate that the interests of family members and paid workers often clash. Low wages and poor benefits keep services affordable for family members who pay out of pocket. But as Ai-Jen Poo, the director of the National Domestic Workers Alliance, notes, good care cannot flourish in substandard working conditions, and only by making common cause can the two groups persuade our society to value care properly.[9] Partly because many workers flee for better jobs in other fields as soon as possible, worries about a growing labor shortage have increased since 1990.[10] More than a quarter of direct care workers are immigrants, many of whom leave family members without care in their home countries.[11] Policies that curtail immigration restrict family members' access to supportive services and reduce the number of available workers even further.[12]

The growing awareness of the global dimensions of US caregiving has been accompanied by a heightened appreciation of the diversity of the caregiver population. Most early studies of caregivers relied on samples with disproportionate numbers of white and middle-class people, and most interventions were directed to that group alone.[13] By the beginning of 2020, thirty percent of family caregivers identified as people of color, a proportion that is expected to grow rapidly in the future.[14] Health-disparities research has proliferated since the 1980s, demonstrating how systemic injustice translates into what epidemiologist Nancy Krieger calls "embodied harm."[15] Although caregivers and recipients who are people of color tend to have higher levels of disability than their white counterparts, they have less access to both acute and long-term care. African American family caregivers are more likely than whites to provide over forty hours of care a week and to assist someone with dementia who lives below the poverty level or is eligible for Medicaid.[16] Latinx caregivers devote more hours a month to caregiving and provide a broader range of services than do non-Latinx whites.[17] Immigration status disqualifies some caregivers from all public services, exacerbating inequities.[18]

In addition, the context within which care is delivered has undergone transformation. As in the larger healthcare system, profit has become increasingly dominant as for-profit corporations, including private investment firms, have taken control of nursing homes, assisted living facilities, and home health agencies, with serious consequences for access and quality.[19] Medicaid, the primary public funding source for long-term care, shifted its focus from institutional care to home- and community-based services. As a result, nursing homes increasingly have focused on private-pay chronic patients as well as those recovering from acute illnesses and surgeries, who can rely on Medicare, which pays more than Medicaid.[20] Although assisted living facilities have expanded rapidly since the 1990s, they primarily serve an affluent population.[21] Low-income caregivers thus often have difficulty finding decent care in either kind of institution for the relatives they tend.

Family structure, too, has changed. The emergence of new familial ties, including egg and sperm donors, surrogates, donor siblings, gay and lesbian communities, blended families, and other forms of chosen kin, has raised new questions about who has a duty to care.[22] Policy makers who refer to the family as the unit of care must determine who counts as family and who gets to decide. More and more individuals assume caregiving responsibilities for relationships beyond those approved by heteronormativity and the state.

Finally, personal experience enlarged my own perspective. When I began research for my 1991 book, *Who Cares for the Elderly? Public Policy and the Experiences of Adult Daughters*, I assumed, as the title suggests, that women caring for aging parents deserved the most attention. Having recently read Elaine M. Brody's landmark article, "'Women in the Middle' and Family Help to Older People," one of the first to highlight the conflict between women's paid work and caregiving responsibilities, I listened with new attentiveness to the anxieties middle-aged friends expressed about caring for their aging parents.[23] My focus changed when I entered my seventies. Then I started hearing stories that jolted me into an awareness that caregivers of elderly spouses or partners were a far more vulnerable group than children caring for parents. Living with the care recipients, spousal caregivers provided many more hours of care each week and reported greater detriments to their health.

I also ceased to be a detached observer. In 1992, my mother was diagnosed with lymphoma and turned to her five children for emotional, practical, and occasional nursing assistance during the five months she suffered from the disease. Her death left me and my siblings responsible for my father, who had suffered from a series of disabling strokes for more than a decade. As his health deteriorated over the following six years, we not only shared his direct care but also hired several immigrant aides to tend him in our absence, thus participating in what has been called "transnational circulations of care," in which workers move frequently between their home countries and the United States.[24] In addition, in 1993 I was diagnosed with cancer and experienced care from the other side as I underwent six months of grueling treatment.

Throughout this book I pay special attention to care for people with dementia. That term refers to a decline in memory and cognitive abilities that is caused by abnormal brain changes and is serious enough to interfere with daily activities. Alzheimer's disease represents between 60 and 80 percent of the cases. Other common forms include vascular dementia and lewy body dementia.[25] Although deaths from stroke, heart disease, and prostate cancer recently declined, the number of deaths from Alzheimer's disease dramatically increased and is expected to reach 13.8 million by 2050.[26] Dementia sufferers constitute a significant proportion of all participants in both institutional and noninstitutional services.[27] They also impose special challenges on family caregivers.[28] Unlike people with most other serious chronic diseases, those with dementia primarily require supervision and help with routine daily activities, not medical services. Family members rather than doctors and nurses thus provide the great bulk of help. After caring for her husband (a former New York Times editor) with Alzheimer's disease for more than two years, Linda McK. Stewart reflected on the futility of their regular physician visits: "Why did we return again and again for 'evaluation'? Common sense told us loud and clear that 'out there' was nothing of any use to us. No magic pill, no surgical intervention, no physical therapy whereby what was lost could be recovered. Still, every few months, there we would be."[29] Between those widely spaced visits, she had little assistance from health professionals. Dementia caregiving illustrates in the extreme the problems all family caregivers encounter.[30]

The first four chapters of the volume focus on issues that have gained new salience in the United States in the past three decades and need further exploration. The second five draw on an online support group for dementia caregivers to examine their perspectives on many of those issues. Chief among them is the extent to which caregivers receive the supportive services they need. The wrenching comments posted on the message boards provide insight into the anguish and horror many caregivers experience.

Chapter 1 notes that although insights from the humanities and social sciences have helped scholars broaden their concerns far beyond stress, that concept continues to dominate the gerontology-caregiving literature. After thirty years I found it easier to recognize that the linkage of stress with caregiving was historically contingent: popular concern about both phenomena emerged in the same period. The passage of time also helped to clarify both the advantages and the disadvantages of the proliferating stress research. The emphasis on stress has enabled researchers to produce statistical knowledge that can be used to highlight the costs of caregiving, evaluate interventions, and assess family members' physical and mental health. Because the stress-research literature relies heavily on quantitative methods, however, it suffers from the drawbacks of quantification in general. Studies assign precise definitions to amorphous words and concepts, simplify complex phenomena, and ignore both the particularities and the broader context.

Chapter 2 discusses the new understanding of dementia that emerged in the 1990s and challenged the medical framework that underlay the emphasis on caregiver stress. Although advocates and researchers had defined sufferers as bodies without any sense of self, British researchers began to argue that people with dementia retained a sense of personhood. In his pioneering 1997 book, *Dementia Reconsidered: The Person Comes First*, psychologist Tom Kitwood defined personhood as "a standing or status that is bestowed upon one human being by others, in the context of relationship and social being."[31] No longer interpreting patients' behavior solely as the symptoms of a deteriorating brain, researchers encouraged health providers to look for cues in the sufferers' past experiences. A common belief is that the personhood model of dementia is especially appropriate for family caregivers. Relying on a reanalysis of two data sets I collected for previous studies, the chapter demonstrates that family members take elements from both the medical and personhood models of dementia, that their understanding of how to promote personhood differs significantly from that of researchers, and that individuals vary enormously in the extent to which they use one framework or another.

The following two chapters provide different perspectives on what has been called the "elder care crisis." Chapter 3 notes that pundits erroneously point to four factors to argue that care for older people is more difficult than ever before.[32] Those include an aging population, the growing proportion of chronic diseases, increasing numbers of women entering the workforce, and the shift of much skilled medical care from hospitals to the home. But it is all too easy to wax nostalgic about caregiving in the past. Drawing on material originally collected for my 2000 book, *Hearts of Wisdom: American Women Caring for Kin, 1850–1940*, the chapter demonstrates that the word "crisis" is a misnomer to the extent that it suggests that normality suddenly has been ruptured. The reality of nineteenth-century caregiving was very different from our idealized image of it. If previous generations of women had fewer responsibilities for elder care, obligations to sick, disabled, and dying people of all ages were constant and unremitting.

Chapter 4 argues that the term "elder care crisis" is appropriate in the sense that we have reached a moment when it is essential to offer radical alternatives to the status quo. Because repeated calls to support family caregivers have gone unanswered, publicly funded long-term care helps a small slice of the population. Many caregivers cannot find relief from obligations that threaten to overwhelm them. The crisis also stems from the plight of direct care workers, most of whom are women and members of marginalized groups and who receive little respect, remuneration, or job security.

Drawing on Alz.connected, an online support group for people caring for spouses and partners with dementia, the next three chapters discuss caregivers' experiences of long-term care services. In 1991, I noted that a critical demand of family caregivers was respite services, which provide temporary relief from the burdens of care. Since then, the number of those services has significantly expanded. Chapter 5 explains why many caregivers fail to take advantage of the ones available to them. Chapter 6 explores the long and tortuous process by which caregivers decide whether to move spouses to institutions. Chapter 7 analyzes the advice support group members give each other and asks what the forums tell us about the likelihood of caregivers engaging in political action to demand greater public support.

Relying again on Alz.connected as well as on published and unpublished reports, the final two chapters examine the impact of the CO-VID-19 pandemic in 2020. Chapter 8 describes how caregivers watched in horror as nursing homes became deathtraps and then locked their doors. Terrified by the possibility of relatives in nursing homes contracting the disease or suffering from loneliness, some caregivers brought them home. When visits resumed, many others were stunned to discover how much their relatives had deteriorated. Chapter 9 discusses the pain caregivers experienced when leaving relatives with severe cognitive impairments at the hospital door and the difficulties of sheltering in place with people who could not understand safety regulations or articulate their symptoms. Overwhelmed with their own troubles, caregivers exhibited little compassion for direct care workers compelled to work in unsafe conditions or leave the labor force.

The conclusion places the issues examined in this volume in a broader context. The pandemic shone a bright light not only on the deficiencies of the elder care system but also on the weakness of the entire care infrastructure. Simultaneously, the disaster provided an impetus for change and helped activists and scholars develop a vision of a future in which care is central to social life.

1

Reformulating Stress and Burden

The concept of stress dominates the research by gerontologists on family care for people with dementia, the supportive services caregivers are offered, the advice they receive, and the advocacy campaigns waged on their behalf. Few recognize, however, that the linkage of stress with caregivers is historically contingent. Popular concerns about both stress and caregiving emerged in the same period. Although the emphasis on the stress of caregiving has many advantages, it limits our understanding of an extremely complex activity. Caregiving exacts serious, often calamitous costs, but it is also a profound human experience and cannot be neatly subsumed under the term "stress."

The story of stress typically begins with Hans Selye, a Czech physician and biochemist who fled the Nazis in the early 1930s and found employment at McGill University a few years later. The theory he formulated in a 1936 letter to the editor of the journal *Nature* and then elaborated in his many later articles and books derived from his experiments with rats. He argued that organisms responded to adverse conditions in three stages, first the "Alarm Stage," when endocrine glands released hormones that had deleterious effects on the body, then the "Resistance Stage," when organisms successfully reversed the physiological damages that had occurred, and finally the "Exhaustion Stage," when the organisms lacked all energy for adaptation, leaving them vulnerable to various forms of disease and even death.[1]

After military studies demonstrated that humans as well as laboratory rats could suffer the consequences, physiologists applied the notion of stress first to members of the armed forces and then to civilians. In 1967 psychiatrists Thomas H. Holmes and Richard H. Rahe devised "The

Social Readjustment Rating Scale," based on the premise that such ordinary life events as "death of a spouse," "divorce," "marriage," and "personal injury or illness" could engender difficulties analogous to those
that arose from combat. The scale permitted individuals to rate their
own susceptibility to stress.[2] A popular 1974 book, *Type A Behavior and
Your Heart*, by two cardiologists, Meyer Friedman and Ray Rosenman,
argued that white men in high-status positions experienced the highest levels of stress and thus were especially vulnerable to cardiac disease.[3] Subsequently, however, studies began to report that workers in the
poorest-paid jobs experience the highest levels of stress.[4]

"By the 1980s," historian Elizabeth Siegel Watkins writes, "'stress' had
become an established term in the American vernacular, used to describe feelings of pressure and tension and to explain the source of some
diseases."[5] A signal event was a June 1983 *Time* magazine article. The
cover of the issue screamed "STRESS!" and displayed the photograph of
a man's face contorted in agony. The article highlighted the deleterious
effects of stress on the body: "Stress is now known to be a major contrib-
utor, either directly, or indirectly, to coronary heart disease, cancer, lung
ailments, accidental injuries, cirrhosis of the liver and suicide—six of
the leading causes of death in the U.S." Stress also caused serious mental
health problems, especially depression and anxiety. Two-thirds of visits
to family doctors in the 1980s were stress related.[6]

During the same period, Americans became familiar with the notion
of burnout, a state of complete exhaustion caused by severe, chronic
stress. The term is often attributed to Graham Greene, whose 1960 novel,
A Burnt Out Case, describes Querry, a famous architect, who arrives at
a Congo leper colony after losing all sense of the meaning of life.[7] In
1974 psychologist Herbert Freudenberger used the label to describe the
experiences of workers in free clinics, women's centers, and hot lines.
Because staff members were either low-paid or volunteers, idealism and
dedication were essential. "But it is precisely because we are dedicated,"
he wrote, "we walk into the burn-out trap."[8] In 1988, Freudenberger expressed his astonishment at the speed with which the term had become

part of "the daily argot of our society." "Burnout" had become "a buzz word, used to convey a great number of personal and social problems."[9]

By that time, attention had begun to shift from systemic problems to individual psychological ones. In the 1970s, Richard Lazarus, a prominent Berkeley University psychology professor, argued that the way individuals appraised and coped with difficult events and circumstances mattered far more than the stressors themselves. The most promising interventions thus involved personal change. As early as 1981 the Institute of Medicine called attention to the "wide range of best-selling books [that] assert that people can avoid developing hypertension, heart attacks, depression, anxiety, and many other disorders by changing their lifestyles in ways that reduce stress."[10]

That was the context in which caregiving suddenly was discovered. Although family members historically have delivered the great bulk of care to sick and disabled people, the topic did not attract the attention of researchers, policy makers, and the public until the early 1980s. One reason was what some critics have called "apocalyptic demography," alarmist reports about the social and economic consequences of population aging.[11] The elderly, who constituted 4 percent of the population in 1910, increased to 8 percent by 1950 and 12 percent in 1984. The rate of increase of the very old, who are most at risk of illness and disability, was even greater. The number of those eighty-five and over rose 165 percent between 1960 and 1980 and was expected to increase even more rapidly by 2050. These "old old" constituted the fastest-growing segment of the population.[12]

Perhaps more than any other factor, a new understanding of Alzheimer's disease helps to explain the growing visibility of family caregiving. No longer conceptualized as senility, age-related cognitive decline was redefined as a specific disease with distinctive symptoms and pathological processes.[13] In 1976, Robert Katzman, a neurologist at the Albert Einstein School of Medicine, wrote a widely cited editorial in the *Archives of Neurology* warning that Alzheimer's disease was a "major killer." Distinguishing the condition from the "mild form of defect in memory storage or recall" that was common among elderly people, he concluded that Alzheimer's was a disease "whose etiology must be determined, whose course must be aborted, and ultimately a disease to be prevented."[14]

Three years later, a group of neuroscientists, officials of the National Institute of Aging, and family members established the Alzheimer's Disease and Related Disorders Association (ADRDA, later the Alzheimer's Association), dedicated to increasing public awareness of the condition. Seeking to convince politicians of the desperate need for funds for medical research, association leaders presented Alzheimer's as an unmitigated disaster. In a series of mass media articles and widely publicized congressional hearings in the early 1980s, they emphasized the prevalence and economic costs of Alzheimer's disease. Lewis Thomas, the famous physician, biologist, and essayist and an ADRDA board member, declared Alzheimer's "not a disease-of-the-month but a disease-of-the-century." It was "responsible for most of the beds in the country's nursing homes." The cost then exceeded $10 billion but would reach $40 billion within a few years as the population continued to age rapidly.[15]

The portrayal of people living with Alzheimer's was unremittingly negative. The first witness called in the 1980 US Senate hearing on Alzheimer's disease was Bobbi Glaves, an ADRDA founder. She began by relating her "own personal tragedy, not to exploit what happened to our family, but because it is typical of thousands of families who may be crying silently for help." Using a phrase that became increasingly widespread, she said that her experience was "like a funeral that never ends." Her husband was "a handsome, vital, athletic man, a civic leader, a public speaker, a highly respected businessman." Now he was merely "a statistic." He had been hospitalized for the last four years, "not knowing his family or speaking a word" and requiring "total care, as the physical deterioration [took] its toll." Glaves still had a husband, but she referred to him "in the past tense." He had become "a shell that simply breathes."[16] Glaves spoke for many when she described an Alzheimer's sufferer as a body lacking all sense of personhood. A woman caring for her mother-in-law asked in the ADRDA *Newsletter*, "What has happened to her humanity? . . . her soul? She exists in oblivion but has an amazing tenacity for life. A mere shell that breathes, she 'lives' on and on."[17] In "Death in Slow Motion: A Descent into Alzheimer's," a *Harper's* magazine article, Eleanor Cooney wrote that she grieved for her mother "exactly as if she'd died. She's gone. I've lost her."[18] A popular advice book for caregivers was titled *The Loss of the Self.*[19]

Advocates pointed out that the disease also wreaked havoc on the lives of caregivers. Alzheimer's was "the worst of all diseases," Thomas wrote, "not just for what it does to the patient, but for its devastating effect on families and friends."[20] Although Glaves's husband might have received assistance from the Veterans Administration, he could not tell her about his eligibility. As a result, she accumulated "living expenses, hospital costs, relocating costs, legal expenses, until we had no reserve." She was in an "unreal world," with "no sense of belonging." When embarrassing situations occurred, she could not explain them to strangers, and people "turned away." And with a "24-hour vigil," she became "totally exhausted, physically and emotionally. I felt I must be prepared for any emergency night or day. It became frightening, living with this stranger who might push me or twist my arm, or throw things at the television." She, too, was on the brink of becoming a "nonperson."[21] Others portrayed family members as the ones enduring the greatest suffering. As anthropologist Lawrence Cohen commented, "The continually reiterated discovery of Alzheimer's journalism is that it is the caretaker who is the *real* victim."[22]

The language of stress served ADRDA's campaign well. At a time of increasing anxiety about the toll that emotion inflicted on health and well-being, advocates and experts emphasized the high stress levels caregivers routinely sustained. *The Hidden Victims of Alzheimer's Disease: Families under Stress*, a 1985 guide book for practitioners written by three gerontologists, explained that "caregivers experience stress either when they cannot manage the patient's behavior or when they feel isolated and unsupported." The authors recommended interventions for family members that follow a "stress management model."[23]

Because family caregivers represented a potential new market for its products and services, the stress-management industry was eager to help. Soon an array of books, articles, workshops, personal coaching services, and web pages appeared, reinforcing the association of caregivers with stress and burden. Family members learned to monitor themselves for the warning signs of stress, including anger, irritability, loneliness, and exhaustion. Advice givers noted that especially serious symptoms include sleeplessness, abuse of alcohol and drugs, compulsiveness, depression, and shortness of breath. Too much stress is hazardous because it can not only undermine health but also cause burnout, thus making further caregiving impossible and leading to premature nursing home placement. The advice continues that caregivers have various ways to manage stress. Frustration and anger diminish when family members acquire information about dementia. Once they realize that many of the most irritating behaviors are disease symptoms, caregivers can employ tips for handling common problems and forestall major crises. Caregivers also must engage in various forms of self-care. Because stress so easily can lead to sickness, they must guard their physical health, eating nutritious food, sleeping well, and exercising regularly. Frequent breaks can help to restore equanimity. And caregivers should seek additional help from other family members and friends, community services, and, eventually, institutions. Support groups are especially important because they relieve stress not only by countering isolation but also by providing an opportunity for members to express unpleasant feelings rather than keep them under tight control. Finally, and perhaps most importantly, according to advice givers, caregivers should cultivate positive attitudes.

A rapidly expanding research enterprise helped to explain why caregivers need that advice. Leonard I. Pearlin, a key player in the field, wrote with his colleagues, "It is difficult to imagine many situations that equal—let alone surpass—the stressfulness of caregiving to relatives and friends with severe chronic impairments." As a result, caregiving "acted as a magnet in attracting the interests of stress researchers."[24] The fact that the concept of caregiver stress easily lent itself to quantification was an incentive for investigators who had not previously focused on stress to do so. Numerous researchers began to devise survey instruments about events typically considered stressful. The first was Steven H. Zarit's 1981 "Burden Interview," which has been cited twenty-eight hundred times and translated into other languages. Although other surveys have since appeared, it remains the most widely used.[25] After Pearlin developed a "stress process model for care," studies became more complex and nuanced. According to Pearlin, that process has three components: stressors are demands or conditions that exceed a person's ability to cope; outcomes are the consequences of the stressors, including physical and mental health problems and early nursing home placement; and moderators are the resources summoned to buffer the impact of stressors. One of the most prominent illustrations of the use of that model is *Profiles in Caregiving: The Unexpected Career*, a major study by Carol S. Aneshensel, Leonard I. Pearlin, Joseph T. Mullan, Steven H. Zarit, and Carol J. Whitlatch (hereafter referred to as Aneshensel et al.).[26] Cited 1,688 times, the book has been accompanied by a vast research literature.[27] According to PubMed, the number of biomedical articles with the key words "caregiver," "dementia," and "stress" published each year grew from one in 1985 to 16 in 1990, 35 in 2000, 108 in 2010, and 170 in 2019. By the end of that year, a total of 2,064 articles had appeared.

The word "burden" is closely akin to "stress." Although family members rarely use the term to describe their experiences, it appears even more frequently than "stress" in the research literature.[28] Some commentators use the two terms interchangeably; some use "burden" as a synonym only for subjective feelings of stress; and some reserve it for the consequence of accumulated stresses. The yearly number of articles with the key words "caregiver," "dementia," and "burden" rose from one in 1983 to 17 in 1990, 32 in 1999, 155 in 2010, and 325 in 2019. The total number of articles with those words published between 1983 and 2019 was 2,981.

The notion of stress also continues to figure prominently in the advocacy campaign around Alzheimer's disease. Because numbers are endowed with special authority, the statistical data researchers produce is especially useful for advocates. An example from occupational health helps to illustrate that point. Sociologist Michelle Murphy explained why the women office workers' movement in the 1970s and 1980s decided to use stress surveys to promote their cause, replacing the experiential knowledge on which advocates previously had relied: "By objectifying and quantifying, surveys translated the nonspecific nature of office pathology into a scientistic format and bureaucratic language socially invested with the power to measure and give shape to the material. . . . A press release might announce '4 out of 5 workers describe their jobs as somewhat or very stressful.'"[29] Similarly, the Alzheimer's Association reports that 80 percent of caregivers for people with Alzheimer's disease state that they often experience high levels of stress, and nearly half suffer from depression.[30] A 2015 report issued jointly by the National Alliance for Caregiving and the Public Policy Institute of the American Association for Retired People found that caregivers who lived with the care recipient, felt that they had no choice in assuming the role, and performed the most demanding services reported the highest stress levels.[31] Alzheimer's.net, which defines itself as an online education and advocacy community, publicized the findings of a nationwide survey demonstrating that caregiver stress undermines physical health, although caregiving responsibilities force many family members to skip medical appointments.[32]

The caregiving-stress literature has other practical applications. Several researchers have evaluated various interventions, including respite services, counseling programs, support groups, and educational and training programs, in terms of their potential for reducing stress.[33] In addition, researchers have produced scales health providers can use to measure caregivers' stress. The American Medical Association urges physicians to try "to mitigate potential stress, burnout or harmful behavior for caregivers by encouraging them to take breaks, maintain a healthy diet, seek preventive health care and join support groups." The first step is often to "conduct a systematic assessment to identify needs, strengths, and resources for family caregivers."[34] Assessment tools also can help to convince caregivers that they are not entirely taken for granted. Because most surveys are short and quick, they can be administered within brief office visits.

In short, the emphasis on stress has enabled researchers to produce statistical knowledge that can be used to call attention to the costs of caregiving, evaluate interventions, and measure family members' health status. But the stress literature also has serious drawbacks, some of which stem from the reliance on quantitative methods.[35] As historian Theodore M. Porter writes, "Quantification is a technology of distance."[36] As such, it may be inappropriate for understanding an activity involving intimate personal relationships.

Many researchers impose preexisting templates on data. The first phase of research by Aneshensel et al. involved conducting qualitative interviews with caregivers. Rather than drawing theories from the rich knowledge they gathered, however, the investigators analyzed the content, in their words, "from the vantage point of universalistic theory pertaining to the origins and impact of chronic social stress."[37] Many other researchers forego qualitative interviews, relying instead on measures that others have developed. Indeed, focusing on stress may appeal to researchers precisely because they can use ready-made measures, thus avoiding the arduous task of creating new ones.

One of the most common concepts researchers use as a moderator of stress is mastery or self-efficacy, taken directly from the stress literature.[38] Aneshensel et al. assessed mastery with statements such as, "I can do anything I really set my mind to do; what happens to me in the future mostly depends on me."[39] Those are quintessential American sentiments, but they may have little place in the context of care. By its very nature caring for people with dementia often extinguishes a sense of mastery and control. Anthropologist Arthur Kleinman recalled that when his wife was diagnosed with early-onset Alzheimer's disease, experts assured him it would advance in a predictable way, through a series of clearly defined stages. Presumably by understanding the stages, he could experience caregiving mastery and thus reduce his stress level. He soon discovered, however, that the progression sometimes "felt almost completely random. The story constantly looped back on itself, filled as it was with fits and starts; with lessons learned, then unlearned, then relearned again; with experiences of tragedy and victory that occurred over and over again, like a suite of unresolved themes and variations." Just as he began to believe he could manage, "things would seem to fall apart once again." He concluded that caregiving "teaches one humility: you learn that no matter how hard you try to make things go well—stuff, bad stuff, is going to happen, and often you have no control at all over it."[40] Kleinman's experience suggests that more than a sense of personal control, caregivers need an ability to tolerate change and uncertainty and accept the inevitability of human fragility.

In addition, stress researchers give little attention to the particularities of individual experiences. Because each family has its own economic challenges, internal dynamics, and idiosyncratic culture, every story is unique. It is thus perhaps unsurprising that, according to a 2012 study, caregivers complain that assessment surveys fail to capture the complexity of their experiences and thus misconstrue their needs. As a result, interventions based on the survey results are often inappropriate.[41] The impersonality of quantitative research undermines the usefulness of the assessment surveys in another way as well. A growing number of observers fault medicine for ignoring the human dimensions of care, including treating patients as whole people, listening closely to their concerns, and responding empathetically to their pain and suffering. Caregivers, too, often want health providers to comprehend their predicaments. To be sure, asking family members to measure their stress levels represents an enormous improvement over ignoring caregivers' needs entirely. But caregiver assessment scales may do little to enable health providers to engage authentically with family members. It is perhaps unfair to compare the standardized questionnaire a busy doctor distributes to caregivers with the writings of Rachel Hadas, a poet and literary scholar. Nevertheless, Hadas's memoir of caring for her husband, a musicologist, offers clues about the kind of understanding some caregivers may seek.[42]

Juxtaposing Hadas's comments with items on caregiver questionnaires exposes the limitations of the latter. For example, the Caregiver Self-Assessment Questionnaire prepared by the American Medical Association asks respondents to rate their overall level of stress on a scale of one to ten. In addition, it asks caregivers to answer "yes" or "no" to several statements that "were found to be predictive of stress." One statement reads, "During the past week or so, I have felt lonely."[43] "Loneliness" is also a central concern to Hadas, who uses the word over and over. Noting that Philip Larkin was a "specialist in loneliness," she quotes from one of his poems on the subject, which she now reads "with special attention."[44] Hadas also writes her own poem about loneliness and then asks, "Does everyone's loneliness share a certain savor, or is each person's loneliness peculiar to them?"[45] She realizes that the "peculiar savor" of her feeling stemmed from the fact that her husband was physically present but almost entirely silent. Some help comes from a book entitled *Ambiguous Loss*, far more from recalling the figure of Penelope in the *Odyssey*. "Is she wife or widow, naïve or sly, calculating or lost? All in turn? All at once?" Hadas wonders. "How could I fail to see that facets of Penelope were parts of my story, too?"[46]

A question on the Kingston Caregiver Stress Scale asks, "Do you have feelings of being confined or trapped by the responsibilities or demands of caregiving?" Respondents are instructed to indicate the extent of the stress on a scale of one ("Feeling NO Stress, Coping fine, 'No problems'") to five ("Extreme Stress, Feeling at 'end of rope,' health at risk").[47] Hadas, too, is familiar with the concept of entrapment. After her husband's diagnosis, she "felt trapped in a situation I hadn't asked to be in. Struggling against that situation or accepting it seemed equally useless and demoralizing."[48] This time she turns to Greek mythology: "When it comes to the no-win situations, mythology furnishes what it is no exaggeration to call classic examples of indigestible choices." She thinks of "Agamemnon faced with the alternatives of disbanding the army and slinking home or sacrificing his daughter. 'Which of these is without evils?' he asks." Her resemblance to Agamemnon seems especially striking when he puts on "the yoke of necessity."[49]

The point is not that doctors must master some branch of literature or enroll in one of the proliferating medical humanities programs in colleges and universities, but rather that questionnaires may do little to convince caregivers that physicians understand the truth of their situations. When the writer Eula Biss experienced severe chronic pain, she was given a scale that asked her to rate her pain between zero ("no pain") and ten ("the worst pain imaginable"). Her physician father explained that a major goal of the scale was "to protect doctors—to spare them some emotional pain. Hearing someone describe their pain as ten is much easier than hearing them describe it as a hot poker driven through their eyeball into their brain."[50] Reliance on the disembodied number a questionnaire produces similarly relieves doctors of the need to listen to caregivers and respond to their specific concerns.

A few researchers have begun to use biomarkers to assess the level of caregiver stress, replacing self-reports with objective indicators of physiological processes. Yin Liu and colleagues, for example, obtained saliva samples provided at scheduled times over nine days to assess the extent to which adult day services reduced the level of family members' stress, captured in measures of cortisol. In such studies, the caregiver's complex subjective experience effectively disappears, hidden behind numbers only experts can interpret.[51]

As a "technology of distance," quantification also may make it easier to position family members as objects to be manipulated in the pursuit of economic efficiency.[52] Some policy analysts do use evidence of caregiver stress to caution against imposing additional obligations on individual households. Taking the needs of caregivers as the starting point, they urge that the government acknowledge greater responsibility to care for its elderly citizens. Many other policy analysts, however, argue that we should encourage increased family caregiving. Pointing to studies that report that the timing of nursing home placement is related more to the intensification of caregiver stress than to changes in the condition of the care recipient, this group also seeks to alleviate the stress of family members. As we will see, however, they do so to prolong family caregiving, not to promote the well-being of caregivers as an end in itself.[53]

Alleviating the level of caregiver stress may not always be conducive to good care. Some studies suggest that men caring for elderly relatives experience less stress than women because they adopt a more managerial approach and focus on providing instrumental services.[54] To the extent that we believe that emotional support and personal attention are important components of caregiving, we may hesitate to rely on stress reduction as the major outcome.

Another difficulty is that quantification simplifies complex phenomena. Studies measure some variables but not others. Three omissions are especially serious. Several researchers have pointed out that the emphasis on stress has obscured the important gratifications caregiving can confer, including gaining a sense of worth and accomplishment, establishing a closer relationship with the person in need of care, and even attaining wisdom from the confrontation with illness and death.[55] Others have noted the absence of attention to cultural differences.[56] My own research suggests that studies should focus more on guilt, which may be even more pervasive than stress.[57] As of December 1, 2020, PubMed listed 11,505 publications with the key words "caregivers and stress" but just 485 using the words "caregivers and guilt." Guilt, however, is what family members discuss over and over. In her 2007 memoir, *Caring for My Mother: A Daughter's Long Goodbye*, Virginia Stem Owens catalogued some of the reasons she felt guilty:

> I can conceive of countless ways by which, on any given day, I could have done better at this job, could have discovered some play therapy or language adaptation technique that would have helped my mother to communicate better. Offered some stimulation to her remaining senses that

would, if not restore or salvage her damaged faculties, at least have entertained her. The foam football I brought for games of catch in her room at [the nursing home] lay in the chest of drawers, another failure. She didn't touch, after a few months, the sketch pad and colored markers with which she once labored to fill in the corners of stenciled figures. Surely I could have been more inventive than that. . . .

What never goes away, doesn't wear out or disappear, is the feeling—no, the certain knowledge—that I could have done more, done better.[58]

A wife posted a message on an Alzheimer's Association online forum for spouses and partners that read,

> I feel guilty—guilty for not being patient enough with my husband. Guilty for resenting the fact that he has this disease which has destroyed all our retirement dreams. Guilty for mentioning how hard it is to people who really don't understand and think I am exaggerating. Guilty for wishing I had made different decisions in my life which wouldn't have taken me to this destination. Guilty that I don't feel close to my husband anymore because he has changed so much. Guilty that he does seem to still want to be close to me. Guilty that I am not a better person in dealing with this awful, awful disease. Guilty that I complain to my step-mom, who is always there with an ear to listen, but who I know must get sick and tired of hearing about my day to day struggles. Guilty, guilty, guilty. That seems to be the only word that comes to mind when I think of myself these days. And I hate it! I simply hate it![59]

Many other caregivers experience guilt about their ultimate powerlessness; they could not halt or even slow the progress of relatives' dementia. Chapters 5–7 discuss the overwhelming sense of guilt that assailed caregivers when they enlisted home- or community-based services for relatives or moved them to institutions. Several considered themselves answerable for any deficiencies in the medical or social service programs they arranged.

Caregivers can find various tips for alleviating guilt—be compassionate with yourself, have realistic expectations, take time for yourself. But guilt may be even less amenable to individual solutions than stress. Psychologists note that, like other "moral emotions," guilt derives from deviations not only from universal standards but also from culturally specific ones.[60] Although people in most countries believe that families have an obligation to care for their own, that belief may be especially pronounced in the United States, which provides less social protection than other industrialized countries. As sociologist Sandra R. Levitsky writes, most US caregivers "wrestle with serious long-term care dilemmas without ever questioning the assumption that family should bear exclusive responsibility for care provision."[61] Is it possible that researchers pay more attention to stress because its relief can postpone expensive nursing home placement while alleviating guilt might encourage family members to demand more government assistance?

Yet another major problem is that quantitative studies assign precise definitions to amorphous words and concepts. "Making numbers requires categories with strong boundaries," write two sociologists, "a clear sense of what is or is not an instance of something."[62] But for months and often years, many caregivers find it difficult to distinguish between the signs of normal aging and the symptoms of Alzheimer's. "The disease crept into my father's life slowly and silently," Nicci Gerrard, a British journalist, recalled, "no broken windows or alarm bells shrilling, just occasional rustles in the night, a creak on the stairs, odd things missing from their usual place but not missed. I don't know when he suspected and I don't know when we did either, or which came first."[63] Because her father had always been absent-minded, it was easy to believe that trait had simply become more noticeable. Unable to determine the onset of disease, Gerrard was unsure when her role as a caregiver began. No single event marks the end of caregiving. Should it be when the relative enters a nursing home? When death occurs? When grief abates?

Some family members are unfamiliar with the term "caregiver." Although it is becoming more widely used, it is by no means universally accepted. An American Medical Association guide for physicians notes that "many people are confused when thrust into the role of caregiver. It can be difficult for a person to separate her roles as a caregiver from her roles as spouse, lover, child, friend, etc."[64] A 2012 study of In-Home Supportive Services, a California means-tested program, reported that many "family caregivers say that they are just doing 'what families do.'"[65] A 2016 study found that African American family members were especially loath to consider themselves caregivers because taking care of older people was an important part of their culture. The researchers quoted one interviewee: "So many in our community if you ask if they are a caregiver they'll respond no. Because the role of a caregiver . . . what's a caregiver? They're taking care of someone but I don't think they are assigning themselves that title of caregiver."[66]

Several researchers note that "burden" has multiple meanings and the concept is not clearly defined in some studies.[67] Few researchers, however, acknowledge the elusiveness of the notion of stress. "While we intuitively recognize when we are stressed," historian Mark Jackson writes, "we have as yet no precise or consistent definition of the term 'stress,' only a partial understanding of how stress is generated or moderated, and limited insight into the complex mechanisms by which it affects our mental and physical health."[68] And even the eponymous American Institute of Stress writes, "Stress is not a useful term for scientists because it is such a highly subjective phenomenon that it defies definition. And if you can't define stress, how can you possibly measure it?"[69] In addition, some researchers now question whether Alzheimer's is a single disease with a distinct pathology.[70]

Finally, quantitative studies abstract caregiving from the context that gives it meaning. Although researchers indicate the race, gender, and economic status of the people they study, they ignore the larger processes that explain why those statistics are important. The inequitable division of domestic labor between the genders helps to explain why women represent three-fourths of all caregivers, why they are more likely than men to quit their jobs to provide care for both spouses and parents, and why women rather than men typically perform the most intimate personal tasks.[71] The ideological commitment to privatization explains why a long-term care system barely exists in the United States. Structural racism explains why many privileged women are able to "buy out" of their responsibilities by hiring African American and immigrant women from Asia and Central and South America as aides and attendants. Medical triumphalism, the belief that medicine ultimately will find a cure for every affliction, helps explain why political leaders responded to the discovery of Alzheimer's disease with research funds but little support for caregivers. Passing a resolution in 1983 to designate November "National Alzheimer's Disease Month," Congress expressed hope that "an increase in the national awareness of the problem of Alzheimer's disease may stimulate the interests and concern of the American people, which may lead, in turn, to increased research and eventually to the discovery of a cure."[72] It said nothing about the people currently living with the disease and the family members caring for them. And today, many Americans still place their faith in the magic bullet they assume medicine soon will produce to eliminate Alzheimer's disease and possibly other dementias.[73]

* * *

The prominence of the notion of stress in discussions of dementia caregiving results not only from the nature of that endeavor but also from historically specific conditions. Americans became aware of the disease just when they were beginning to understand that stress was widespread and could inflict serious physical and mental health problems. Focusing on stress also served the interests of advocates who believed that exaggerating the costs of Alzheimer's to both patients and caregivers would persuade political leaders to fund research for a cure. And because stress was amenable to quantification, it was an attractive object of study.

Few people can care for relatives with dementia for long periods of time without experiencing some stress, and many welcome interventions designed to alleviate it. But as subsequent chapters note, stress is only one of the many responses family members have to providing care and is not always their central concern. Policy makers who assume that relieving the stress of caregivers will induce them to delay institutional placement may have limited understanding of their wishes or needs. First, however, we turn to the personhood perspective on dementia, which undermines assumptions built into the stress model in two ways. It posits couples as members of a dyad rather than as two separate individuals, one of whom imposes burdens on the other.[74] And it suggests that the goal is not to relieve stress but rather to preserve the dementia sufferer's sense of self. Relying less on instrumental strategies than on emotional involvement, that approach tends to increase caregiver stress.

2

Challenging the Medical Model of Dementia

For more than two hundred years, medicine has been marked by contestation over what knowledge should count as authoritative.[1] Throughout the nineteenth century, physicians valued personal relationships with patients as a source of medical knowledge. Believing that disease arose from the interaction of people with their environments, doctors sought information about individual patients and the contexts of their lives. At the turn of the century, however, discovery of the bacteriological causes of specific diseases made it more acceptable for physicians to maintain distance from patients and treat them as fungible. Biological reductionism rendered irrelevant the patients' emotional and moral state, interaction with providers, and physical surroundings. The shift to offices and hospitals further increased the impersonality of care by preventing doctors from observing patients' homes and family relationships. Medical schools emphasized the importance of maintaining emotional distance from patients, not cultivating intimate ties. As the number of nursing schools rose, nursing leaders, too, defined their occupation in terms of technical skills and abstract knowledge.[2]

Nevertheless, the dominance of medical expertise was never complete. Historians examining the processes by which medicine expanded to establish authority over childbirth and mothering in the first part of the twentieth century show that African American, Native American, and European immigrant women often resisted the messages of medical advisors; many expressed contempt for knowledge derived from formal education rather than personal experience.[3] Even many women who welcomed the new advice produced by medicalization viewed it as a resource to be used selectively.[4]

Competing concepts of dementia today illustrate the persistence of tensions between particularistic and universalistic knowledge. According to the medical perspective, dementia proceeds inexorably through a series of predetermined stages, damaging and then ultimately destroying the sense of self. In the past thirty years that view has been increasingly challenged by the personhood perspective, which assumes that people with dementia retain a sense of personal identity and that social interactions can retard disease progression and possibly even restore functioning. The most famous definition of "personhood" in this context is that of British psychologist Tom Kitwood—a "standing or status that is bestowed upon one human being by others. It implies, recognition, respect, and trust."[5]

Kitwood directed his comments to the staff of long-term care facilities, and until recently, most studies of person-centered care have focused primarily on formal providers.[6] We might assume that the personhood perspective is especially appropriate for family caregivers because they deliver care within the context of an intimate relationship and emphasize the need to foster dignity. Some observers look to family caregivers to teach the staff of nursing homes and home- and community-based services how to recognize and respond to individuals' wishes and feelings and foster self-respect.[7] But to what extent and in what ways do family members view themselves as promoting the personhood of people living with dementia?[8]

I seek to answer that question by drawing on two data sets I originally collected for other purposes and reanalyze here. For my 1990 book, *Who Cares for the Elderly: Public Policy and the Experiences of Adult Daughters*, I conducted lengthy, in-depth interviews with thirty-eight women caring for parents with dementia in the Los Angeles area.[9] To protect the anonymity of the respondents, I refer to them as daughters rather than by name. For my 2017 book, *Living in Death's Shadow: Family Experiences of Terminal Care and Irreplaceable Loss*, I read twenty-three book-length narratives by family members of people with dementia. They included fifteen daughters, four sons, two wives, and two husbands. Four appeared between 1995 and 1999, sixteen between 2000 and 2009, and three after 2010.[10] I also use three memoirs published after *Living in Death's Shadow* appeared, one by a wife, another by a granddaughter, and the third by a husband. Although professional and popular understandings of dementia have changed markedly since the daughters were interviewed and some of the memoirs were published, the fundamental issues the family members faced remain the same. To what extent should they accept medical descriptions of people with dementia and to what extent give credence to their own understandings of their relatives? Both the interviewees and the memoir writers were primarily white, well educated, and relatively affluent. As social inequality grows, the experiences of members of different groups increasingly diverge. Many of my generalizations thus may apply only to people with relatively high social status.

Adhering to the Medical Model

Virtually all family members in this study described the recipients of their care at least partly within a medical framework. The diagnosis of some form of dementia thus represented a critical turning point. Some caregivers referred to it as "the verdict" or a "death sentence." Those who had hoped that the elders had a treatable problem, such as depression or alcohol- or drug-induced dementia, were shocked to discover that they suffered from an irreversible condition. But the diagnosis also could be a source of reassurance. One adult daughter explained why she and her siblings had insisted that their mother undergo an evaluation: "We suspected, and we didn't think we had a right to suspect without a professional opinion. . . . We used to swap stories of 'guess what mother did now?' and it wasn't cruel." The diagnosis "reconfirms that it's not you, because sometimes when you're in with someone who's not dealing with things properly, you begin to feel, 'Was it me? Did I hear that? I don't believe she said that.'" The novelist Sue Miller was able to convince her siblings that something was the matter with their father. "I had noticed his failing early on," she wrote in her memoir, "but no one else in the family shared my perception. 'He's fine with *me*,' my brother would say, and I would feel accused of imagining things or of responding to Dad in a way that was somehow *responsible* for making him seem vague." She thus felt "guilty relief" when a doctor diagnosed Alzheimer's disease. Although "real sorrow" intermingled with that relief, "the diagnosis signaled the end to the nameless anxiety that I'd felt had been mine alone for years, and for that, no matter what, I was grateful."[11] Once elders were labeled sick, family members could make sense of unusual behavior and consider the best way to provide care.

The initial step for many caregivers was consulting the advice literature to learn more about their relatives' impairments. The first manual for caregivers appeared in 1981, soon after the reconceptualization of Alzheimer's disease and the establishment of the Alzheimer's Disease and Related Disorders Association (ADRDA). *The 36-Hour Day: A Family Guide to Caring for Persons with Alzheimer's Disease, Related Dementing Illnesses, and Memory Loss in Later Life*, by Nancy L. Mace and Peter V. Rabins, contained a wealth of information about dementia, the major problems family members face, strategies for dealing with those problems, and the type of assistance available.[12] One adult daughter stated, "I had a lot of hostility toward [my father] in the beginning because I just got so furious that he wouldn't take care of himself and he wouldn't make decisions." But after reading *The 36-Hour Day*, she changed her attitude. "I used to get really angry at him, because I didn't realize that he couldn't do all these things," she continued. "After I realized he couldn't do them, I just accepted it." Another daughter had a similar experience caring for her mother:

> I took [my mother] to the doctor, and he's the one who told me about the book, *The 36-Hour Day*. I went and got that book, and I read it from cover to cover. And after I read that book, I started to understand some of the things that were happening to me. I started to understand why it is when she calls me and I would have her come here that she would want to go home again. It was because she felt totally uncomfortable, she wasn't

in surroundings that she's used to, she would forget where rooms were. Just all these things started to come together and I would understand. . . . When I read the book, I realized that she was just like a model case. I mean, all these things that were in this book were happening to her. I was seeing that she can't help it, and I think once I realized in my own mind that, yes, this is what is happening to her, then our whole relationship and my attitude toward her changed.

Now in its fifth printing, *The 36-Hour Day* continues to sell well, and several memoir writers referred to it. But since the 1990s caregivers have had access to a much wider advice literature as well as to medical information on the web. Like the adult daughters quoted above, John Daniels wrote in his memoir that understanding the genesis of certain behaviors enabled him to gain more control over his emotions. When his mother exhibited the first signs of failing memory, he moved her from Maine to Oregon, close to his home. Before he understood his mother's condition, he thought she was being "purposely evasive. I wanted to hear about her work, her college life, stories about me [and my brothers], her final thoughts about my father and the life they had shared. What I got instead, most of the time, were repeated comments and questions about the appearance of trees she spent hours looking at through the windows, about the arrangement of the furniture or the placement of a picture, about the food we ate." Those remarks "recurred with maddening frequency."[13] His anger began to fade when he learned that his mother's actions were not deliberate. Aaron Alterra wrote that after consulting the *Merck Manual*, he understood why his wife hardly noticed his absence when he left for a week to visit other relatives.[14]

Interpreting relatives' disturbing behaviors in light of the disease, both the adult daughters and memoir writers were able to learn techniques for dealing with them. One daughter, for example, noticed that the staff members of the day care center her father attended touched elders who were upset. "They give them a hug, or a pat, or hold their hand. . . . Lovely, lovely. And I've learned to do that with my mother.

When she's real agitated, if I just sit down and put my arm around her, she calms right down."

Caregivers of people diagnosed with Alzheimer's disease rather than other forms of dementia were especially likely to learn about the typical course of the condition and to believe that knowledge could dispel uncertainty, a condition that frequently fuels anxiety.[15] One daughter explained how she was able to prepare for the future: "At the hospital, there was a wonderful doctor, and he said: 'Watch for these signs. When you come to pick her up and she has to brush her hair or brush her teeth, she's beginning to deteriorate. And then watch for her doing this and wandering off and not being able to get home.' So we watched for all the signs to come." Others had learned the symptoms associated with the different stages of disease and carefully noted when their relatives reached each one. Sue Miller was able to forgive herself for failing to halt her father's decline. "I think this is the hardest lesson about Alzheimer's disease for a caregiver: you can never do enough to make a difference in the course of the disease. Hard because what we feel anyway is that we have never *done* enough. We blame ourselves. We always find ourselves deficient in devotion. . . . In the end all those judgments, those self-judgments, are pointless. The disease is inexorable, cruel. It scoffs at everything."[16]

Caregivers also adhered to the medical template when they described how disease had transformed their relatives. The presence of the elders served as painful reminders of their former selves. "The person I loved isn't there," one daughter commented. "It's just a body sitting there. The terrible thing is that she looks like the same person, but she doesn't share my joys or my sorrows or anything. It isn't the same person, but I still have to look at that person that looks like the mother I loved. And it just tears me apart." Another daughter talked about her mother's steady decline: "Having just lost my dad, I'm real grateful she's still alive, but it's sad. It's hard to have a positive attitude, just watching her get frailer and more forgetful. In a week or two you can see the difference, that's she's walking with more difficulty, and she remembers less. It's hard to see at such close quarters." Caregiving highlighted the extent to which the old relationship had been radically disrupted. Aaron Alterra could feed his wife only by pushing her head up so he could force a spoon into her mouth. "More than other duties that some might find more troubling," he wrote, "it seemed to me that feeding her that way diminished her far beneath her remaining considerable humanity."[17]

In a few cases, the changes wrought by dementia were not all painful. As a child, Floyd Skloot had suffered from the terrible abuse his mother inflicted. But she was "almost tame now, her rages burned down to a heap of dying embers."[18] When he moved her to a nursing home close to his home in Oregon, she became "special to the nurses and aides because she didn't complain, didn't snap at them (my mother!) Now, of all times, she was mellow."[19] Another memoir writer had fought with her father throughout her childhood. As his "aggressiveness" and "belligerence" diminished, she gradually forged a close relationship with him.[20]

Far more commonly, however, family members witnessed the disappearance of cherished traits. Virginia Stem Owens wrote that her mother, "who had been so fastidious about her person, the icon I had watched dressing for work in her starched white blouses and pearl button earrings, now wandered from the kitchen to the bedroom in slovenly smocks, hair askew, refusing to bathe sometimes for days."[21] Eleanor Cooney had "once loved to show off [her mother] because she was so much cooler and smarter than anyone else's mother. Now I scrambled to cover up the gaps, compensate, and before long, hide her."[22] The woman Madeleine L'Engle had "experienced only as a loving and gentle mother" began to make "her desires known in no uncertain terms" and was "not above using her cane as a weapon."[23] And John Thorndike's father, "once so knowledgeable about the history of Western civilization," was "now trying to keep track of what meals he has eaten."[24]

Fostering Personhood

Although only the rare caregiver explicitly mentioned the personhood perspective, most illustrated it in various ways. Memoir writers typically began by describing the elders' lives before dementia struck, not only to emphasize how much had been lost but also, perhaps, to demonstrate that the relatives remained worthy of respect. In addition, caregivers focused on the singular aspects of their relatives that persisted long after dementia descended. A daughter who described her mother as "a very strong person" stressed that "even in all her dementia . . . that personality of hers was still there, like I'd help her down the stairs, and she'd pull back." Some asserted that the disease had exaggerated or uncovered lifelong personality traits. Another daughter told the following story:

> When my mother's brother was visiting, my father had no idea who this man was. My mother left the car lights on in the car, and my uncle said, "Give me the keys and I will go and turn them off," but my father said no. He told my mother that she had to go out, that she was the one who had left them on, and she was going to have to turn them off. This kind of behavior was a side of him always, but it was not always so naked in front of my uncle. He would not have been totally unconscious about it. He would have veiled it in the past.

On the other hand, she added, "He never was a good person to get along with. It's hard to tell now when his personality is deteriorating whether or not it is the crankiness they talk about or the nastiness related to Alzheimer's disease or if it is just him."

If caregivers deviated from the medical model of dementia, however, they also departed from the personhood model various scholars and researchers describe. The personhood literature emphasizes the qualities elders retain and the importance of responding to them as they are now. According to Sam Fazio, director of quality care and psychosocial research at the Alzheimer's Association, and his colleagues, a fundamental of person-centered care is to "recognize and accept the person's reality."[25] Many family members, however, viewed themselves as guardians of the people they remembered. To be sure, past and present could not always be neatly differentiated. Advocates of person-centered care often acknowledge the importance of knowing the elders' history and biography.[26] Fazio and colleagues continue, "It is important to know the unique and complete person, including his/her values, beliefs, interests, abilities, likes, and dislikes—both past and present."[27] The staff members of a nursing home observed by anthropologist Ingunn Moser were able to relate better to one resident after learning that he had been a professional football referee and continued to see himself in that role. The primary goal, however, was to recognize the man's current self, not seek to restore the past.[28]

Like researchers who embrace the personhood model, family caregivers stressed the need to foster the dignity of the people they tended, but they defined that term very differently. Rather than attend to the wishes and needs the elders currently expressed, family members spoke in terms of honoring the self-respect of the people they knew in the past. Thus, even when dementia was very severe, they refused to enroll the elders in activities they previously would have considered demeaning, tried to keep their surroundings the same, and dressed them in the outfits they once might have chosen. Striving to create the illusion that the old relationship remained intact, family members camouflaged their own contributions (thereby forfeiting the appreciation many craved).

Some caregivers not only tried to shield the elders from any awareness of how their former relationship had changed but also continued to view themselves as operating within it. Recent studies promote that orientation by proposing interventions that strengthen the "couplehood" of partners and people with early-stage dementia rather than addressing the needs of each separately. Researchers argue that such interventions can benefit both members of the dyad. According to Justine McGovern, a professor of social work at New York University, "Life partner care partnerships provide opportunities for ongoing relatedness and psychoemotional growth that can offset some of the losses experienced with progressive cognitive impairment."[29] Other researchers argue that because women's "identity is formed and judged within the contexts of relationships," wives of people with dementia may be especially likely to seek to preserve a sense of the marriage "to retain their own status and sense of self."[30]

But maintaining old relationships does not serve all caregivers equally well. Many adult daughters I interviewed reported that caregiving brought them into intimate contact with their mothers for the first time since adolescence. Issues they believed had been fully resolved suddenly reemerged. Several women lapsed into old modes of interaction and reexperienced feelings that were more appropriate to childhood or adolescence. Three female memoir writers caring for mothers similarly had difficulty translating medical information into what they considered appropriate emotional responses. Madeleine L'Engle could not entirely protect herself from hurt when her mother withdrew emotionally: "I know that it is a classic symptom of an atherosclerosis, this turning against the person you love most, and this knowledge is secure above my eyebrows, but very shaky below."[31] Reeve Lindbergh "knew intellectually" that her mother, Anne Morrow Lindbergh, had lost her ability to speak as a result of a series of strokes. Nevertheless, when Anne remained silent despite Reeve's efforts to converse, she started "thinking very fast, and the thinking is childish and irrational: she does not talk to me anymore because she no longer loves me. I know it isn't exactly true or is irrelevant . . . but the thought speeds into my mind, and before I can protest, it turns into another one: she is not talking to me because I am not worth talking to."[32] When Lauren Kessler brought her four-month-old daughter on a visit to her mother's nursing home, her mother recoiled, saying, "What *is* that thing. . . . Get that thing away from me." Knowing that Alzheimer's disease "often removed or muffled inhibitions," Lauren feared her mother "was revealing something long buried, something that had been layered over by civility and propriety. *What is that thing?* Could this annoyance, this distaste, this aversion, really be my mother's true feeling about babies? And not just babies, of course, but *my* baby. And not just my baby, but me, her first baby."[33] The negative stories the mother had told about Lauren's infancy now assumed a darker hue.

Pretending nothing had changed could create other difficulties as well. Several adult daughters had difficulty establishing control over their mothers. One woman confiscated her mother's car keys only after her mother had had three accidents. A second hesitated to hire an aide to tend her mother although she suspected that her mother occasionally lost her way when returning home from shopping. Moreover, as one daughter said, "You gradually realize that you are trying to maintain the status quo for yourself because it may not matter to them anymore." Another daughter remarked that furniture had always been a large part of her mother's life. She "loved antiques" and "got much of her pleasure driving around Palm Beach and then going into her house and saying, 'Isn't this a nice place, my this is nice.'" The daughter thus had her mother's furniture shipped across the country when she moved to a Los Angeles facility. "But there was a three-week delay in getting her furniture to where she was staying, and she'd forgotten it all. There was just that much progression of degeneration in that time. . . . I was still making decisions on the basis of what I thought she would want. I didn't want to have to acknowledge that she's no different from X, Y, or Z who also has Alzheimer's, that there's no individual distinction making her the mother that I knew."

Eleanor Fuchs had a similar experience. Despite pressure from physicians and other family members to find a nursing home bed, her "only plan" for nine years was to keep her mother "somehow in a normal life and then, a simulacrum of a normal life. I didn't question the decision or even know it was a choice."[34] Key to that enterprise was hiring aides who could help her mother remain in her beloved apartment. When the mother returned home after two weeks away, however, she had forgotten she had ever lived there and had no desire to do so again. "I have to ask myself," Fuchs wrote, "for whom have I been keeping her going in this tinseltown, this dumbshow of a life? In a sickening moment I suspect that this years-long effort may not have been for her at all, but for me, only for me, because should she—or her simulacrum—cease to exist in this place . . . should it all be dispersed, my own history would just dematerialize into a dream."[35]

Some caregivers do eventually appreciate the elders just as they are. After living with and caring for his father for six months, John Thorndike wrote, "I've grown closer to him. . . . It's brutal to watch your father slide into oblivion—and to imagine your own decline to come—but day after day I still want to be here in his house. I lay my hands on him, I listen to everything he says, and every morning I'm glad to see his face."[36] Others learned to savor the present. Fourteen months after beginning to care for her mother, Reeve Lindbergh commented, "I am growing accustomed to having her alive, not the way she used to be, but exactly as she is. I am beginning to like our life together, right now. I don't understand this at all, but for the time being it makes me happy."[37] In a similar vein, anthropologist Janelle S. Taylor wrote, "Sometimes in Mom's company, I am able to slow down enough to gain a new appreciation of the moment. A few days ago we spent a half hour looking out my mother's bedroom window to where a woman sat on the sidewalk outside, next to her baby in its stroller, blowing bubbles. The breeze caught the bubbles and carried them up, whirling and dancing, catching the afternoon light in brief rainbow flashes. It was the kind of thing I would not normally watch—and it was beautiful."[38] And Floyd Skloot, who confronted his own health problems, realized his mother could teach him how to live within limitations. Watching the joy she found in her relationship with a man she met at her assisted living facility, Skloot wrote, "My mother . . . is still giving something vital back to me, reflecting the change she endures with genuine grace something of the changes I am trying to endure as well."[39] Far more often, however, family members focused on the past, mourning their losses and working hard to repair them.

Individual Variations

Both the adult daughters and memoir writers varied considerably in the extent to which they illustrated the personhood model of care. Barry R. Peterson, a CBS News correspondent, clung so closely to the medical framework that his account of caring for his wife, Jan, another journalist, appears almost like a parody. After Jan's diagnosis of early-onset Alzheimer's disease, Petersen was "forever reading books or checking the latest website on Alzheimer's." When Jan began to decline, he "realized how the personal toll on me was building. I was now the living embodiment of the Alzheimer's book title: *The 36-Hour Day*. The days felt like they were 36-hours long, or more . . . I needed a break to get back my own energy."[40] One reason he later placed Jan in an institution was that many people warned that he was "being dragged down in ways which will start affecting my health and well being, if it hasn't already. This is not unusual for caregivers, and studies show that being an Alzheimer's caregiver to a loved one can shorten your life rather dramatically."[41] He also quoted frequently from the "Seven Stages of Alzheimer's Disease" by the Alzheimer's Association. Writing to inform family and friends that Jan would enter an assisted living facility, he noted that she had reached the sixth of seven stages and thus had become too disabled to live at home. When he encountered resistance, he continued to invoke expert advice, organizing a meeting and inviting a social worker to speak. The social worker arrived "with charts and pictures and explained in graphic and uncompromising detail how Alzheimer's attacks, physically alters, and destroys the brain. . . . She was teaching her version of Alzheimer's 101, because if you do not know The Disease and have not lived with it for years or decades, it can fool with ease." Her lecture persuaded some, though not all, of Jan's friends and family that Petersen had made the right decision.[42]

Judith Levine was one of the few caregivers who mentioned the emerging literature on the persistent personhood of people with dementia. Drawing on that theory to understand the progression of her father's Alzheimer's, she ridiculed the mental tests her mother trusted. "Mom organizes and substantiates her own observations of Dad's slide with expert assessments," she wrote. Determined to resist "the medical standardization of dementia," Judith tossed "away the chart of stages" and took note of what was "stable in Dad, even flourishing." Her major complaint, however, focused not on the content of the advice but rather on the use her mother made of it. The reigning caregiver narrative, she asserted, had encouraged her mother to exaggerate her burdens to justify divesting herself of responsibility. Judith had little sympathy with her mother's complaints about loneliness and lack of assistance. She challenged her mother's assertion that she had devoted the past ten years exclusively to caregiving and expressed disbelief when her mother insisted that all affection for her husband had vanished. When her mother announced that she had been dating "Sid," whom she had met in her support group, Judith feared that a new relationship with a "fully functioning peer" made her father's deficits "loom larger" than they actually were. "I'm determined not to let Mom represent herself as the victim of circumstances as scripted by the official Alzheimer's story," she wrote. The conflict escalated when the mother said she wanted to place her husband in a nursing home. Judith accompanied her mother on tours of possible facilities but insisted that her father still loved his home and could receive good care there. She thus protested when her mother began the process of institutionalization by applying for Medicaid and arranging the assessments the facilities demanded. At the end of the memoir, the mother went to live with her boyfriend, leaving her husband in the apartment with full-time aides. The issue of nursing home placement remained unresolved.[43]

Other caregivers who wrote within the personhood framework were less dismissive of expert advice. After a brain injury left Alix Kates Shulman's husband with serious cognitive impairments, she chastised "certain friends who think I should arrange for his care [outside the home] and get on with my life, as if his self had perished and he could be reduced to his disabilities." She stressed that "not only has he daily stretches of lucidity, calm, and sweetness, lasting anywhere from moments to hours, . . . but the enduring combination of traits that always distinguished his self from another's—his sunny optimism and charm, his aesthetic passion, his deep-rooted modesty, sincerity, courtesy, and generosity of spirit, as well as his diffidence and reserve—keep breaking through the fog." Nevertheless, she found comfort in reading "*The 36-Hour Day*, with its useful tips on how to cope and its descriptions that render the strange familiar." Scott's challenging behavior was "revealed as typical of his condition, as my responses are all too typical of mine. That book has nailed us."[44]

Caregivers also varied in the extent to which they viewed their relatives as having lost all sense of self as death approached. Mary Gordon imagined her mother's life as "mostly a blank, perhaps an empty screen occasionally impressed upon by shadows."[45] L'Engle wrote that by the end, her mother was "lost somewhere in the subterranean self." "No longer the integrated person" L'Engle remembered, she was "a dark shard, broken and splintered."[46] Having been "enfeebled by several years of strokes and seizures," Lucette Lagnado's mother "lost any semblance of an identity." In the nursing home, she was "simply a woman against a wall."[47] By contrast, Lynn Casteel Harper wrote that, rather than disappearing as he became disabled, her grandfather "persisted, a complex conglomeration of the past and his new present. . . . The essences behind his previous life endeavors seemed intact in Jack until the end—in subtle shades, often known only to those who spent time with him—while the activities that once embodied them had fallen away."[48]

The Soul of Care: The Moral Education of a Husband and a Doctor, by the well-known medical anthropologist Arthur Kleinman, is instructive in another way, demonstrating that the personhood perspective can endow caregiving with meaning. The book is simultaneously a caregiving memoir, an indictment of the medical profession, a loving tribute to his wife, and a meditation on the meaning of care.[49] Because it chronicles Kleinman's long struggle to become the kind of family member who could recognize and attend to the personhood of a dementia sufferer, I describe it in considerable detail.

The first chapter begins, "Not much in my youth signaled a future of caregiving."[50] Born in Brooklyn in 1951, Kleinman describes himself as a headstrong and willful youth. His parents presented a model of irresponsibility, spending their entire inheritance. Because they employed both a housekeeper and a cook throughout his childhood, he never had a chore. The following few chapters trace his meteoric rise in medicine and academia. Anxious to escape his home, he fled first to Tufts and then to Stanford for college, graduating with highest honors in 1962. Because his childhood doctor had taken an interest in him and encouraged him to become a physician, he entered Stanford Medical School, where he graduated in 1967. After an internship at Yale–New Haven Hospital, he was a research fellow, first at the National Institutes of Health, then at the US Naval Medical Research Unit in Taipei, Taiwan, and finally in the Department of the History of Science at Harvard University. While a psychiatry resident at Harvard, he earned an MA in social anthropology. In 1976 he became a tenured professor in the Department of Psychiatry and Behavioral Sciences with an adjunct position in anthropology at the University of Washington.[51] There his career and reputation flourished. By the end of his six years in Seattle, his "star was on the rise, and I chased after it with everything I had." The child psychiatrist Leon Eisenberg, who had profoundly influenced him at Harvard, "lured" him back with tenured professorships in Harvard Medical School and the Harvard Faculty of Arts and Sciences.[52] Now his career began "exploding in every possible direction." He chaired and held named professorships in two departments and "cranked out books and articles at an alarming pace while serving on boards, committees, panels, and organizations all over the world." In addition, he saw private patients at night and served as a clinical professor in a hospital affiliated with Harvard. Although the pace was "relentless," he "did not want it any other way."[53]

Kleinman was able to dedicate himself to his career because his wife, Joan, took care of the rest of his life. Looking back, he realized his privilege had been "incredible."[54] Joan raised the two children and did all the housework. (Kleinman knew the location of the washing machine but not how to use it.) She also helped him through various crises. When his frenetic work pace destroyed his health in Seattle, she "would tend to me as if she had another child in her care."[55] Left on his own for a month in

China, he developed a cascade of life-threatening symptoms and lost 20 percent of his body weight. Once back home, "it took months to recover, but Joan was fierce in her efforts to care for this broken man. She pulled me through."[56] She was there for him again when he experienced a panic attack, devoting herself to his care, "slowly, imperceptibly, rebuilding my confidence over the months that followed."[57] She also was the one who developed close relationships with his colleagues and students. People who came to talk to him about academic problems turned to her for personal ones. Often they "just wanted to sit with her and soak up the love that washed over them in the form of care."[58] And she gradually smoothed his rough edges, convincing him to treat others more considerately and appreciate the family she had created around him. Thus, when Joan received a diagnosis of early-onset Alzheimer's disease in her late fifties and gradually became the one in need of care, he had a model on which to draw.

His own interests and academic pursuits also served him well. To some extent, Kleinman had spent his life preparing for his role as a caregiver. Even as a boy he had enjoyed listening to people's stories. The first patients he saw as a medical student taught him that care involved far more than diagnosis and treatment. He studied anthropology because he chafed at the narrowness of his medical education and then spent the rest of his career finding ways to infuse clinical practice with insights gleaned from the social sciences and humanities. One of his most popular and influential books is *The Illness Narratives: Suffering, Healing, and the Human Condition*, published in 1988, which urged physicians to listen to patients' stories to understand better how they make sense of their troubles.[59] That book helped to generate a flowering of personal narratives of illness and disability as well as works by health professionals and scholars in various fields seeking to illuminate the patient's point of view.

Feminist scholars insist that care is a skill anyone can acquire, not an essential aspect of women's nature. The second half of Kleinman's book examines the decade he devoted to Joan's care. By his own account, he was an empathetic and compassionate caregiver, honoring her personhood in various ways. Knowing her intimately, he was able to plan special occasions for her. Several ended in near-disaster. His most ambitious outing was a trip to New York to see Verdi's *Don Carlo*, an opera she had always loved. Although her disruptive behavior enraged the audience around them, he insisted they stay to the end. "Her face was so alive with enjoyment, I wanted her to hear the most beautiful singing. . . . Didn't she deserve some happiness in the midst of the horror of her disease?"[60]

Rather than clinging to a fixed image of Joan, Kleinman responded sensitively and tenderly to her needs as they changed throughout the course of her illness. When she lost her sight, he became her guide: "I took her by the hand, kissing it and her cheek, first just to remind her of how deeply loved she was, and later on . . . to assure her it was really me."[61] He also performed work such as bathing and toileting that was fraught with disgust triggers. When his son reprimanded him for ignoring Joan on one occasion, he took the criticism to heart and tried harder to engage her in family conversations. Like many family members, Kleinman delayed institutionalization long after he might reasonably have been expected to consider it. And when he finally decided to place Joan in a nursing home, he searched for one he believed could care for her with special warmth and attentiveness. He visited every evening.

Kitwood highlighted collaboration as an example of a "positive interaction" between caregivers and recipients.[62] Although Kleinman found caring for Joan frustrating, agonizing, and at times almost unbearable, he portrayed her as a critical member of their partnership rather than as a separate individual who imposed a terrible burden on him. As long as she could, she remained concerned about his well-being. "Emotional and moral reciprocity underwrote nearly every caregiving interaction. Without it there would have been little or no trust."[63]

Like many other memoir writers, Kleinman eventually began to focus more on loss than on continuity. Joan's final years "felt like the next circle of hell. . . . She would alternately become sad, agitated, and easily frightened; every once in a while she displayed flickers of suspicion bordering on paranoia."[64] Kleinman insisted that he was able to endure that period because caregiving had made him a better person. As his mother told his children, he had become "human."[65] Slowing down, he learned to enjoy the present. Although Kleinman rarely refers to stress, he notes that adherence to the stress-management advice for caregivers improved his health. Gradually he viewed himself becoming "a reflection of Joan, taking on many of the defining characteristics of the person she was before Alzheimer's disease took hold." He had "absorbed the best parts of her persona—the caring, the calming, the attention to details."[66]

Caring for his wife also sharpened Kleinman's critique of the medical profession. Although the primary care physicians he and Joan saw took an interest in their ongoing lives, the neurologists remained distant and impersonal, viewing dementia exclusively within a medical framework. We saw in the last chapter that they assured Kleinman that Joan's illness would advance in distinct stages. As a result, they asked only for information that would reveal the progression. When Kleinman mentioned anything else, they indicated he had transgressed the appropriate boundary between doctors and patients.

Kleinman acknowledges that every caregiving story is different; his own "reveals only so much."[67] He and Joan had not only distinctive personalities and dynamics but also multiple advantages. As a medical professional, he knew how to navigate the healthcare system. Although he never found a neurologist he liked, he understood medical technology and could find whatever other specialists Joan needed. He was surrounded by a loving family and could count on his children, mother, and occasionally other relatives for support. He also had significant financial advantages. One reason that caring for people with early-onset Alzheimer's disease tends to be especially difficult economically is that family members are often forced to retire prematurely.[68] Kleinman not only kept his well-paying job at Harvard but also received special accommodations. When Joan was still well enough to go to Harvard with him, the university provided aides to tend her—a gesture that must seem incredible to every parent who has ever needed employer-provided childcare. When she no longer could spend the day in his office, Kleinman had enough money to hire a professional caregiver to watch her at home five days a week. Although Joan originally resisted Sheilah's presence, the two women gradually formed a close relationship that Kleinman credits with slowing dementia's advance. And when the time came to look for nursing home care, he could pay for the best facility he could find.

Kleinman ignores other privileges he had long enjoyed. For example, although he notes the myriad ways Joan facilitated his career, he says little about other ways his gender contributed to his professional success. In 1960, two years before he entered medical school, women represented just 7 percent of medical students nationwide.[69] Few women at either the undergraduate or graduate level had male mentors who could launch their academic careers the way several senior professors catapulted Kleinman's. Like Joan Kleinman, many women who came of age in the 1940s and 1950s devoted themselves to childrearing for many years, regardless of any ambitions they may have had.[70] A common assumption is that women care more easily for elderly spouses and partners than do men because they have spent most of their lives as caregivers. *The Soul of Care* suggests that the opposite may equally be true. For Kleinman, attending to his wife's needs was a novel experience, allowing him to express the values he had espoused throughout his career. Women who have forfeited careers to care for children and other family members may view responsibilities for spouses and partners near the end of life as trapping them in a role they had long wanted to escape. Nevertheless, Kleinman demonstrates that the personhood perspective can benefit the caregiver as well as the recipient and presents a model of compassionate care practices others can try to emulate, even in less favorable circumstances.

Conclusion

Although advocates of the personhood model of dementia care look to family members as exemplars of best practices, families are not all of a piece. Not only do they differ in the extent to which they adopt the personhood perspective, but they also face a problem that has been common since the rise of scientific medicine and the new understanding of disease specificity at the end of the nineteenth century. To what extent should they view sick and disabled relatives as whole and unique individuals and to what extent as a configuration of symptoms? Because a diagnosis of dementia can call into question individuals' sense of personhood, that issue emerges in a particularly stark form for their caregivers. We have seen that although family members resist reducing relatives with dementia to their symptoms, caregivers cling to the diagnostic label and medical definitions of progression for various reasons—to muster resources for dealing with the problems that arise, develop techniques for coping with disturbing behaviors, and gain critical emotional distance from them.

Family members encounter another dilemma as well: How can they disentangle their desire to return to the past and enact old roles from the need to recognize and respond sensitively to current needs and wishes? Several caregivers in this study gradually realized they were trying to preserve a set of conditions that no longer had any meaning for their relatives. I personally experienced that issue in another way. In chapter 5, I discuss Jasmine Mehta, the pseudonym of the Trinidadian Indian woman my siblings and I hired to care for our father after our mother died. As he became more and more impaired, Jasmine gradually became the closest person to him. During his final hospitalization, my siblings and I realized that she was able to offer a type of sympathy and reassurance that greatly surpassed our own. When a question arose about where our father should spend his last weeks, we realized that Jasmine was more important than any of his children and that he had to remain where she could see him every day. We could reminisce and relate to him as our father, but she responded to him on the basis of the life they shared together. Near the end of his final hospitalization, she reminded him that it was time to plant the window boxes on the fire escape outside his apartment, as they did every spring, and asked him what colors he would like this year. Slowly, he responded, "Red, white, and blue." "OK," she said. "Soon we'll go home and plant red, white, and blue flowers." That was his last conversation. In this case, a formal service provider rather than a family member rendered the kind of care many advocates of the personhood perspective consider most appropriate.[71]

3

Looking to the Past

What the Nineteenth Century Can Tell Us

Several pundits recently have declared a "care crisis" in the United States.[1] Although they focused first on childcare, they increasingly have expanded their purview to include elder care as well. Commentators who sound the alarm about our care crisis often point to several factors to argue that family care for elderly people is more challenging than ever before and is thus more likely to inflict serious physical and mental health problems.[2]

The first is the demographic transformation. The elderly, who constituted 4 percent of the population in 1900, increased to 8 percent in 1950 and then to 16 percent by 2019.[3] The rate of increase of Americans eighty-five and over has been particularly dramatic; the "old old" are the fastest-growing segment of the population.[4] Although most people sixty-five and over can tend themselves and their households without assistance, the prevalence of disability rises steeply with age.[5] Caregivers, too, are often older than they were before; many must cope simultaneously with their own age-related health issues. And the caregiver support ratio is expected to drop. In 2018 there were seven people ages forty-five to sixty-four for every person eighty and over, but that ratio will decline to three to one by 2050.[6]

Second, the major causes of death are now chronic diseases (heart disease, cancer, and stroke) that often inflict years of infirmity. Although physicians can now save the lives of many people who previously would have died quickly from those conditions, the survivors frequently endure severe disabilities over extended periods. As a result, caregiving often lasts a long time. In 2015, more than half (60.5 percent) of primary caregivers provided care for four years or more.[7] Moreover, many elderly people suffer from multiple chronic ailments, including Alzheimer's disease and other cognitive impairments.[8]

Third, caregivers often face competing demands. Fifty-seven percent of women had paid employment in 2017.[9] Those who relinquish their jobs, reduce their hours of work, rearrange their schedules, and take time off without pay to provide care experience serious financial penalties.[10] As a result of delayed childbearing, many women care simultaneously for children and aging parents. Nearly 46 percent of female caregivers and 40 percent of male caregivers can be considered members of this "sandwich generation."[11]

Fourth, the average length of stay dropped after the establishment of a prospective payment system for hospital care under Medicare in 1983. A substantial amount of care, including skilled care, was then transferred from hospitals to families.[12] Family caregiving today thus includes much more than providing assistance with activities of daily living (ADLs), such as bathing, dressing, and eating, and instrumental activities of daily living (IADLs), such as shopping and managing finances. *Home Alone*, a 2010 report from the AARP and United Hospital Foundation, revealed that nearly half (46 percent) of caregivers also perform medical and nursing tasks once considered the exclusive domain of trained healthcare providers, including medication management, wound care, and operation of specialized medical equipment.[13] *Home Alone Revisited*, issued seven years later, examined the difficulties of furnishing that kind of care and the serious consequences for family members.[14]

But is caregiving today really more difficult than it was in the past? Can we even compare different eras in terms of the costs of delivering family care? Two prominent researchers conclude that nineteenth-century caregiving was much easier than it is today. Harold Braswell, a healthcare ethicist, focuses on the end of life. Noting that death often arrived suddenly, he writes, "The role of the familial caregiver was not to dramatically reduce the dying individual's pain, since pain reduction was impossible prior to the advent of anesthesiology. Rather, the role of the caregiver was to tend to the dying person's body as ably as possible while bearing witness, preferably in the company of a religious advisor, to their transition to the afterlife. This primarily religious standard of care made family caregiving relatively accessible."[15] It is true that the concept of *ars moriendi*, or the art of dying, spread widely in the nineteenth century, reaching people of various social and religious backgrounds. The basic elements of the good death were consciousness and lucidity, resignation to God's will, and fortitude in the face of physical pain and emotional suffering. The moment of death was the ultimate test, and family and friends searched for evidence that the dying person had passed it well and therefore could hope for eternal salvation. But if nineteenth-century writing emphasized the state of the soul, the body demanded attention. Men and especially women administered medications to dying people, applied poultices, watched for dangerous symptoms, changed dressings, and cleaned up vomit, excrement, pus, and blood; after death occurred, friends and family washed the body and laid it out.

In a section titled "From Sitting to Surgery," sociologist Mignon Duffy does note some of the work of care performed throughout the disease course: "[Professed] nurses, along with the mothers, daughters, and wives they assisted, were responsible for tasks as varied as changing bandages, applying leeches or plasters, preparing special foods or tonics, and 'sitting' with patients to monitor their condition and to provide emotional support."[16] But she implies that because those tasks were far removed from the "complex diagnostic and treatment processes in health care today," they imposed relatively few burdens. In what follows, I argue that caregiving responsibilities were constant and unremitting and often inflicted serious costs on women.[17]

Caregiving Obligations

Because mutual aid was often a requirement of participating in social life as well as a form of insurance in the nineteenth century, responsibilities extended very broadly. Women in isolated rural areas sometimes cared for strangers who needed assistance far from home. When George Cutter was wounded in a battle in 1856, he was taken to the home of John and Sarah Everett, who nursed him for more than six months.[18] Women moving west from the east coast stopped to assist strangers they passed along the way. Charlotte Stearns Pengra, a traveler on the Overland Trail, rode with women from other parties to help a woman afflicted with "camp colic": "I thought her case almost hopeless, but after applying numerous remedies we succeeded in relieving her."[19] Frances Sawyer, another woman who made the trip west, wrote in her diary, "Tonight we visited an adjoining camp to see a lady and her daughter who had turned over in a carriage today with coming down a steep mountain-side."[20]

Many women also cared for an extensive network of kin and neighbors. In 1867, Laura Stebbens explained why she could not join her friend in reform work: "My eldest Aunt, almost eighty, is so very frail and feeble, that I ques[tion] very seriously the propriety of my leaving—both [aunts] are very helpless and in sudden illness—or of accidents, they might suffer much; and then I should reflect upon myself exceedingly."[21]

A diary written by Nannie Stillwell Jackson in 1890 and 1891 portrays women's neighborhood obligations in unusually rich detail. The wife of a small farmer in Arkansas, Nannie saw her close friend Fannie Morgan as often as four times a day. In addition, Nannie frequently exchanged goods and services with at least twenty other women, both white and African American. Care for sick and dying people was embedded in this collective female life. When Mrs. Dyer "was terribly afflicted with boils," Nannie visited her, along with several other women. Both Nannie and Fannie spent time at the home of Mrs. Caulk when her baby was ill. When Nannie herself fell ill, Fannie cooked breakfast for her; Mrs. Gifford and Bettie Newby came by in the evening. Sickness at the Archdale home required a range of services from several women. On March 22, Nannie "set a while" with Mrs. Archdale's sons Bill and Lee, both of whom had pneumonia. She continued to visit the house regularly over the next few days, reporting on March 28 that the sons were better but that the daughter had contracted the disease. On April 8 Mrs. Archdale became ill and sent for Nannie; Nannie, in turn, summoned Fannie, and together they gave Mrs. Archdale "a dose of oil and turpentine and some gum camphor." Various other women spent the next few nights with the patient. On April 13, Mrs. Archdale took a turn for the worse. Nannie visited her "5 or 6 times," and she and Fannie spent the night. When Mrs. Archdale died the following day, several women "dressed her and laid her out."[22]

Two obligations of neighborliness were especially onerous. Because infectious diseases were rampant, infants and children frequently required nursing care. Common nineteenth-century killers included pneumonia, typhus, typhoid fever, diphtheria, scarlet fever, measles, whooping cough, and dysentery. A high proportion of the sufferers were infants and children. During epidemics, women moved continually from house to house in the community, exposing themselves and their own families to disease. In February 1859, Emily Hawley, the daughter of Michigan farmers, noted in her diary that her sister was "real sick with scarlet fever. Mrs. Wiley's little girl died with it last night." The following month Hawley wrote, "Not hardly a day but we hear of a death, sometimes more. There were five funerals . . . last Sunday." Five days later she reported, "Attended the funeral of Mrs. Wiley's little boy . . . now all their children are dead, sad, sad."[23]

Large families required women not only to care repeatedly for very sick children but also to lend assistance at frequent deliveries. Because childbirth was extremely hazardous, attendants often had to assume responsibility for critically ill newborns and women. Some women completed their work by laying out the infants they had helped to deliver. On January 9, 1890, Emily French recounted the events of the previous night: "Mrs. Sloans sick all the night, I up with her, the child a girl still born at 8 this morning. . . . Her Annie, 16 months is her baby yet. I put all away as best I could, got a place for the child, a nice smooth box."[24] Common maternal complications included hemorrhage, convulsions, and puerperal fever. Announcing the birth of her first grandchild in October 1861, Mary

Ann Webber expressed thanks that her daughter was spared and then explained, "We thought Saturday morning that she would die or at least we very much feared the event, but God saved her. She is not yet out of danger, although she now is as comfortable as could be expected."[25] And if fewer caregivers had to deal with their own age-related health problems, many were pregnant themselves. Emma Reid wrote to her father from Idaho territory in 1881, "For three weeks preceding my confinement, we had six children down at once, five of ours and one of the Warrens who had come to help us. Twenty nights I took my turn sitting up half the night, then when I knew that I, too, must soon be a care, I finished the night. And the next day, just across the hall from my little boys moaning in their delirium, I gave birth to twin girls."[26]

Chronic Disease

Chronic illness has always been with us. Tuberculosis, or consumption as it often was called, is an ancient scourge. In the early nineteenth century, it was the fifth major cause of death.[27] Robert Koch's discovery of the tubercle bacillus in 1883 galvanized the world but produced neither a vaccine nor a cure. Although some sufferers enjoyed periods of remission after symptoms appeared, permanent cure was impossible before the 1946 advent of antibiotics. Caregiving thus often extended over years. Martha Shaw, a woman in Topeka, Kansas, had been married to her postman husband, Johnny, for two years when he showed the first signs of tuberculosis in 1893. His sickness required her to provide nursing care for many years. Especially in the later stages, patients coughed and vomited frequently, soiling themselves, their beds, and sometimes even the walls around them. Caregiving also included traveling frequently in search of a cure. In the late nineteenth century, it was widely believed that the western climate had a beneficial effect on TB sufferers. The Shaws traveled twice to Colorado for periods of several months and then in the fall of 1992 departed for Los Angeles. Although notorious for its polluted air today, the metropolis once billed itself as a health resort. The couple arrived back in Topeka three months before Johnny died.[28]

Although we tend to think that the shift from acute illnesses to chronic disorders as the major cause of death is a recent phenomenon, it occurred more than a century ago. As early as 1914, the New York Academy of Medicine announced that "more people die from chronic disease than from acute."[29] More precise information came from Louis I. Dublin, the chief statistician of the Metropolitan Life Insurance Company. Drawing on data collected between 1911 and 1922, he reported in 1925 that the cancer death rate had significantly increased. "We are now confronted with a new situation," he wrote. With "the reduction in the mortality from other conditions . . . [and] with every improvement in the condition of life in the early ages, more and more people will approach the later period [of life] when the population is exposed to the cancer menace."[30] By 1940, cancer caused 165,000 deaths annually in the United States.[31] Despite his initial focus on cancer, Dublin was well aware that other chronic conditions added even more significantly to the death toll. Heart disease was the leading killer, responsible for 385,000 deaths in 1940; hypertension and arteriosclerosis accounted for an additional 144,000.[32]

Chronically ill patients, however, had low status. Private general hospitals admitted people with long-term ailments only when they qualified for curative treatment. Those who failed to improve were dispatched to public hospitals as soon as possible. Interviewed by the Federal Writers' Project in 1939, an intern remarked, "City Hospitals get all the 'crocks' . . . this is patients who are really what we call chronics."[33] And dumping did not end when patients reached the public system. After receiving chronically ill people from private facilities, public acute-care hospitals sent them to chronic-disease hospitals with miserable conditions. As historian Daniel M. Fox writes, policy makers "regarded the management of chronic illness and disability as mainly a problem for people with the lower incomes. The needs of the chronically sick or injured poor would be met by state mental hospitals, by the sanatoria and general hospitals run by the city and county government."[34]

In the 1930s, Dublin belonged to a small group of doctors, statisticians, and public health officials who argued that the growing prominence of chronic disorders demanded a shift in medical priorities. Criticizing "the fetishism of the acute," they campaigned for increased funding for research into the causes of chronic afflictions and better care for the sufferers.[35] Those calls went unanswered. The healthcare system that developed in subsequent decades was heavily biased toward acute conditions. But if health policy makers ignored chronic care, family members could not. Caregivers have long had to care for people with conditions that lasted for weeks, months, or even years.

Competing Responsibilities

During most of the nineteenth century, caregiving was more likely to conflict with domestic labor than with paid employment. Household work for most women was extremely arduous. Although the manufacture of textiles, soap, and candles moved into the factory early in the century, indoor plumbing did not reach most households until the twentieth century. Laundry alone was a day-long ordeal, demanding that women carry gallons of water, lug pails of wet clothes, scrub and rinse each item, and hang it on the line, exposing their hands in the process to lye and other caustic soaps.[36]

When women left their homes to respond to pleas for help, their housework accumulated in their absence. Nannie Jackson and her husband watched a sick woman throughout most of one night. When they returned home, Nannie's husband "laid down and took a nap." Her work, however, could not wait. "I churned and cooked breakfast and had it ready before daylight," she wrote in her diary. A week later, she noted that she had spent most of the day caring for another sick friend and, as a result, had "done no work."[37] A mission of mercy had serious economic consequences for Effie Hanson, a North Dakota farm woman.

Writing to a friend about the assistance she and her husband rendered when her mother-in-law was dying, Effie noted, "We lost some chickens [during] those cold spells as we wasn't home to take care of them as we should."[38]

Some of the tasks women performed when family members fell ill were indistinguishable from their routine household labor. But sickness also imposed extra burdens, such as cooking custards, gruels, and broths, preparing special tonics, and washing blood- and sweat-stained sheets and clothes. Because hospitalization rarely was an option, women had to provide personal care, even for critically ill patients. "It is hard to have the care of a poor sick man day after day, week after week," wrote Mary Ann Webber, a Vermont woman, to her son in 1871 when her husband lay dying. Dressing him, getting him in and out of bed, helping him walk, and bathing him consumed time and energy she previously had devoted to her daily chores. As he grew progressively weaker, her burdens multiplied. Although she was familiar with heavy farm work, lifting a bedridden man several times a day taxed her strength.[39] Marian Louise Moore, an Ohio homesteader, remembered her experience nursing her mother: "In the Spring of the year 1872 . . . she was sick three months, part of the time helpless [with] typhoid inflammatory rheumatism. . . . This sickness of hers brought more work upon me, washing and other work, then I had more work of my own than I could possibly do well."[40]

Women who left home to seek paid employment were often forced to return when family members fell ill. After Malenda Edwards quit her job in the mills to care for her parents, she wrote to a friend that she was serving as "physician and nurse too" and would travel west were it not for the need to provide care.[41] Velma Leadbetter had learned dressmaking in hopes of achieving economic independence. Her work separated her from her family in Nanticoke Valley in New York, but she was recalled periodically to assist during sickness. Her daughter later wrote, "The maiden woman in a country family belongs to everybody in case of illness . . . Call on her and she'd come home and take care of the mother or the father who was ill. So Mother would have to hang a sign out, saying 'I'm sorry but I've gone up to my father's.' . . . They thought *nothing* of calling her out like that."[42] Even entry into a profession did not excuse single women from the duty to care. Mary Holywell Everett was a successful physician when her sister became ill. A male colleague to whom she had written counseled her this way: "Even at the risk of losing your practice entirely, duty commands you to remain by the side of your old mother and help her to carry the burden." Writing to Everett about her absence from her practice, a patient commented, "Being that you have no husband, your dear mother has the first claim to you."[43]

The history of nineteenth-century women teachers is filled with stories of women who left their posts to nurse family members. Lettie Teeple had just begun her first teaching job in Michigan in 1848 when she "was hurried away from school by [family] sickness."[44] Sarah Gillespie was nineteen and had just begun her teaching career when her mother, Emily, fell ill in the fall of 1884. As Emily's health deteriorated, Sarah increasingly was torn between her responsibilities as a daughter and as a teacher. After a visit home in June 1885, Sarah expressed her concerns about leaving her mother with only a "hired girl" to help: "Ma has the dropsy to her body. . . . She did not sleep she said her feet & legs pain her so badly—Now if I was there I'd rub them for her—But there is nothing done for her at all." On May 16, 1886, Emily suffered a stroke, and Sarah resigned her job. She was able to return to school in November, but when a new term began in April 1887, she deferred opening the school to stay home an extra week. Instead of boarding in the community, she traveled the nine miles between home and school each morning and evening in order to tend her mother. When the term ended in June, Sarah returned home and devoted herself to her mother's care. Even when Emily lay dying in March 1888, the offer of a new teaching job sorely tempted Sarah, much as she tried to convince herself otherwise. "No—I can not teach no use to think of it now," she wrote nine days before her mother's death.[45]

Enslaved women faced the cruelest conflict between work and care. A host of illnesses, including dysentery, typhus, diarrhea, rheumatic fever, diphtheria, and whooping cough, ravaged slave communities. Quarters were overcrowded and lacked proper sanitation and ventilation; hard physical labor, combined with inadequate rest, diet, and clothing, heightened vulnerability to disease. In addition, disabilities frequently resulted from accidents and brutal punishments. Unsurprisingly, enslaved people had higher rates of mortality than whites. The conditions of the slave quarters, which abetted the spread of disease, also made caregiving a herculean endeavor. A cabin consisted of one room with a dirt floor, no window, cracks in the walls, and a chimney made of clay and twigs. Two or more families frequently shared such cabins, which measured between ten and twenty-one feet square. The great majority of families lacked privies and any sanitary means of garbage disposal. Enslaved women could eke out time to care for their families only when they returned at night, exhausted from work in the fields or big house. Care for sick members of owners' families had to take precedence over care for enslaved women's kin.[46]

Medical Care

The great majority of nineteenth-century women delivered care without the help of formal services. In 1873, the nation had only 120 hospitals, most of which were custodial institutions for poor people. Middle-class patients rarely entered them.[47] Although low-income people had fewer options, most families were reluctant to entrust sick relatives to such facilities. After hearing that her husband had been wounded in battle, Harriet Jane Thompson wrote to him, "Dear William, do take care of yourself and not go into the hospital if you can possibly avoid it for there you are apt to get disease and not be taken care of."[48]

Doctors also were scarce. Many families could not afford the fees physicians charged. Without telephones or automobiles, summoning physicians involved considerable time and effort. Women who did rely on doctors typically resorted to them only after exhausting their own remedies. According to a history of nursing in nineteenth-century Kansas, when epidemics of diphtheria, scarlet fever, smallpox, whooping cough, and typhoid fever swept through the state, families sought "professional advice so rarely that when a physician was called it was understood that death was probably imminent."[49] Moreover, physician care did not replace neighborhood assistance. During both sickness and childbirth, female friends and kin continued to make major treatment decisions and exercise medical skills after doctors arrived.

Most caregivers had even less contact with nurses. Although nursing did not begin to organize into a profession until late in the century, many women worked as "professed nurses." But their cost was prohibitive for many families, and those who could afford to pay for nursing care often chose not to.[50] Louisa May Alcott claimed that she intended to hire a nurse during her mother's long illness but could find none who met her standards. She later employed a nurse to care for her father, but only because her own poor health prevented her from caring for him herself.[51]

Because formal health practitioners could not claim special competence, they had little to offer. We take for granted an enormous chasm between professional and lay knowledge and skills, but throughout most of the nineteenth century little distinguished the ideas and practices of physicians from those of family caregivers. Lacking special diagnostic tools, doctors were restricted to therapies that could elicit swift and dramatic symptomatic change. Family members as well as doctors could observe the results. In an account of her husband's death in 1855, Mary Ann Owen Sims wrote, "He requested me to examine the blister (that the Drs. had put on his thigh during the night) . . . I told him it was not drawing [blood]."[52]

In many cases, doctors and family members assumed similar responsibilities. Before the advent of asepsis and antisepsis at the end of the nineteenth century, surgical care consisted largely of dressing wounds, setting broken limbs, and lancing boils. Many women felt competent to perform these procedures on their own. In 1884, Emily Gillespie, a farm woman, wrote that her son Henry hit his thumb with an axe and "cut it nearly off." "Deeara-me it is too bad," she wrote. "He held it on while I done it up. I hope it will grow on again without leaving too bad a scar."[53] Two weeks before Emily Gillespie died four years later, her daughter Sarah wrote in her diary, "Her bedsores are very painful—one which is a trifle better now is 3 in. deep and 2 ½ in. in diameter. I have to cut out the 'puss' and cleanse them often and it fairly makes my veins refuse to carry the blood sometimes."[54] When Martha Shaw cared for her husband with tuberculosis in 1890, she was responsible for his surgical wound although "it looked so badly," she could "not bear to touch him."[55]

The overlap was even greater in the area of pharmaceutical care. Doctors carried powders in their saddlebags and concocted different remedies at their patients' homes. But physicians did not have a monopoly on the administration of medications. Many women kept a stock of herbs, which they picked up in the woods or from their gardens during the summer and "put up" each fall, along with preserved foods. One of the first tasks of women who migrated west was planting the "starts" they brought with them. Like many other forms of production, drug manufacturing gradually moved out of the home. Even such potent medications as mercury were available in many local stores and could be administered without physician oversight. "I expect this will smell of calomel, oil, etc.," wrote Abby Bright in her journal, soon after arriving at the home of her brother and his family in Indiana in 1871. "The children have been quite sick with lung fever, are a little better but very restless." By the turn of the century, an enormous variety of patient medicines were available.[56]

The Costs of Care

Although nineteenth-century women often derived important gratifications from delivering care, the work also exacted a heavy toll. Many women attributed their own ill health to the burdens of care. Six weeks before Emily Gillespie died, her daughter Sarah complained about back problems, which she blamed on the strain of lifting her mother. Because she had little time to eat, she lost weight. Constant chores and lack of sleep left her exhausted. She considered herself an invalid in the year following the death. We saw that Mary Ann Webber complained to her son about her exhaustion when caring for her husband. Louisa May Alcott wrote five months after her mother's death, "I too have been ill and still am ordered to keep still for some months. Too much nursing last summer was bad for me."[57]

Conclusion

Anthropologist Elana D. Burch writes, "Discussions of care and aging sometimes tend toward orientalism and nostalgia for places and times before modernity, globalization, and capitalism when families cared for their elders. Yet many of these care arrangements depended on forms of gender socialization and coercion because, in previous eras as now, women were disproportionately recruited to provide elder care."[58] Some family members and policy analysts use romanticized images of the nineteenth century to justify the present state of affairs. But there was no golden age of family caregiving. The need for care kept nineteenth-century women tightly bound to the home, imposed overwhelming burdens on them, and increased their risk of disease. If they had fewer responsibilities for older people, they had far more obligations for sick and dying children and parturient women. Rather than limiting caregiving to immediate family members, women cared for extended kin, neighbors, and occasionally even strangers. Women also faced competing demands on their time and energy. Very few women entered the labor force, but the intrusion of caregiving on household work often had serious consequences. Although most nineteenth-century women responded to relatively brief events (births, acute illnesses, and deaths), some rendered care over long periods of time. And women delivered what was considered medical care. To be sure, such care is very different today. As a result of advances in various specialties, medical care is far more complex and technologically sophisticated than ever before. Isolated in individual houses, caregivers cannot depend on friends and community members for assistance. And they must follow distinct protocols, not rely on their own expertise. Nevertheless, this history rebuts the notion that this generation of caregivers is the first to provide care for the kinds of problems we now consider the exclusive province of trained professionals.

4

The Elder Care Crisis

The Tyranny of the Family-Responsibility Ethic

Acknowledging that certain patterns are long-standing is very differ-ent from concluding that they are inevitable or immutable. Although caregiving is not more challenging than ever before, many present-day family members have difficulty fulfilling their obligations. Rebecca Sol-nit reminds us that the medical definition of a crisis is "the crossroads a patient reaches, the point at which she will either take the road to recov-ery or to death."[1] In that sense, "elder care crisis" is an appropriate term; we have arrived at a moment when it is critical to find radical alterna-tives to the existing situation. The crisis results from policies based on an ethic of family responsibility that not only imposes unsustainable burdens on family caregivers but also contributes to the dismal employ-ment conditions of direct care workers.

Family Responsibility and Long-Term Care Policies

Sociologist Melinda Cooper argues that, since the late 1970s and early 1980s, neoliberals and social conservatives have joined forces to attack welfare programs by invoking the ethic of family responsibility. Neo-liberals seek to shrink government control by relying on the market for benefits. Social conservatives want to bolster the traditional heteronor-mative family structure, and especially women's role in it, which they view as having been under siege since the 1960s. In times of trouble, both groups assert, individuals should look to their kin rather than the state for support.[2] Here it is important to note that widely shared normative beliefs assume that caring responsibilities arise from family relationships. Although we may exempt people with family histories of abuse and exploitation from that duty, we expect family members to care for their own in most instances. The question is how far that responsibility extends and who gets to decide.[3] In the United States, which offers less generous long-term care services than most other Organization for Economic Cooperation and Development (OECD) nations, policy makers focus on family responsibility to justify parsimonious public funding.[4]

In his 1981 inaugural address, President Ronald Reagan declared that "government is not the solution to our problem; government is the problem." His administration then proceeded to cut various social programs, forcing individuals to rely on families for assistance. The next four administrations followed his lead. Indeed, as Cooper notes, Clinton's welfare reform act of 1996 finally realized "Reagan's dream of a fully federalized system of familial responsibility."[5]

Cooper says little about family caregiving for sick and disabled people, but the family-values crusade had perhaps its greatest success in that area. The Tax, Equity, and Fiscal Responsibility Act (TEFRA), passed by Congress in August 1982 and signed by Reagan the following month, added hospice as a covered benefit under Medicare. Most observers agree that the primary motivation was to transfer care work to families in order to contain healthcare costs. Alarmed by the amount of government money spent on caring for elderly people in their final months of life, legislators were eager to find a way to reduce that expense. Growing popular support for hospice ideals undoubtedly facilitated the passage of the benefit, but that outcome was ensured by a report of the Congressional Budget Office concluding that the government could save as much as $1,120 for each Medicare beneficiary who enrolled in hospice. A sunset clause limited the benefit to a three-year period; renewal would depend on a report on the program's cost effectiveness.[6]

Legislators capped hospice payments at 75 percent of the average cost of caring for Medicare beneficiaries in hospitals in the last six months of life, subsequently reducing it to 40 percent, far too low, many hospice leaders argued, to enable them to provide high-quality services. The savings were to come primarily from the continued reliance on unpaid kin. Robert Dole, who introduced the hospice provision in the Senate, later asserted that its passage "was possible because many believe, as I do, that it is less costly to care for a patient at home, foregoing expensive hospital treatment." Andrea Sankar, an anthropologist who studied family members helping people die at home during the late 1980s shortly after the passage of TEFRA, found that although the work could be extremely rewarding, it also made enormous physical and emotional demands: "Common actions and activities that people take for granted can become overwhelming problems and ordeals for patient and caregiver. Eating, sleeping, taking a pill, drinking a glass of water, elimination, taking a bath, keeping the patient clean, turned and free from bedsores, going outside—all represent major undertakings for both." Procedures caregivers frequently were expected to perform included suctioning, catheterization, disimpaction of bowels, administration of enemas, and injections.[7] Nevertheless, the burdens of caring for dying patients at home received little attention in congressional hearings on the Medicare provision. To many advocates of the hospice benefit, families appear to have represented primarily a cheap form of labor.[8]

Some family members praise hospices for fulfilling their goal of delivering holistic care for people at the end of life. Historian Sara Evans, for example, wrote that "Solace" was "a good name" for the "wonderful facility" where her mother spent her final days. "From the moment she arrived she was enfolded in a community of caregivers whose sole purpose [was] comfort on every level—physical, emotional, spiritual."[9] But many others complain that the amount of help hospices offer is seriously inadequate. "Even the most astute caregiver," wrote Kathryn Temple, a professor of English, "might have difficulty getting past the hospice promotional literature to discover just what the limits of the promised 'care' might be." Journalist Hillary Johnson recalled that as her mother "deteriorated, her care became exponentially complicated and demanding. A hospice nurse would visit each day, but for the remaining twenty-three hours, we were on our own."[10] Diane Meier, a physician and professor of geriatrics and palliative care, used similar words: "We send very very sick, complicated patients home under the care of family members who are not trained professionals. . . . They are on-call 24/7 and have to be alert to changes at all times. They don't get to go home after an eight-hour shift." Although hospices provide some assistance, it tends to be very paltry. "Ninety-nine minutes out of 100," Meier concludes, "the family is on its own."[11]

As the last chapter noted, families also have more care work earlier in the disease course. Soon after passing the hospice legislation, Congress established a prospective payment system for hospital care under Medicare, resulting in a drop in the average length of stay. A 1989 study found that in the first five years, that policy transferred twenty-one million days of care work from hospitals to families.[12] Patients arrive home sicker as well as quicker, increasing the intensity of services family members must deliver. In many cases high-tech equipment follows patients out of the hospital. Technologies recently adapted for the home include dialysis, ventilators, cardiac and apnea monitors, feeding tubes, and infusion pumps for administering narcotics, antibiotics, and chemotherapy. Some technologies must be constantly monitored, and many require families to perform tasks that previously were considered the exclusive domain of trained nurses.[13]

In the early 1980s, escalating nursing home costs caused even more alarm than rising hospital expenditures. Reagan administration officials were thus especially anxious to transfer responsibility for long-term care from institutions to families. Many older Americans assume that Medicare covers nursing home stays, but that program is tilted toward acute care and pays less than 15 percent of nursing home residents. Medicaid, a joint federal-state, means-tested program, is the primary funding source, covering 63 percent of residents.[14] Eligibility rules differ among the states, but only people with little income and no assets other than a home, car, household goods, life insurance, and burial funds can qualify. Those with too much money can "spend down" their resources to the eligibility level.[15] Although originally intended to assist poor women and children, Medicaid directed more than 40 percent of its funds to nursing homes in the early 1980s.[16] A 1980 report prepared for the Health Care Financing Administration (HCFA, later the Centers for Medicare and Medicaid Services) was one of the first to examine the dimensions of the problem. "Total expenditures for nursing home care under the Medicaid program [had] increased drastically" (from $800 million in 1967 to $6.4 billion ten years later) and showed "no signs of abating." The government therefore had to find a way to control the costs. The authors rejected the idea that families be required to pay part of the expense of nursing home care. Although that practice was consistent with welfare policy dating back to the Elizabethan Poor Laws in Britain, it had been prohibited in the United States in 1971. The solution was thus to provide incentives to encourage family members to deliver additional care.[17]

Medicaid initially had been biased toward institutional care, funding a negligible amount of home- and community-based services (HCBS). The HCFA article noted that correcting that imbalance could enable family members to delay or avoid nursing home care. The authors insisted that "there must be caution not to widen too broadly the use of funds for home care purposes other than those related to cost containment." Upholding the principle of family responsibility, the authors declared that access should be limited to persons "at imminent risk of institutional care." (That measure was intended to counter the "woodwork effect," the propensity of people who do not need institutional care to come out of the woodwork to demand HCBS and thus drive up the total cost of care.) Determination should rest not with family members but rather with professionals, who are uniquely equipped to assess the level of disability and the amount of care relatives "can reasonably and fairly be expected to give."[18] The principles embedded in that report have continued to underlie public policy today: family members cannot be entrusted with deciding how much care they can provide, and noninstitutional services can be justified only insofar as they substitute for institutional ones and thus help to contain overall costs.

The year that report appeared, the Department of Health and Human Services launched the National Long Term Care Demonstration (also known as the Channeling Demonstration), a massive social experiment spanning ten states. The goal was to determine whether community services could be a cost-effective alternative to nursing home care. The projects began in 1982 and ended three years later.[19] The results were disappointing: the infusion of funds for care outside institutions failed to save money by postponing expensive nursing home care. There was, however, one positive finding: additional funding for home- and community-based care did not encourage family caregivers to withdraw their services. "The best news in the findings for advocates of increased community care benefits," wrote Rosalie Kane, a professor of social work and public health, "was that family members made no major reductions in the care and attention they gave the sample members. The dropoff in informal care was slight, occurring mostly among distant relatives and friends rather than close relatives and, arguably, could be said to have been appropriate." The government could thus expand noninstitutional services, safe in the knowledge that family members would continue to serve as the backbone of the long-term care system. Kane noted that caregivers who had access to services were more likely "to feel confident in the care their relative was receiving." But that benefit "was unlikely to impress legislators as worthy of a high price tag."[20] The evaluators also found some improvement in caregivers' well-being, another finding that was deemed unimportant.[21] The goal was to cut expenditures, not improve the quality of life of either caregivers or their recipients.

The Medicare Alzheimer's Disease Demonstration, conducted between 1989 and 1994, replicated the Channeling Demonstration but focused on dementia. The results were equally discouraging. Case management and funding for community care did not significantly reduce caregivers' burden and depression, the number of hours they spent helping relatives, and the rates of nursing home placement.[22]

Because both studies examined a relatively modest range of services, they left open the possibility that a more robust set would have a greater effect. The government thus slowly began to increase funding for home- and community-based services in the early 1980s, most notably through a provision allowing states to apply for waivers to include more HCBS under Medicaid.[23] The proportion of Medicaid funds directed to non-institutional services grew from 11 percent in 1988 to 27 percent in 2000 and then to 45 percent by 2018.[24] Because most disabled elderly people want to remain home, humanitarian as well as economic concerns may have helped to drive the change. Another major impetus for that shift was the 1999 Supreme Court decision in *Olmstead v. L.C.*, holding that disabled people have a right to services in the community and cannot be compelled to enter institutions.[25]

Despite the assurances from the National Long Term Care Demonstration that family members were not eager to surrender caregiving obligations, policy makers continued to worry that publicly funded services would replace those now provided "free." A host of researchers sought to lay those fears to rest. As a study of the Texas Medicaid program between 2006 and 2008 reported, "Medicaid policy makers need not be overly concerned about a potential adverse effect of expanded coverage for formal care on the level of informal care available to adults and older persons."[26] That conclusion can be explained in various ways. One is that family members must devote considerable time and attention to mediating between elderly relatives and formal service providers. Especially when older people have cognitive problems, family members are responsible for applying for Medicaid, a cumbersome and lengthy process that can last several months.[27] Family members tend to have even more obligations in the growing number of consumer-directed programs. Although credited with empowering participants, those programs often rely on relatives to hire, train, supervise, and in some cases fire homecare workers.[28]

Moreover, caregivers typically adhere to the same cultural values as policy makers. Viewing the delivery of care as a family responsibility, they hesitate to search for whatever public services are available. Many support-group leaders in Los Angeles interviewed by sociologist Sandra

R. Levitsky said that part of their job is encouraging family members to get help.[29] Those who do contact service agencies tend to make more modest requests than professionals deem appropriate.[30] In addition, the fear that family members will withdraw when public programs are available rests on the assumption that the two are interchangeable. Family members, however, view caregiving as a complex, intimate relationship, not as a series of discrete tasks.[31] That may be especially true for women, who still dominate this activity. Various studies indicate that men and women experience personal relationships very differently. Fathers are more likely than mothers to take an instrumental approach to their children, focusing on a series of specific activities and remaining more distant and detached. Mothers are more likely to emphasize the relational aspects of care—to experience closeness and connectedness with their children and express empathy. Recent research suggests that those generalizations apply to elderly men and women who care for spouses or partners.[32]

Finally, both federal and state Medicaid programs have erected safeguards to ensure that family members do not relinquish services. Following the recommendation of the Health Care Financing Administration consultants, the federal Medicaid program restricted HCBS to people at risk of institutional placement. By then, families typically have been providing care for long periods of time. In addition, many state programs authorize only those services family members cannot provide. Oregon's Medicaid program offers one example. Eligible individuals can choose to receive home- and community-based services from either a home health agency or the Consumer-Employed Program, hiring a homecare worker on their own. In both instances, case managers conduct initial assessments to determine how many hours and what kinds of services the individual needs. According to instructions on the published assessment tool, case managers should look first for "natural supports" (NS), a term implying that publicly funded supports are unnatural. NS can include family, neighbors, friends, roommates, and members of community groups. The instructions provide the following example to illustrate how conversations with NS should be conducted: "You said you assist your mother with one of her two showers each week. Can you continue to provide those showers? The [homecare worker] has been authorized 13 hours per month to bathe your mother the 2nd time each week." A note then reads, "Without the NS the consumer would be eligible for up to 25 full assist hours. Because the consumer has a NS providing for ½ the bathing hours each week, the conversation would start at the point of what hours the individual is 'authorized,' not that the rule permits up to 25 hours if a NS wasn't part of the service." The Consumer-Employed Program allows NS to receive pay as homecare workers but only if they first explain why they no longer can provide services for free. Under the heading "Pitfalls," the instructions continue, "Do NOT ask leading payment questions! For example, do not ask: 'You are now providing care without being paid. Did you know you could be paid to do these tasks?'"[33] To some extent, programs supported by state funds help to supplement Medicaid services for low-income, elderly people. Most, however, offer a narrow range of services, cover few people, and seek to complement rather than replace family care.[34]

The public services we have examined never were intended to reach more than a tiny slice of the population. Although wealthy families can pay privately for chronic care, most people risk economic ruin if they attempt to do so.[35] Despite hopes that the private insurance market would be able to cover the expenses, only approximately 7 percent of people over fifty had long-term care insurance in 2020, a figure that represents a significant decline from the previous decade.[36] In 2017, the median income of elderly households was $42,113. The median cost of a home healthcare aide for thirty hours a week was $33,540. At a daily cost of $70, the median annual cost of adult day services five days a week was $18,200.[37] Some elderly people go without crucial services. Some overburden family members. Some qualify for Medicaid after exhausting their resources on care.

But even Medicaid recipients often fail to obtain adequate care. States differ in the extent to which they provide Medicaid HCBS, and most programs have long waiting lists.[38] A 2005 study reported that more than half (58 percent) of people eligible for both Medicare and Medicaid had unmet needs for help with daily activities. As a result, a high proportion had fallen, wet or soiled themselves, and been unable to bathe or shower as often as they wanted.[39] Four years later, researchers examining In-Home Supportive Services, a California personal assistance program supported by Medicaid, reached a similar conclusion. Some older adults were "not receiving the type of care that would be most responsive to their needs, while others [were] simply not receiving enough help and would benefit from additional hours of care."[40]

I conclude this section by addressing one of the most serious consequences of the family-responsibility ideology. Elderly people who are estranged from kin, childless, divorced or widowed, or who spent their lives outside families often find themselves bereft of essential care. Because women have a longer life expectancy than men, often marry older men, and are less likely than men to remarry after divorce or widowhood, they are especially likely to lack a relative to provide care. Elderly women also are more likely to have fewer financial resources because they have fewer pensions and lower lifetime earnings (often the consequence of withdrawal from the labor force to provide care).[41] Women thus are doubly disadvantaged by the reliance on family responsibility. I have noted that, like other forms of domestic labor, care for older people continues to be allocated on the basis of gender. Although men provide more assistance than they did before, women still represent the majority of caregivers. But after lifetimes of caring for others, many women have no one to turn to when they are most in need.

Direct Care Workers

The care crisis stems from the plight of paid caregivers as well as unpaid ones. The nearly 4.5 million US direct care workers have an enormous, though largely unexamined, place in the experiences of family caregivers.[42] Especially when race, class, culture, immigrant status, and generations divide the two groups, their association is often fraught. Nevertheless, they are inextricably related. They interact frequently and depend heavily on each other to provide good care; each group must compensate for the deficiencies of the other. Projections of a dwindling supply of family caregivers increase the importance of direct care providers. The population of adults sixty and over is expected to double between 2016 and 2060, from 49.2 million to 94.7 million. During the same period, the size of the population aged eighteen to sixty-four is expected to remain stable.[43] With fewer family members available to care for the growing elderly population, the role of front-line workers will become especially critical. And the two groups confront similar issues. The refusal to accept care for the elderly as a social responsibility and the low value attached to all types of care explain not only why so little support surrounds caregivers but also why a living wage eludes the workers.

Providing hands-on care to people with disabilities, direct care workers hold various job titles, including nursing assistants, home-health aides, homecare aides, and personal attendants. As long-term care services increasingly move out of institutions and into homes and the community, the number of home-health and homecare aides rapidly expands. The homecare labor force more than doubled between 2009 and 2019, from 973,000 to 2.4 million.[44] Just one-third of direct care providers work in nursing homes and assisted living facilities; two-thirds are employed in private homes.[45]

Those statistics undoubtedly underestimate the homecare sector because they exclude the large numbers of workers hired by middle-class and upper-class families in the "gray market." In my 1991 study of relatively affluent daughters caring for elderly parents in Los Angeles, a city with a large pool of immigrants, I found that just fifteen relied on a home health agency but twenty-eight hired helpers through ad hoc, informal arrangements.[46] Caregivers follow that route for several reasons. Although agencies take responsibility for paying taxes and vetting workers, their services are far more expensive. Many caregivers prefer to make their own personnel selections. And some want to avoid agency regulations. When Elinor Fuchs, a professor in the Yale School of Drama, asked an agency director to find a worker who would have a car and could take Fuchs's mother shopping and to the movies, the response was, "No, these are *home-care* companions, for *care* in the *home*, we cannot assume the risks of car inspection, driver certification . . ." Fuchs also rejected the director's offer to do a needs assessment, on the basis of which the agency would send a trained aide who would be supervised through periodic visits and assessments. "Oh, I see," Fuchs wrote, "it's a business! I should have realized."[47] Family members recruit independent homecare workers in various ways. Some go through medical channels, asking doctors and nurses for recommendations. A social worker helped Arthur Kleinman locate Sheilah, the Irish American woman who cared for his wife. My mother found Jasmine Mehta, the Trinidadian Indian introduced in chapter 2, by following a more common route, asking friends' housekeepers if they had relatives who needed work.

Middle-class people are not the only ones who hire homecare aides on their own. I have noted that, largely as a result of advocacy by people with disabilities, a growing number of Medicaid-funded homecare programs allow clients to employ independent providers rather than those supplied by agencies.[48] Family members not only frequently hire, train, and supervise the workers but also represent a high proportion of the paid providers.[49] These consumer-directed programs employ a combined total of approximately one million independent providers.[50]

Regardless of their job title, the setting in which they work, and the way they are hired, direct care providers share certain characteristics. Their average age is forty-one. The overwhelming majority (86 percent) are women. Most (60 percent) identify as people of color. More than a quarter (27.5 percent) are immigrants from Asia, Africa, the Caribbean, and Latin America.[51] (That proportion is higher in states with large immigrant populations.)[52] Sociologist Evelyn Nakano Glenn demonstrated that white, middle- and upper-class US women have long created what she calls a "racial division of reproductive labor" by transferring care work to women of color.[53] Rhacel Salazar Parreñas, another sociologist, extended that argument by adding an international dimension. Women from the global South migrate to the global North to relieve privileged women of caring labor.[54] Many leave children behind in the care of grandparents and other kin. Although they can stay in contact through email and Skype, those who are undocumented face overwhelming obstacles when they try to travel home or bring their children to the United States. Fearful of deportation, undocumented workers also are especially wary of complaining about employment conditions.[55]

Interacting with families is a large part of direct care work. Anthropologist Nancy Foner studied aides in a New York City nursing home. Because services provided by family caregivers help to relieve the aides' heavy workload, Foner assumed she would find that the workers welcomed family involvement. Instead, she learned that the "aides tended to be annoyed, occasionally deeply angry," with family visitors. "The general view is that [they] are another source of pressure on the job." According to the aides, families demand a level of care the aides cannot possibly provide and "spoil" their own relatives with special favors. Foner intentionally chose a "typical" New York nursing home, where most patients and family members were white and the workers overwhelmingly women of color. Racial differences contributed to the social distance aides felt from both the residents and their families.[56] A study of nursing homes in an Illinois city reported that three-fourths of the aides had experienced racism from residents, family members, and other staff.[57]

Especially when clients live with family members, homecare aides have intimate contact with them. Although some workers appreciate the relationships they develop with families, others have serious complaints. Marlene Chapman, a worker interviewed by Ai-Jen Poo, the director of the National Domestic Workers Alliance, spoke about the special difficulties of dealing with the families of people with dementia: "Some of [the clients] lie—accusing you of things to their families. Some families believe them and think the worst of us; some don't. It takes a lot of patience."[58] A study of the Cooperative Home Care Associates, a pioneering worker-owned agency in the South Bronx, reported that "when asked what is the most difficult aspect of the job, many home health aides reply that it is dealing with difficult patients and family members." Some blamed families for aggravating clients' problems, giving cake to those with diabetes, smoking and cursing, and in general creating too much noise and commotion.[59] The homecare workers whom sociologist Clare L. Stacey studied in California and Ohio similarly cited examples of negligent kin. One aide was especially censorious of the family of a client with both dementia and epilepsy; no one helped her take her medications, repaired her smoke detectors, or removed the many boxes that could easily make her fall. Although the family lived close by, the client called the worker when she needed something or just wanted company.[60] When we read in the following chapter the list of grievances caregivers have about workers, we should remember that criticism was mutual.

Stacey also found that relationships with clients (and occasionally families) could be a source of pride. Providing services to a vulnerable population enhances the workers' self-esteem and allows them to display the unique skills they possess.[61] I noted in a previous chapter that by the end of my father's life, Jasmine Mehta had become the closest person to him. Marlene Chapman, the worker quoted above, reported a similar experience. The doctor she cared for "didn't want to die with anybody else around but me. He didn't want to be in that place with nobody else. We had gotten so close and he loved me. I put my whole self into it. I took care of that man with my life."[62]

Whether or not direct care workers value their relationships with families and clients, their jobs have serious disadvantages. Although often required to perform medical tasks, the workers receive very little training.[63] The work is extremely hazardous, involving heavy lifting, needle punctures, and assaults. Nursing home assistants report more injuries than workers in any other occupation, including construction and truck driving.[64] And remuneration is paltry. Benefits are either inadequate or nonexistent. In 2015, nursing assistants earned an average of $18,729 a year; the average annual earnings for homecare workers was $13,361.[65]

Sociologist Matthew Desmond described the life of Vanessa Sullivan, a Puerto Rican single woman with three children who had diabetes and was employed as a homecare aide in East Trenton, New Jersey. She liked the work. "I get to help people," she told Desmond, "and be around older people and learn a lot of stuff from them." But between managing her illness and caring for her children, she could work only twenty to thirty hours a week. Even with public assistance, she could not make ends meet. She recently had found an apartment in public housing. Before that she and the children had slept in a motel room when she had enough money and in her Chrysler when she did not.[66]

Aides who can work longer hours also have problems getting by. Many can find only part-time jobs that pay minimum wage and offer neither security nor benefits. As a result, they must piece together several jobs, often working far more than forty hours a week. A September 2020 *New York Times* article cited the example of Sheryl Carlos, a fifty-six-year-old woman who worked at three jobs seven days a week in Post St. Lucie, north of West Palm Beach. In addition to part-time employment in both a nursing home and assisted living facility, she cared for a few people in their homes. "Let me tell you something, I don't have a life," she remarked while driving home one morning after finishing a nine-hour shift. "If some jobs were paying you enough, you wouldn't have to be working like that."[67]

In addition to receiving lower wages than their counterparts in institutions, homecare aides face special challenges. Like other domestic workers, such as cleaners and nannies, they are isolated and invisible. Without coworkers, they have no one who shares their complaints about the jobs and can help them assert their rights.[68] They also lack basic job protections. Three major pieces of legislation—the Civil Rights Act of 1964, the Americans with Disabilities Act of 1967, and the Age Discrimination in Employment Act of 1971—do not cover those in jobs with single employees. The Occupational Safety and Health Act of 1970 explicitly excludes workers in private households.[69]

Because employment in the gray market is operated "off the books," compensation varies according to employers' whims. My own family experience again may be instructive. During the five months my mother battled lymphoma, Mehta was less a home health aide than a cleaner. After my mother died, Mehta continued to provide the same kind of assistance to my father. But as his health deteriorated over the next six years, her responsibilities grew. After beginning to dress, bathe, and cook for him, she became the case manager, providing information to, and negotiating among, the many different specialists involved in his medical care. When he started to need night and weekend care, she helped locate new aides (through her extensive contacts within her immigrant community), interviewed those not known to her personally, and then trained and supervised the entire staff. But her remuneration did not immediately match her new job description. For a year after our mother's death, my siblings and I simply continued her arrangement. Finally we realized that we were the employers and should pay taxes (such as Social Security, unemployment compensation, and workers' compensation) and provide paid vacations, sick leaves, and annual raises. As Mehta's responsibilities mushroomed, we tried to revise her pay scale to reflect her expanded job description. Our desire to be good employers, however, clashed with other pressures. As we watched our father's savings dwindle away, we worried that he would outlive his ability to pay for help, especially as he began to require around-the-clock care. And we could not help but be aware that Mehta's pay steadily reduced the size of our inheritance. Although her wages helped her and her husband buy a house, they still faced serious, ongoing financial difficulties. Because Mehta's husband stayed home during the day to care for their children, he was restricted to night work, which paid poorly and was unstable and dangerous. Once, he was badly hurt in a mugging when he returned home at 4:00 a.m. and afterward could not work for several months.[70] As a result, their household income dramatically declined.

Although some family members benefit from keeping wages low, all suffer when poor employment conditions drive workers from the field. Between 40 and 60 percent of direct care providers leave each year for better jobs, often in restaurants and retail.[71] Low retention rates upset clients with dementia, who require stability, exacerbate the labor shortage that limits access to services, and undermine workers' ability both to rely on the knowledge and skills derived from experience and to provide the person-centered care most family members demand.[72] As we will see, family caregivers often complain about the difficulty of repeatedly recruiting and training new homecare aides.

Conclusion

The United States experiences a care crisis not because caregiving is harder than ever before but because the nation tries to care for its elderly citizens on the cheap. Invoking the ideology of family values and stressing the need to constrain costs, the government provides little assistance to caregivers of elderly people. As a result, caregiving too often involves enormous personal sacrifice. The ability of wealthy individuals to buy out of their responsibilities may exacerbate the situation. Just as many affluent people who can afford to educate their children privately oppose efforts to subsidize public schools adequately, so caregivers who hire aides and attendants in the gray market may have little concern about the impoverishment of the government-funded long-term care system.

The exploitation of workers who are overwhelmingly women and members of marginalized groups contributes to the elder care crisis. The next chapter demonstrates that family members anticipate that direct care workers will provide compassionate and dignified care, understand recipients' needs, preferences, and idiosyncrasies, and establish affective bonds with them. Employment conditions limit the ability of workers to fulfill those expectations.

5

"That Was No Respite for Me!"

Using Services at Home and in the Community

Viewing caregivers in terms of cost efficiency, policy makers worry that they will unload their responsibilities on the state, astronomically increasing its burdens. Because the government foots the bill for most nursing home residents, policy makers assert that it is vital to provide the support family members need to alleviate their stress and thus postpone or prevent institutional placement. At the same time, the argument continues, it is crucial to ensure that home- and community-based services do not substitute for the care family members now provide for "free." There is no evidence, however, that caregivers think in similar terms.[1]

Internet forums provide a window on their perspectives.[2] In 2011, the Alzheimer's Association launched several peer-led, online support groups for people affected by dementia. By August 2020, the groups had a total of ninety-nine thousand members.[3] Some posted regularly, others just once or twice. Although the conversations are public, members alone can post threads and responses. Membership requires establishing an account with a screen name. Members are invited to provide additional personal information, but most decline to do so. Rather than supplying self-portraits, many send photographs of pets or flowers. I have noted that memoir writers often open their accounts with long descriptions of relatives before dementia descended, to differentiate them from other individuals with similar conditions. The forum participants have other concerns. Looking for company, they seek to establish commonality with other members. As a result, they typically introduce their relatives by stating the diagnosis and, in the case of Alzheimer's, the stage of the disease, rather than highlighting any distinguishing characteristics. Most memoirs, moreover, describe relatives who died some years earlier, and writers have had time to consider how to present the deceased's struggles with dementia. Seeking help with urgent, ongoing issues with living people, support-group members often provide extremely intimate details without much reflection and thus want to conceal the relatives' identities as well as their own. The use of screen names and lack of distinguishing features helps to preserve anonymity.

According to the association, women are overrepresented, as they are in other support groups.[4] Although the association has no statistics about race and class, the posts suggest that the members are more diverse than those discussed in chapter 2. Most of those who note the occupations they or their relatives held mention professional and managerial ones. Several, however, cite working-class jobs (truck driver, security guard, building supervisor, hotel worker, crane operator). The writing indicates that the majority of participants had relatively high levels of education.

The Alzheimer's support groups reveal that many people begin the caregiving journey with no idea how to obtain assistance. Despite all the new attention to death and dying, few family members anticipate caring for someone with a chronic terminal disease, much less one that devastates cognitive abilities. Moreover, little information is available about resources for families.[5] A sixty-four-year-old woman wondered if the term "assisted living" meant that an elderly relative could live at home with help from others and then asked, "Am I way off base? I know I have a lot to learn yet" (November 12, 2013). Other forum participants asked such questions as, How do you know when it is no longer safe to leave people with dementia home? Should you hire homecare workers privately or rely on an agency? What about moving a person into the house to provide care? When are people ready for day care? What does it cost? How can you find quality care? How can you find a worker to care for someone at home? Does Medicare cover long-term care services? How does one apply for Medicaid? Do you need a lawyer? What does "memory care" mean? How do you know when it is appropriate? How do you decide whether relatives should be in assisted living facilities or nursing homes?

This chapter relies on the posts on two forums between December 1, 2011, and April 1, 2021, to examine both the benefits and problems of home- and community-based services for caregivers. The Spouse or Partner Caregiver Forum has an average of two thousand posts from two hundred participants a month.[6] By December 31, 2020, it had received a total of 198,094 posts on 18,149 topics. With a total of only 306 posts since 2011, the forum for LGBT Community and Allies is much smaller. Caregivers who post messages on that site are informed that they should go to the Spouse or Partner Caregiver Forum, which has participants in various forms of partnerships. LGBTQ community members offer the same advice. In response to a woman who wrote that she had enough stress without dealing with homophobia, Selma commented, "I've been with my wife for over 40 years, married since it became legal, and yes, at first I didn't tell people because it is hard enough being gay." She felt welcomed on the Spouse-Partner message board: "People there are kind and non-judgmental. Certainly we are all going through what no one should have to go through" (April 19, 2019). Nevertheless, the LGBT Community and Allies Forum remained important. Roberta wrote that although she had received "a tremendous amount of support on Spouse/Caregiver forum," she checked the LGBT forum "once in a while, because living in a same sex marriage presents its own challenges" (October 14, 2019).

I emphasize caregivers of spouses and partners because, although occasionally sighted in doctors' waiting rooms, they are largely invisible. They also rarely appear in accounts about family caregivers of older people, which focus overwhelmingly on adult children (usually daughters) caring for parents (typically mothers). *The Age of Dignity: Preparing for the Elder Boom in a Changing America*, by Ai-Jen Poo, director of the National Domestic Workers Alliance, devotes a chapter to the sandwich generation, "squeezed, pulled, and torn between the demands of their children and the needs of their parents," but says little about elderly care-

giving spouses or partners.[7] Announcing his commitment to addressing the needs of caregivers, candidate Joe Biden wrote that his "plan
is about easing the squeeze on working families that are raising their
kids and caring for aging loved ones."[8] The headline of a *Washington
Post* article about the problems of caring for elderly people in their own
homes reads, "Adult Children Pay the Price of Keeping Aging Parents
at Home."[9] A well-known, nationwide referral service for placement in
long-term care facilities is called A Place for Mom. The title of a prominent advocacy group is Caring across Generations.

Statistics appear to justify that bias. Adult children represent half of
the caregivers of people sixty-five and older as opposed to spouses and
partners, who represent just 20 percent.[10] But spousal caregiving is more
difficult than parental caregiving along several dimensions. Caregivers for
spouses or partners tend to be older and thus more likely to have their
own physical health problems. Living with the care recipient, they provide
more hours of care than other caregivers.[11] They also remain in the caregiver role for longer periods of time. In 2015, approximately 64 percent of
spousal caregivers had furnished assistance for four years or more.[12]

Caregivers of spouses and partners with dementia are an especially
vulnerable group. Their average age is seventy-one. Although women
account for three-fourths of all people with dementia, they also represent the majority (63 percent) of the caregivers.[13] (Evidence suggests
that the reason is not only that women tend to marry older men but also
that a significant proportion of men but extremely few women leave
spouses diagnosed with dementia.)[14] They provide approximately fifty-
six hours of care a week (more than twice as much as other dementia
caregivers), often helping with bathing and dealing with incontinence.
Although 92 percent undertake medical and nursing tasks, just 8 percent
have received instruction in performing them. A third (33 percent) rate
their health as fair or poor, and 44 percent state that it has worsened as
a result of their caregiving role.[15] Research confirms those self-reports.
Spousal dementia caregivers are at high risk for physical health problems, cognitive decline, and even dementia.[16]

Lisa Freitag, a pediatrician and medical ethicist, has coined the phrase "extreme caregivers" to describe parents of children with special needs. Freitag acknowledges that health professionals also provide care for that population, but they receive compensation, have medical training, do not work 24/7, and rarely develop the same emotional intimacy as parents do. Extreme caregiving, she writes, "can be complicated by medical complexity, and it often involves juggling multiple time-consuming tasks. The work must be carried out while maintaining a home or career (or both) and is usually done without respite. And, most importantly, extreme caregiving is performed for a person with whom the caregiver has an intense and personal relationship."[17] As we will see, care for spouses and partners with dementia has many of those attributes.

Abbreviations suggested by the Alzheimer's Association and commonly used in the posts include the following: DH for dear husband; DW for dear wife; LO for loved one; and MC for memory care. Given the nature of the sample, quantification is not appropriate. I use pseudonyms instead of screen names to protect confidentiality.

Respite Services

The language changes when we examine noninstitutional services from the point of view of caregivers rather than recipients. No longer "home- and community-based services," they become "interventions" or, more commonly, "respite services."[18] Respite services take three forms. Caregivers are most familiar with home care and tend to enlist it first when relatives no longer can be safely left alone.[19] As we have seen, some hire aides, homemakers, and other helpers on their own, in the "gray market." Others rely on agencies, which are far more expensive but have the advantage of vetting workers and taking care of insurance and taxes.[20] The for-profit sector has grown rapidly since 1980.[21] By 2016, approximately 80 percent of homecare agencies were profit maximizing.[22]

The two other forms of respite services (adult day care and overnight respite care) emerged in the 1980s and expanded rapidly as a result of pressure from advocates.[23] The National Adult Day Services Association defines adult day care as "a professional care setting in which older adults, adults living with dementia, or adults living with disabilities receive individualized therapeutic, social, and health services for some part of the day."[24] By 2016, the United States had more than 4,800 centers, serving more than 280,000 clients on any single day.[25] Approximately 90 percent of the centers provide cognitive stimulation, and nearly 80 percent offer memory-training programs; most also furnish transportation and meals.[26] The centers are not tightly regulated at either the state or the federal level.[27] Approximately 50 percent were for-profit entities in 2016.[28] Overnight respite occurs in institutions that allow short stays (usually a few days or weeks). Because relatively few assisted living facilities and nursing homes offer this service, it is used less frequently than the other forms of respite care.[29]

Caregivers can obtain financial assistance for respite care from various sources. Created in 2000 under the Older Americans Act, the National Family Caregiver Support Program provides block grants to states to offer respite care as well as a few other services. (Because the funding level is low, the program reaches only a fraction of the caregivers who need that assistance.)[30] Six years later Congress passed the Lifespan Respite Care Act, providing a small amount of funding for respite services.[31] Caregivers of recipients of veterans' benefits are eligible for thirty days of overnight respite care a year. Under the Medicare Hospice Benefit, caregivers can place recipients in a Medicare-approved facility for five days at a time. And caregivers of recipients of Medicaid can obtain respite care under the waiver program.

Although a few writers mentioned that they relied on public funding and a few others complained about the cost of care, most did not indicate how they paid for services. A lesbian, however, described the special difficulties she faced applying to In-Home Supportive Services, a California program funded by Medicaid:

Judy and I have been happily married for 21 years. Judy was diagnosed with dementia and has rapidly progressed through the five stages . . . I am dealing with an agency called In-Home Supportive Services to see if I can get some help with Judy—even a few minutes so that I can take a breather. Unfortunately, the case worker that they assigned to us is homophobic. When I introduced myself as Judy's spouse, the woman became livid. She asked inappropriate questions, like sleeping arrangements and told me I would have to jump through hoops to even get an hour's care. Well, I jumped through those hoops and crossed all the T's. I've been waiting for several weeks to see the final papers only to find out that they "lost" the information I sent. I'm just really frustrated and don't want to fight the fight but that means I won't get the help. (September 28, 2014)

Several quantitative studies suggest that respite services can reduce caregivers' stress levels, raising hopes among policy makers that they may have the potential to ward off institutionalization.[32] Popular advice for caregivers frequently focuses on the need for a break. The Family Caregiver Alliance, for example, warns, "Without respite, caregivers are susceptible to burnout."[33] Caregivers request respite care more often than any other form of assistance.[34] And many testify to its benefits. Writer Alix Kates Shulman explained why she began to "sink" when the aide who had cared for her husband suddenly quit: "Those behaviors that I was able to take in stride when I had five hours to renew myself each day—his asking the same question a dozen times, exploding when I try to correct him, elbowing pedestrians who walk too close, unplugging the lamps from the walls instead of turning off the switches, insisting that we are in London and must try to get home—now push me over the edge."[35] Nevertheless, when respite services are available, they tend to be underutilized.[36] This chapter can help to explain why.[37]

Like many other caregivers who have been studied, the forum participants indicated that respite care often provided the relief they sought.[38] Responding to a wife who described herself as overwhelmed by caregiving and wondered "what to do to keep the stress from flaring up," a man advised, "Respite. Respite. Respite." He learned to become "a darn good caregiver" for his wife "because I also took care of myself" (February 2, 2012). After depositing his wife in overnight care, Thomas looked forward to his Alaskan cruise. But first he "sat in our beautiful backyard and just drank in the peaceful feeling. I don't think I've felt this peaceful since this ordeal started exactly 5 months ago" (August 19, 2014). Linda was an eighty-three-year-old woman whose husband had serious heart and kidney problems as well as Alzheimer's. "I was at my wit's end Tuesday," she wrote.

> I had chased John down the street twice and brought him back home. He was constantly trying to get out and needed 24/7 attention. He was so bored but didn't watch TV, couldn't read, couldn't really do anything.
>
> My daughter just showed up and we decided to check out a Day Care for Alzheimer's that opened recently. We had checked out another day care weeks ago and decided it was not up to our standards. We were very pleasantly surprised this time. We really liked the administrator and everything was immaculate.
>
> So for the first time John shuffled out of the car into Day Care on Tuesday and I had FIVE WHOLE HOURS! I hardly knew what to do!!!! (July 4, 2013)

A woman whose husband had both Parkinson's, which affects movement, and lewy body dementia wrote, "Today I dropped off my hubby for his first stay at an Adult Day Care Session . . . *I am so thankful that the first visit went well, and that I will be able to have this option to take a few hours of 'me' time.* Hope that others can take advantage of this service or something similar to take a much needed break from the endless tasks and caregiving job that we fell heir to" (August 22, 2014). Patricia wrote that the sixty dollars she spent for two days per week of day care for her husband in the two years before he died was "WORTH EVERY PENNY. Sometimes I just went home and slept while he was there. Sometimes

I'd go sit at McDonalds and cry in my coffee. Sometimes I would grocery shop or do Dr. appts. It was just my free time to do what I needed whatever that might be" (February 22, 2020). Day care was especially crucial for a security guard whose wife attended two days a week: "It's really helpful not to have to attend to her during that time, so I can get a few things done, unwind and get ready for bed (since I work nights, I have to sleep during the day)" (June 20, 2013). Yet others referred to day care as a "godsend," a "blessing," or "heaven" (January 3, 2013, January 22, 2017, February 2, 2017).

But relief was not the only emotion caregivers expressed. Several also reported feelings of guilt.[39] In some cases, guilt arose from actions over which the caregivers had little or no choice. One woman, for example, felt guilty when she put her husband in overnight respite so she could go to the hospital for surgery, another when she hired an aide because she had to go to work. We will see that another woman was enraged when she found her husband sick with bronchial pneumonia after overnight respite care. She blamed herself most severely: "I am so scared he won't make it and it's all my fault. I should never have trusted his care to someone else" (November 21, 2013). Day care also provoked guilt. "Well, I put my husband into a day program 2 days a week," wrote Deborah. "I must admit it is nice when I have some time but I find I go and pick him up early because I feel guilty. He didn't want to go" (July 29, 2013). June was looking for a day care program for her husband because she no longer felt safe leaving him home alone. She felt "guilty doing it but I know I have to do what is best for him" (November 13, 2014). Robert similarly assumed enrollment in a day care program was for his spouse's benefit. Because his wife no longer had any interests or activities apart from walking the dog, he hoped a program would provide stimulation. Nevertheless, after leaving her for the first time, he was "surprised at the amount of guilt I am having" (July 21, 2014).

Service use also made caregivers painfully aware of the extent to which dementia had diminished their spouses. "Wow," wrote Maria, "I am at home and the [caregiver] aide is giving my DH a shower for the first time. It is more traumatic than I thought it would be. He is doing fine and I guess that's what is sad. Just like when I found out that at the day care, aides were helping him in the bathroom. It's a privacy thing, that now so many people can help him and it's okay to be seen naked and in your most basic needs. It's just making me cry because I see the decline and it becomes more real" (January 6, 2015). After other writers expressed similar sentiments in response to her post, Maria wrote again: "The first time the bus picked him up for day care, I cried because of the meaning of it. My strong, macho man is now a toddler and I wanted to throw up watching him get on the bus, going off to school" (January 7, 2015). Another woman wrote that her husband, "an educated, super intelligent/successful man," enjoyed a day care program once the staff convinced him that he was a volunteer helper. He seemed unaware of the difference between that work and "anything he was doing only a few short years ago (as a managing director of a firm, serving on numerous boards, etc., etc.)." This wife described herself as "happy he is happy there, but also sad and depressed that this man who was so successful, bigger than life, and a beloved leader in our community is actually at a level where this is acceptable entertainment to him" (July 11, 2019).

Moreover, relief was not the only reason caregivers enlisted services. Overnight care enabled family members to have a back-up plan in case they became ill and test a facility they hoped to use later. Both in-home care and day care provided companionship as well as supervision. Kathleen wrote that day care gave her husband "a distinct purpose to get out of bed in the morning, take a shower and dress and then we would both get in the car—where I would drop him off before taking myself to work. He considered it his 'job.' He enjoyed the social aspects of seeing other people, interacting with different people and just doing something different everyday" (January 22, 2017). Like Linda above, a woman whose husband was diagnosed with Alzheimer's soon after her father died from the same disease planned to enroll her husband in a day care center because "he seems so bored" (February 22, 2017). Homecare workers talked to relatives, took them on walks and to the movies, and played games with them.

Respite services did not always provide as much relief as family members had hoped. As we have seen, most family members view caregiving as a complex, intimate relationship and an overwhelming responsibility, not as a series of discrete tasks.[40] One woman explained why she felt little relief when she relinquished specific chores: "24/7 care is very demanding, even with other caregivers helping you. You cannot turn off your concerns when someone else takes over" (August 5, 2012). A second woman made a similar point: "I think the reason respite feels so unsatisfying is that the caregiving is only part of the load. The other parts—grieving the partner we have lost and feeling trapped and lonely—are always with us" (March 29, 2014). In addition, family members spend enormous amounts of time engaged in what Italian sociologist Laura Balbo defines as "servicing," mediating "between the family's human needs and the external resources regulated by the logic of market profitability and state power."[41] Forum writers described in considerable detail the work of locating and arranging for services, convincing elderly relatives to attend them, monitoring them, and assessing their quality. Some had conducted long searches to find day care programs they deemed acceptable. Sandra had interviewed "around 12 different home health care agencies and 100 different caregivers" in the previous five years. "The whole experience of hiring, firing, and training caregivers has been a total 'nightmare' for me!" (February 1, 2016).

Access problems were also common. A home health agency told Karen that few workers were available in her area. "I hate the fact our choices for the aides is so limited," she wrote. "That adds stress to both of us making us feel like we have to take what we are given because it's 'slim pickin' around here. Exhausting. Sickening. UGH!" (December 12, 2012). Another woman in a rural area wrote that the closest day care center for her husband was sixty miles away—too far for a round-trip drive twice a day. Because the demand for day care centers exceeds the supply, spaces were not always available, even in cities.[42] And admission was not automatic. Aides refused to work for people who were physically aggressive or verbally abusive; they also were rejected by both day care centers and overnight care facilities. An inability to communicate disqualified one woman's husband from day care (June 28, 2018); incontinence barred another writer's husband (July 10, 2014). Yet another woman wrote that she and her husband got only as far as the nursing station of a facility offering overnight care before being told he could not stay (June 25, 2014).

There were other difficulties as well. The hours of day care centers did not align with the caregivers' workday. Carla, the wife of a man with many health issues in addition to dementia, wrote, "I am now looking at a day care center and am trying to figure out how to cover the 1 hour gap in the morning from the time I need to leave to work and the Day Care center start time" (July 19, 2015). And one size did not fit all. Writers worried that spouses with early-onset Alzheimer's disease would feel out of place in centers with clients who were decades older. William had hired aides to tend his wife at home when he worked half-days at his office. He would have preferred sending her to day care but wondered if it was "REALLY an option for a 54 year old woman, who doesn't admit to having a problem, and would recognize she is being left somewhere?" (February 1, 2013). One wife decided not to suggest day care to her husband because he would consider the activities—sing-alongs, day-time television, bingo, and crafts projects—too demeaning. Another woman hesitated to find a day care program for her husband, who never had been a social person.

The most serious problem for many writers was that their spouses fiercely resisted any form of outside help. "How can I get DH to accept an in-home caregiver when he gets upset and tries to scare away anyone but family or close friends he's known for years?" asked a woman who then elaborated, "We've had to have an appliance repairman in and DH is agitated the entire time they're in the house. He starts out OK but if he thinks they've been here a bit too long he starts getting upset and gets rude" (May 20, 2012). Other writers complained that relatives barred the door to aides, insulted those who gained entry, and forced them to leave. Michael wrote from Florida, "7 years as sole caregiver to wife. She refuses any outside help. We have been through a dozen nurses all this time, she insults them and throws them out as soon as I leave house. Granddaughter just moved in. She is going to college here locally. Thought I would pay her part time as a companion. Wife is now throwing her out" (September 2, 2014). Ann noted that her husband had been diagnosed with a rare form of dementia after retiring from the navy. At the end of a particularly grueling day she wrote,

> This morning the caregiver came. She was the cutest, young lady. She was sweet, bubbly kind and very happy I stayed with them for about an hour and a half. Everything was fine when I left.
>
> About 30 minutes later, the caretaker called. Gary was upset and crying. I talked to him and he was alright with me being gone for a little while longer. I got another phone call about five minutes later. Gary tried to get out of the house. At first by the front door, then the back. The caretaker was trying to stop him when he took the kitchen door and slammed it backwards, hitting the laundry room door. The kitchen door handle put a hole in the laundry room door.

Ann phoned the police, who took her husband to the hospital. "I am so tried, sore, mentally exhausted, and confused," she concluded. "I thought this would be a good thing, to have a caregiver come to let me have some time to quilt, go to lunch with friends, or whatever. I guess that is the way it goes" (December 16, 2014).

Spouses protested even more vehemently about attending day care. "My question is how to get DH to daycare when almost every morning it is a battle," wrote one woman. "He thinks I am meeting someone when I drop him off at daycare, though I try to reassure him that is not the case. I am sick of the indigestion and stress of trying to talk him into going, yet if he stays home, he spends the entire day in bed, then up all night" (January 18, 2016). Darlene must have desperately needed the break her husband's day care center gave her. She introduced herself as a woman in her seventies whose health "wasn't great." She had had a liver transplant and two heart attacks. But when she took him one morning, he "refused to get out of the car. The girls that work there tried to coax him but he slammed the car door and locked it. I'm so disappointed, it was my only break so now it's back to 24/7" (September 9, 2015). Marcus was happy to find a center with "lovely people nice facility nice activities etc." But his wife went only once: "DW hated hated hated hated hated hated hated hated hated every minute" (January 22, 2017).

Other spouses tried to leave during the day. One woman's husband seemed content when she left him at day care for the first time. "3 hours in I got a call to come and get him," she wrote. "He had gotten hold of a phone and called 911, said he wanted the police because they had him locked in. When I arrived (it is 3 miles away) he was pounding and kicking the door. I could see the door moving. They said that is your husband on the other side" (February 17, 2015). Yet other relatives protested after they returned home. "Such is the life of a dementia caregiver," remarked a woman whose husband came home "upset and angry and pouting" (February 19, 2013). Another woman concluded that "it was worse for me to have him there, at the Adult Day Care Center for 'my respite' and then to have to calm him down for hours on end when I brought him home. That was no respite for me!" (January 19, 2014).

In some cases, providers terminated services. Aides quit when clients verbally abused them or acted aggressively.[43] Day care centers expelled clients whose dementia was no longer in the early, least severe stage and who became aggressive or kept trying to leave. Jan, a nurse married to a retired family-practice physician, asked,

What can I do when MDH [my dear husband] has been released from one Active Adult program & is about to be released from another (after 20 times there) & simply not participating, being verbally abusive, & constantly asking when I am coming to pick him up. I give him a note each time, but it doesn't prevent him from asking many times. He is only there

4 hrs. twice weekly as it is . . . I definitely need some time to myself & if & when Adult Care is terminated, I'm really at a loss about what to do next. Any advice or suggestions would be most welcome. (August 11, 2018)

Rachel described what happened when she went to pick up her husband after his first morning in day care:

I was just pulling up when I see a couple of police cars in the parking lot in front of it, a number of the staff standing around, and right there in the middle my DH serene as if nothing was happening. I felt embarrassment of course, but such feelings are a luxury I brushed aside. Apparently, he had tried to leave a few times and succeeded in the end, bolting through the door and running towards the busy road in the front of the place. The staff told me that he was agitating to leave all day, yelling out some choice words at them in the process. Needless to say, he is not going back there again tomorrow, as I was planning. The day care personnel told me, in a nice way, that I need to medicate him to keep him in a calm state in order to be accepted back there.

Rachel hesitated "to medicate him, simply to bring him to a place to socialize. I don't know how much socialization he can have if he is zoned-out" (March 21, 2012). Nineteen months later Rachel tried to leave her husband at the local Veterans Administration for overnight respite care. "I was so looking forward to my two-weeks vacation from caregiving," she wrote.

I took him there last Monday. Come Thursday morning, I get a phone call at work. Come and get him. What? Why? He is constantly trying to walk out the door and keeps walking around in an agitated state. Duh. No kidding. Does the term dementia mean anything to you? . . . New sur- roundings, with strange people and beeping machines all around were unsettling for my husband and, naturally, he looked to leave and get back home. I guess keeping an eye on him was too much work for them . . . I was, and still am, so mad! Exactly how was he supposed to behave for their liking? . . . They talk a good game, but when the chips are down, they just throw their hands up.

Rachel concluded, "The moral of the story is that we are all on our own and can only depend on ourselves. This is a very lonely experience" (December 17, 2013).

Large numbers of caregivers deemed the quality of services unacceptable. (One caveat belongs here. Disappointed writers may have been overrepresented because people were most likely to seek advice from a support group when programs did not meet their standards. Although quantification was impossible, we should note that some posts expressed gratitude for the quality of care their relatives received.) Jim pointed out that "Adult Day Care programs are not all created equal. Many programs are not much more than glorified baby-sitting, while others have complete programs" (June 20, 2013). Janet discovered that the center she selected did not provide even minimal supervision. Her husband seemed to enjoy day care for a while. Two days before writing, however, she was shocked to discover him at home when she returned in the early afternoon. He had "walked several miles without any outerwear and now is starting to get sick. There are no sidewalks on the roads he had to walk on. I can't believe he made it home!" When she called the center, she discovered no one knew he had left. She asked, "Is this just something that happens at these places?" (January 10, 2013).

Some forum participants faulted homecare agencies. "Over the past few years," one man wrote, "I've come to find out that the agency I've been dealing with hasn't sent me persons specifically trained with dementia at times despite their dementia marketing." He had begun to seek other options after discovering that "specific training for Alzheimer's and dementia is very hard to come by as there isn't a statewide test that a [home health aide] would pass and be certified and you would have the confidence to know they know their stuff. Nor is there a national certification either. Here where we live all someone has to do is take a 4 hour course and magically they're a home health aide. And some of these schools that offer these 'certifications' don't exactly give off a professional vibe." He had "gone through" twenty aides in as many months (November 9, 2020).

Others complained about specific aides. According to family members, they were unreliable, arriving late or not at all. Rather than tending the client, they spent their time in a separate room texting on their phones. Lacking any knowledge about dementia, they repeatedly called family members at work to ask for advice but then disregarded instructions about how to provide care or do housework. One convinced a client to give her money and furniture. After cataloguing the many reasons why she considered the aides she hired unacceptable, a woman exclaimed, "So much trouble we have to deal with this disease!!!!" She decided to rely on a neighbor or even her ninety-three-year-old mother-in-law when she had to run errands (January 12, 2015). Dissatisfaction with aides encouraged other caregivers to move relatives to institutions sooner than expected.

Overnight respite care received the harshest criticisms. Leah had second thoughts about leaving her husband in a memory-care facility when she realized she had been subjected to a bait-and-switch technique:

> We did "the tour" almost two weeks ago and it seemed like the best place. "The tour" showed us the likes of the penthouse suite as a sample room. Every employee greeted us with happy faces. When we got there today, however, we were scolded for being 45 minutes late. Got to his room—it was quite horrible, not at all like what we were shown on "the tour." A teeny tiny room with a teeny tiny cot for a bed. No TV (even though they said ALL their respite rooms had TV's.) Ignored and treated rudely by every staff member we met. I was actually yelled at by a member to SIT DOWN. No standing in the lobby area. The whole experience was so horrible I can't believe it even happened. (October 15, 2019)

DementiaCareCentral, a resource center for dementia caregivers, urges them to "remember that new places and routines can be distressing for persons with Alzheimer's disease or dementia. If you do choose to use overnight respite care, be sure that the facility appreciates your loved one's needs."[44] But one woman discovered that following that advice could not ensure decent care for her husband. "After everyone kept telling me I needed it, I arranged for respite care," Ginger wrote.

> I went to the place three times, did interviews, filled out questionnaires as to my husband's ability and needs. He needs prompting for grooming. He can shower but he needs to be told to go in there and hand him the soap and shampoo. He will brush his teeth, but has to have it explained. And I've been doing all the shaving for him. All this was written out and for good measure, I did a single-page sheet and took it along with him.
>
> I didn't leave town for this visit, but hoped it would work so I could take a little trip later. I called every day to speak to someone about how he was doing and spoke to him twice.
>
> When I went to pick him up he was unshaven, unbathed, in the same clothing he had on when I left him. I'd sent him a new tube of toothpaste—it was still in the box. He looked and smelled like a homeless person. His prescribed skin creams were not used—obviously no one paid any attention to him at all. His clean, folded clothes were untouched, never worn.
>
> When I got home and put him in the shower, his disposable undergarment had been on for some time. It was full of feces and urine and was so heavy it fell to the floor with a thump-plop. . . .
>
> Now I don't trust anyone to take care of him. . . . He's not going anywhere else to live until he is so out of it he won't know, or I am—whichever comes first. It was neither Respite nor Care. What a racket. (June 28, 2013)

Another woman brought her husband, a retired engineer, home after two days because "he was dehydrated, and did not get his medical needs met!!!" (March 10, 2013). When Selma went to pick up her husband from a facility in rural Texas, she found him coughing and disoriented and immediately took him to the doctor, who diagnosed bronchial pneumonia. "The doctor told me that people with Alzheimer's disease plus his complications, that this can happen very quickly," she wrote. "But if I noticed, how could a trained nursing staff not have noticed that something was wrong" (November 21, 2013). Yet other writers complained that the stays were too short to provide a real break and that any benefits quickly evaporated, especially when relatives returned home angry and distraught. "After five years of caregiving I finally took a couple of days of respite," wrote one wife. "It was great to sit on the beach and relax but Charles did not do well and has been a challenge since we got home. I'm not sure the respite time was worth the price I had to pay" (October 9, 2014). The great majority of writers who placed their husband in overnight respite vowed never to do so again.

Conclusion

When I concluded my 1991 book, *Who Cares for the Elderly? Public Policy and the Experiences of Adult Daughters*, I wrote that the greatest need of caregivers was for respite services, which could provide temporary relief from the burdens of care. Now I realize it is not so simple. The number of respite services has grown rapidly in the past three decades, but they remain underutilized. We did not hear from caregivers who rejected respite care out of hand but can learn a great deal from those who contemplated seeking such care but then refused to do so. Some hesitated to confront their spouses or partners with their impairments. We saw in chapter 2 that a primary goal of many dementia caregivers is to foster relatives' dignity by concealing their deficits. Bringing spouses to adult day care or hiring homecare aides to supervise them might defeat that goal.

Another major obstacle was resistance from spouses and partners. The forums provide little information about exactly why so many spouses objected, but we can hazard some guesses. Many men may have assumed that their wives could continue taking care of them, as they had in the past. Both men and women may have regarded an ability to manage on their own an important source of self-esteem, especially when they had experienced major losses. Some forms of respite—adult day care centers and overnight care—would involve spouses associating with people they regarded as far more impaired than themselves. Unfamiliar places and providers terrified some dementia sufferers. And many elderly people share with most Americans the belief that dependence on any social services demonstrates inadequacy. Having internalized a value system that glorifies self-sufficiency, they refuse to accept care even when they desperately need it.

Forum participants who enlisted respite services supported the finding of numerous studies that the lack of training direct care workers receive seriously undermines the quality of care they can provide.[45] Two women whose husbands had been mistreated in overnight care realized that no one at the facility had any idea how to care for them. Others complained that homecare workers called them repeatedly at work to ask how to manage clients with dementia. Staff members' lack of knowledge about dementia sufferers also may explain why many programs rejected those who engaged in challenging and disturbing behaviors—the group whose caregivers had the greatest need for relief.

To the extent that respite services provide relief, they may encourage caregivers to defer institutional placement. But the use of respite services generated not just relief but also sadness and guilt. The many unsatisfactory services may have made institutionalization more rather than less attractive.

6

"They Can't Possibly Love Him as I Do"

The Anguish of Institutional Placement

The belief that respite services can contain costs by delaying or preventing nursing home placement ignores not only the complex responses of caregivers to those services but also the long and often agonizing process caregivers undergo when deciding to move relatives to institutions. Nursing homes evoke the most anxiety. Since their establishment in the 1930s, reports of the poor quality of their care have circulated widely. The US Senate Committee on Aging held a series of hearings between 1963 and 1974, leading to reform of both federal and state regulations. Nevertheless, the Institute of Medicine concluded in 1986 that a high proportion of nursing home residents received "shockingly deficient care." The 1987 Nursing Home Reform Act addressed some, but by no means all, of the problems. Grave concerns about quality persist. In 2008 state surveyors found that 25.6 percent of nursing homes had deficiencies that harmed residents or placed them in immediate jeopardy. A 2019 study reported that 75 percent of nursing homes failed to meet federal guidelines for staffing levels of registered nurses; they were often completely absent on weekends.[1] The growing dominance of for-profit enterprises has heightened quality concerns. By 2008, 70 percent of the 15,720 nursing homes were for-profit; corporate chains controlled more than half.[2] Moreover, the past few years have witnessed a steep rise in private equity investment, from less than six hundred deals in 2004 to more than fifteen hundred in 2019. Staff shortages have increased while safety precautions, including infection control, have languished.[3]

Although most nursing homes are privately owned, the government often pays the bill. Medicaid, public assistance for low-income Americans, is the primary funding source, covering more than half of the residents. The government contains costs not only by restricting the use of public funds for home- and community-based services but also by keeping the Medicaid reimbursement rate for nursing homes very low (in some states, beneath the cost of treating Medicaid residents). That practice has serious consequences. Facilities increasingly seek short-stay patients recovering from acute illnesses who can rely on Medicare, public insurance for those sixty-five years and over, which reimburses facilities at a higher level than Medicaid does. They also give priority to long-term patients who can pay their own way, at least initially. Medicaid recipients thus must often wait a long time to find a bed. Some nursing homes evict residents who apply for Medicaid after exhausting their resources. Facilities with high proportions of Medicaid residents have the lowest staff levels and receive the most citations for healthcare deficiencies. Located primarily in low-income communities, they serve disproportionate numbers of African Americans and other people of color.[4] In addition to Medicaid, some veterans receive institutional care from the Veterans Administration.

Assisted living facilities originated in a grassroots movement in the early 1980s to provide alternatives to nursing homes by granting residents more autonomy and providing less institutional surroundings. As they expanded rapidly in the 1990s, for-profit companies increasingly took control.[5] Today, assisted living is a multi-billion-dollar industry that operates with little federal or state regulation. In 2016, approximately 81 percent of assisted living facilities were for profit; more than 57 percent were affiliated with large chains.[6] Because minimal public funding is available, the industry primarily serves an affluent population. In some cases, fees increase when patients need more assistance. A growing number of critics charge that many facilities fail to disclose the entire rate structure at admission, refuse to fulfill promises that residents can age in place, and provide inadequate care and supervision to an increasingly disabled clientele.[7] We will see that many forum participants are acutely aware of those problems.

Although public policies and private initiatives seek to keep people out of institutions, the caregiving discourse may have the opposite effect, especially for those suffering from dementia. Nearly two-thirds of nursing home residents have some form of cognitive impairment.[8] Over and over, health professionals, books, websites, and support groups remind family members of the following points. Caregivers' physical and mental health is as important as that of their relatives. Too much stress can lead to "burnout," making further home care impossible. Family members who place relatives with dementia in nursing homes are not "failures" and should not feel guilty. Because institutions employ trained and skilled staff, they can offer the most appropriate care and keep people with advanced disease safer than they could be at home. Rather than "dumping" relatives into facilities, most Americans consider institutionalization only as a last resort. But virtually all people with dementia will need to enter nursing homes at some point. Because beds are scarce and people with dementia can adjust to institutional care better before they reach the most advanced stages of their disease, family members should begin to investigate possible facilities early in the disease course.

Like other caregivers, most participants on the spouse or partner forum initially were determined to rely exclusively on home care until a relative's advancing dementia forced them to reconsider.[9] At that point, they confronted numerous obstacles. One was the quality of care. Even caregivers who could afford to pay privately were appalled by what they found. "I visited two nursing homes today," wrote Cynthia, "and to be blunt, I wouldn't board a dog in either one of them. And for this they are charging $72,000 per year" (January 3, 2018). Others could not afford to pay out of pocket. Some who had thought they had done everything right (stayed in school, gotten good jobs, bought health insurance, and saved for retirement) were shocked to discover they had no protection from the cost of long-term care. "We are desperate," wrote Donald. "We don't qualify for Medicaid and we have Medicare but it doesn't cover nursing homes. Private pay is too expensive but we can't continue caring for mom. Every week she has a delusional episode, running away from us, hiding in the woods. What are we supposed to do? Meds don't work. Nothing works. How do we get her into a facility?? Are there any loopholes we don't know about? Help!" (August 28, 2020). After noting how often she was told her husband needed to be in a nursing home, Cheryl wrote, "What planet do a lot of people live on, and who in the world can afford it, if necessary? Sticky Wicket!!!" (December 31, 2013). Frank could not decide whether to send his wife to a nursing home because "the cost is out of pocket and expensive. It will wipe me out in 3 years" (April 20, 2013). Others decided to keep spouses home as long as possible to avoid having to pay nursing home or assisted living facility fees.

Caregivers who applied for funding from Medicaid or the Veterans Administration discovered the process could be cumbersome and protracted. Both required applicants to submit documents that were often difficult to locate. Even with a lawyer's help, Brenda's application for Medicaid for her husband took four months (June 17, 2014). Another woman was shocked to discover that the "nicer" facilities have only a few beds, if any, for Medicaid recipients, and that most require residents to pay privately for one or two years before converting to Medicaid (April 25, 2020). A husband complained that a caseworker "botched the asset evaluation" and repeatedly gave him the wrong information. He hoped he did not have to hire an expensive attorney to prove he was poor (April 4, 2020).

Reflecting on the various reports she read in the forum about applying to the Veterans Administration, Janice wrote in January 2019, "While some applications go smoothly, other applications face numerous ridiculous and absurd frustrations that go on for months." She had experienced those frustrations firsthand: "I've been waiting since July for approval of the Catastrophically Disabled Veteran category 4 status application. Most of the delay is the result of the VA saying it wrote asking for more information, another form, in August, but I never received the letter. That cost three and a half months. Am waiting again now" (January 14, 2019).

Admission to a facility was not guaranteed. The most desirable ones had long waiting lists. A few spouses were rejected at pre-admission interviews. Joyce, who had worked at a biomedical research company, was especially irate: "I spent weeks of sleepless nights making the placement decision for Gregory, time thinking about what to take from the house, setting aside his clothes, lining up someone to move the furniture, gathering pictures of family and friends, writing a brief biography, purchasing some additional pieces of furniture, basically spending tons of emotional capital leading up to signing the contract (all this with many assurances from the Memory Care facility that he'd do fine adjusting). The next step was an in-home evaluation by their nurse to determine what his care charges would be." The nurse's voice was "aggressive and somewhat loud," and she seemed to try to deliberately provoke him. As a result, he picked up a chair near him.

> I received a call from the nurse later in the afternoon to say that the facility would not accept him. WHAT? So this after only a five minute evaluation. They were worried that if the other residents approached him, tried to hug him or touch his puzzle, that he might hurt them. I can certainly understand that concern. But aren't memory care facilities that advertise their expertise in Alzheimer's disease supposed to be equipped to handle these sorts of Alzheimer's behaviors? Or do they want only to take care of easy-going elderly residents whose dementia is only memory-related and not the most difficult symptoms that come with Alzheimer's disease? (November 23, 2017)

Joyce echoed the complaint of many caregivers who used respite care that service providers seemed to know little about managing people with advanced dementia.

And admission could be revoked. A few writers were horrified to learn that many facilities refused to honor promises to keep residents until the end. Some assisted living facilities evicted residents when their dementia reached a late stage. And both nursing homes and assisted living facilities discharged those who began to act aggressively. Termination occasionally occurred abruptly. Rebecca wrote about an incident with her brother-in-law: "My husband and I had just gotten his brother moved to a Memory Care Unit closer to home a month ago. We thought everything was going great and we were never told otherwise. My husband received a call from the administrator today that she was evicting his brother to the hospital psych. [ward] and that he could not return there. We are devastated and do not know what to do" (December 24, 2019).

Placing relatives in nursing homes followed two distinct timetables. Some caregivers had to enroll their spouses in a hurry. After violent episodes, police had taken their spouses to geriatric-neuropsychiatric hospital wards, where doctors insisted that institutional placement follow discharge. Although some hospital social workers offered help, they could find few facilities willing to accept those patients, and the caregivers had little time to canvass possible alternatives. "The decision has been taken out of my hands," wrote Diane.

> Doctors/family/friends all say it is now time to place dh because of his violence & now wandering (he has physically tried to attack myself & our dtr w/a knife which is why he ended up in the hosp) He is currently in a geriatric psych hosp . . . so now trying to find a nursing home that will take him, because of his violence . . . & refusal to take his medics, we are very limited in places. . . . Unfortunately 2 of the places found so far that are close to me have poor reviews so I've eliminated them. We keep going farther away from home but want him to be well taken care of so if I have to drive extra miles then I will, but makes it harder to see him as often especially in the winter. (December 29, 2016)

Pamela wrote, "I feel that the hospital is putting me in a real bind because they don't want to keep him 3 days, and they expect me to put my beloved in basically a kennel for old people. Plus, how can I make a decision of this magnitude in one afternoon?" (May 3, 2018). A woman who had quit her job to care for her husband finally admitted defeat. "Four weeks ago my life became a nightmare," she wrote. "I tried to place my DH in a [nursing home] where he became violent. Cops were called. DH was sent to the ER and was in the hospital for 3 weeks because no facility would accept him. After no other choice I took him home." She was far from reconciled to her lot: "I know this sounds bad, but I just don't know how long I can do this. I thought I was going to get my life back" (June 2, 2016).

A much larger group of caregivers asked for advice because they were agonizing over whether or not to move their spouses or partners to institutions. Several insisted this was the hardest decision they had ever had to make. Caregiving burdens vied with emotional ties, fears of initiating an irreparable rupture, and guilt over sending intimates away. "My DH is a sweet, sweet man," wrote Denise, "yet it is exhausting me to take care of him. How will I know when it is time to commit him to full-time memory care? They can't possibly love him as I do, though I'm sure they would give him good care. Plus, he is male and most of the residents are female. He is big and strong and vigorous physically and also very gentle and kind most of the time. How do I make this life-changing decision?" (June 26, 2016). The contradictions in the post underscored Denise's ambivalence. (Her husband was "big and strong" but also "gentle"; they could not love him as much as she did but would give him good care.) Ronald had left high school teaching to care for his wife with early-onset Alzheimer's disease. Now he wondered if he could bear sending her away from home: "How in the world do you survive dropping your 57 year old wife, stage 6 in assisted living home, youngest person there by 9 years and walk out door and live with yourself???????????" (May 26, 2013).

In many cases, encouragement from others (health professionals, support-group leaders, family members, and friends) added to the mix of considerations. "My husband has gotten so much worse," wrote Sharon. "During his last hospital stay the doctors and nurses kept suggesting nursing home placement. I can't seem to grasp that yet although I'm exhausted. Does that mean I'm not ready to give up?" (February 12, 2014). Two women had to decide whether to leave spouses in facilities originally chosen for respite care. Five weeks before writing, Carolyn had enrolled her husband in an assisted living facility on a temporary basis. Now she wondered whether he should remain there permanently. She was "feeling more at ease" since he left. Moreover, "The Co-Facilitators of My caregiving [group], say that I've done a great job and gone thru so much caring for 1 person in a life time. This includes 12 years of ALZ, also 4 back surgeries and a hip surgery." Nevertheless, she still went "back and forth. How does someone know it's time, or even how to ask Drs. what they think? I'm hurting and so confused" (November 11, 2016). Rose's own health concerns compounded her dilemma. After suffering a small stroke, she had placed her husband in a facility for a two-week respite, hoping to use that time to sleep better and reduce her stress level. When she visited him after the first week, she "felt such overwhelming sadness and wanted to just pack up his things and bring him back home." At one point he said he missed her. "You can imagine how hard that was to hear. We both had tears in our eyes and it took all my strength not to break down and cry. It is so strange to be living alone right now—to have a husband but not be together." Her family and friends tried to convince her to place him permanently, but she remained torn: "I know his care requires constant vigilance on my part and this is physically and emotionally exhausting but I feel so depressed thinking this is where we have come to in our marriage. . . . Yet his care really is a 24/7 job and I don't know how much longer I can do this without having another serious health issue" (August 29, 2015).

Other circumstances also made institutionalization seem attractive. Wanda found it increasingly difficult to lift her husband, who weighed 250 pounds (August 22, 2016). Jean wrote, "I know some of you are determined to care for your LO's until the end, but I am the sole caregiver with no other family to help out" (May 1, 2016). Others were unable to prevent spouses from falling or control their agitation. Nevertheless, those caregivers too asked for advice because they remained uncertain about the correct course of action.

Some support-group members hesitated after completing the application. "Papers all filled out and ready to be submitted," wrote Vicki, "but now I have second thoughts." Introducing herself to the forum six years earlier, she had written that she and her husband were moving from Florida to Michigan, where they had six children who could help provide care. As her husband became more debilitated, however, she realized that her children were preoccupied with their own lives. When she tried home help, he became violent. He then refused to stay in day care. And now her diabetes was out of control. She was getting "headaches more frequently, heart palpitations and other physical pains." Nevertheless, she felt "like I will rip his heart out if I separate him from me and more so from his dog" (August 26, 2017).

Because caregivers received advice to place relatives' names on waiting lists early in the disease trajectory, it is not surprising that many writers remained indecisive when informed of openings. Sheila decided she no longer could care adequately for her sixty-two-year-old husband with advanced Alzheimer's. "Sadly," she wrote,

> I believe he is ready for residential care. He was accepted in a highly regarded memory care facility 45 min. from home. It's breaking my heart to make final decision. He will likely be the highest functioning person there and I have so many mixed emotions . . . I've read here that it is not recommended to "second guess" the decision for additional care. And many of our friends believe this is best for all. I want to make the right decision. Any advice from someone who has had to make this decision? We have lots of support from family and friends, but ultimately I am the one who is accountable and will live with the decision when made. Need to decide by noon tomorrow! Sure would appreciate additional perspective at the 12th hour. (January 17, 2014)

Several other caregivers rejected the beds that became available. Timothy wondered how he could put his "wife of 56 years" in an institution. One of her aides had told him that she needed "24/7 supervision. It is getting hard to even understand verbal instructions. There was an opening at a highly recommended facility and I was all set to take her, but I could not emotionally do it. She is very dependent on me and close to her dogs" (August 5, 2012). Sonia wrote, "I'm sure hoping that I made the right and best decision. They called this morning with an opening if we wanted it. . . . Said it may be 3–4 more months before they get another opening or longer. . . . I passed on the bed right now because my heart isn't ready to move him. The lady did agree with what y'all been saying about them adjusting better when placed earlier than later, so for now I am thinking that I will use this next little bit to better steel my heart for what surely must come" (September 11, 2014). The night before Ruth's husband left home, she confessed, "I am a wreck about all this, putting my husband in memory care facility. I hope I am strong enough to hold it together. I do not even know how I am going to get him inside that building, this is the hardest thing that I have ever done. I am so guilty that I am doing this, it is eating me up inside" (April 30, 2017).

Ambivalence occasionally lingered after enrollment.[10] A few caregivers brought spouses home. Rhonda explained, "I just couldn't stand being without him" (February 10, 2018). Phyllis used similar words but focused on her husband's feelings rather than her own: "I couldn't stand it. It was the wrong place for Alan. He was nowhere near as debilitated as all the other residents and he just refused to eat and cried a lot. My daughter came with me today and took one look and said—let's make a break for it and get him out of here—it's all wrong, and she was right" (January 31, 2015). Scott, however, reconsidered after removing his wife from a facility: "Last spring, after a long decline, I put my DW in Memory Care. It was agonizing. I hated myself for weeks, brought her home, 'just to try one more time,' and failing that, took her back permanently" (September 7, 2019).

A few other writers transferred their spouses to different institutions. A woman whose husband had been a truck driver explained why she moved him to a facility that was farther away: "The Assisted Living Home that Jerry is in is on the opposite side of town to where we live, but I had to place him in a 'quality' home. Most of the Assisted Living Homes around our house that Jerry had been in before, did not give Jerry even the basic care (enough food and water) and in one home, Jerry had 3 injuries in one week!" (March 15, 2014). A second woman found a better nursing home closer to home:

> My love was in what was supposed to be a wonderful nursing facility some distance from me. It went from what I thought was good to unfortunately not so good, and there was an attitude among the aides that showed that some of them didn't want to be doing that job. In all fairness, I probably wouldn't want it full time either, but that doesn't mean they needed to display that attitude.
>
> Happy to report we have been finally able to move LO much closer to a newer facility where the staff seem to like having LO there rather than just tolerating. It is not a line of wheelchair bound residents snoozing in front of the nursing station and most importantly at least for now (fingers crossed) LO is not left in bed half the day with a sleeping pill. . . . We talk, attend activities, and I can see more interaction.

She hoped her good luck would hold, adding, "Please send your prayers that this continues" (October 16, 2012).

The great majority of writers did not reconsider the placement decision. Some described the enormous sense of relief they experienced. Three weeks after her husband's departure, Lori wrote, "I now understand what taking the weight off your shoulders means. I did not realize how stressed I was! I haven't had any chest pain, [blood pressure] is down, I am not reaching for food to console me, and I am sleeping all night . . . I have had several wonderful days with my grandchildren, not having to keep them quiet or away from grandpa. I have had coffee with friends, gone to church, went for long walks. I feel like I am living again. Hardest decision I have ever made but it now feels right" (September 25, 2016). Brian commented that although he was "an emotional wreck" after placing his wife in a nursing home, he quickly became convinced that she could receive better care there. Calling late the first evening, he "learned that they were able to give her a shower and that she was sleeping in her pajamas. I have been unable to get her to take a bath or shower in over 3 years and she has slept in her clothes for 2 years. Just getting her to change clothes or even a wet depends can take me days or hours. Trained staff was able to get her clean in one night. I am told it took two of them to do it. While still grieving I rejoiced" (April 2, 2016).

More commonly, the sorrow that enveloped the writers was unalloyed. Nina, for example, wrote,

Today I placed my dear sweet DH in Memory Care. No Matter how much I prepared myself for this day and how worn out and ready I felt for the transition, I never anticipated the profound sadness I am feeling right now. After I left him, I couldn't bring myself to come home so I drove around for hours. I went to the grocery store and bought dinner for "one." Finally I got up my courage and came home to a dark and empty house. I keep thinking I hear him moving around or calling my name but that's just my imagination. I am alone and that is how it will be from now on. I realize this is all about me and nothing about how sad and scared and confused he might be right now. I will call in a few hours and talk to the nurse. I pray that he is calm and able to sleep tonight. (November 17, 2016)

Guilt was even more widespread. Elaine had just begun to enjoy her new life when her husband asked when he could go home:

Three weeks ago when I put my husband in a Nursing Home in an alzheimers unit I was burned out and unhappy and at my wits end. Since then, I have been happier than I have been in at least 3 years. I am getting a good nights sleep, I am rested, I don't have to pay attention to someone else 24/7. But today my husband wanted to know when I was bringing him home. My heart sunk, he understood when I put him in there that I needed to do this for myself, but now he just gives me that don't you love me anymore look. Have others of you had this experience? How do I deal with my guilt? (October 25, 2018)

Cheryl's husband adopted a different strategy:

After 5 years of 24/7 care for my husband of 59 years of marriage, I had to place him in [memory care]. He became increasingly verbally abusive. Demanding constant attention. Accusing me of unheard things. Our 5 children and my pastor encouraged me to place him in mc. I did not realize the stress, anxiety and back pain I was having came from trying to do it all. The night after I placed him in mc, I slept the night through. My back pain left. . . . He begs to come home. Will find a new wife to take care of him. That I want his money. I didn't know how to care for him anyhow. So many accusations. I hate the thought of visiting. I feel so guilty. (April 22, 2018)

But guilt also could arise even when spouses seemed comfortable in their new surroundings. Victoria, too, had embarked on a new life. "Hubby has adjusted so well to his memory care home," she wrote.

He thinks I live upstairs and is always delighted to see me but has never once complained or asked to come home with me when it's time to leave. I've taken him out a few times and he's always been ready to go home afterward. He seems to have forgotten ever living anywhere other than where he lives now. I've been going to see him every day but I missed a couple of evenings this week. He didn't seem to notice but I felt so guilty. I guess because I was continuing to live my life without him. Survivor's guilt? One night I started working on taxes as soon as I got home (the last

1099 had arrived in the mail) and I didn't notice the time until I looked up and realized he'd be getting ready for bed. The second night I had a church meeting that we'd planned to attend together but getting him after work and bringing him back downtown through traffic would've meant skipping my dinner and spending more than an hour in gridlock and likely being late and frazzled. He didn't remember the meeting or ask about it and it probably ran too long for his current capacity anyway but I sat there feeling guilty that I was enjoying the evening without him.

Those of you who are a few steps ahead on this journey, does this guilt go away? How do you handle it? Next week, I am chairing two evening meetings so I won't be able to get out for a visit before his bedtime nights. It's hard to work full time and honor my few remaining church/community services obligations and also get out to visit him on weekdays. It's at least a 30-minute round-trip drive (much more during peak traffic hours.) . . . Is it okay to just visit every other day? (February 21, 2015)

Like many others, June felt the need to justify her placement decision, which provoked both sorrow and grief:

My loved one was admitted 3 months ago to LTC facility which is very nice with excellent care. So no problem there. The problem is ME. I was relieved of the stress, constant care and taking care of everything plus the dementia behaviors. I did well with admission and have gotten along well, visiting most days, having meals with him but I am heart broken just going to see him. I am getting so that I hate going to see him. I hate being there and I hate coming home and then I feel guilty. I knew in my heart that I could no longer do all that is required and placement was the right answer. He has had this disease for 14 years. I just couldn't continue. (August 4, 2016)

Comparing herself to other support-group members, Marlene felt a deep sense of failure. Both her cardiologist and her geriatrician as well as her children finally had convinced her to move her husband to a nursing

home. "Even tho' I know it's the thing to do," she wrote, "I'm having terrible guilt. So many of you are doing it at home so I figure: 'Why can't I?'
Am I a weak person or selfish or less caring?" (February 28, 2015).

As many researchers and policy analysts note, family members often
view institutional placement as a way to alleviate the stress of care. The
advice they receive from others encourages that perspective. The forum
participants examined in this chapter, however, focused far more on the
guilt they experienced. The following chapter explores the reasons why
that feeling was so pervasive.

* * *

Some disability activists suggest eliminating nursing homes while greatly
expanding home- and community-based services.[11] When we consider
the long history of segregating and isolating people with both cognitive and physical disabilities in institutions, that proposal makes good
sense.[12] But it risks replicating the tragedy of the deinstitutionalization
of mental hospitals. Between 1955 and 1975, the population of the nation's
mental hospitals plunged from 559,000 to 193,000. President Kennedy
was a major advocate of managing mentally ill people outside hospitals, calling for a "bold new approach" based on the establishment of a
vast network of community mental health services.[13] But that promise
remained unfulfilled. One observer notes that "mental health professionals were . . . oblivious to what it might mean for families to replace
the ward staff without the training and resources ordinarily available
in the hospital."[14] Mentally ill people who had no one to take them in
often ended up on the streets, contributing to the present homelessness
crisis.[15]

The proposal to close long-term care institutions also would not
serve the needs of the family caregivers we have examined. Although
this chapter focused on their strong reluctance to move spouses and
partners to nursing homes and assisted living facilities and the sorrow
and guilt they felt after doing so, they faced such intense conflicts precisely because they believed that institutional placement eventually was

essential. Forum participants who could not find a way to enroll relatives in nursing homes or assisted living facilities described themselves as desperate. Very few removed relatives from those facilities. And, as we will see, the writers were virtually unanimous in recommending institutionalization when advising others. Even during the COVID-19 pandemic, when the death rate in nursing homes steadily mounted, the writers urged other caregivers not to bring relatives home. The forum participants wanted the quality of long-term care facilities improved, access to them increased, and their fees reduced, but they also wanted institutions to remain an option when the demands of care overwhelmed them. Eliminating that alternative would make caregivers feel even more trapped than they currently are in circumstances they cannot control.

7

"Oh No, Don't Feel Guilty"

Advising Others and Fighting Back

The forum participants not only articulated their own concerns but also responded to the worries other members expressed. Viewing those responses along with the original messages participants posted enables us to assess the extent to which caregivers are likely to become a force for change. The responses varied enormously. Some forum participants simply sent prayers or good wishes. Some reflected and validated other writers' feelings of sadness and guilt by sharing their own. Some told of troubles that resonated with the ones others had described. And some explained how they had coped with and ultimately overcome similar problems, providing reassurance that strident objections to day care gradually diminished, that aides formed close relationships with the elders in their care, and that, over time, both caregivers and spouses adjusted to institutionalization.

Most responders also offered advice. Despite the diversity of stories, these writers generally agreed about several points. First, rather than allowing the disease to claim two victims, caregivers must care for themselves. For example, they never should tolerate acts of aggression. For their own protection, they must call 911 immediately and ensure that their spouses are taken to the hospital for medication management. (Although numerous reports have pointed to the dangers of overmedication for elders, most writers appeared to be unaware of them.[1] None referred to other approaches, including the one recommended by the "personhood" movement: trying to understand the meaning of behavior problems to the elders and find ways to communicate with them.)

Caring for oneself also includes getting as much help as possible. Various strategies can help caregivers overcome resistance to respite services. They can say that homecare workers are there for their own benefit, not to tend the spouses. They should call day care an adult activity center or club and create the illusion that the clients are there to work or volunteer. They also can ease spouses into programs, staying with them for the first few hours or days. "In my experience," wrote Bruce, "caregivers give up too soon. The director of our daycare encouraged people to give their loved ones at least 3 weeks to adjust. I went through 3 weeks of hell at the beginning, crying and fussing about not going, etc. After 3 weeks, it was like someone had flipped a switch, and it was OK. My wife never looked forward to going, but all the crying and fussing stopped" (January 20, 2017). Others wrote that their spouses eventually enjoyed the programs they initially resisted.

Despite the many negative reports of overnight care, one woman received overwhelming encouragement when she announced that she planned to use that form of respite to attend her brother's eighty-fifth birthday. The comments were even more enthusiastic after she reported that she and her husband had visited the facility, and he seemed to agree to spend two days there. The posts read, "I am so happy you found this and will be able to get away for a few days"; "I so love that you're being proactive in finding respite care"; "Good for you. It sounds like you have a good plan worked out"; "There is nothing more therapeutic than a 'break' from what we have to deal with on a 24/7 basis. All I can say is GO FOR IT!!!! It will only make you a better caregiver"; "Way to go!"; "Do it! Do it! Do it!" (September 22, 2014).

Second, because dementia advances inexorably, family members should learn what is in store and plan for the future. In response to a woman who wondered how long she could keep her mother living with her and her family, Kim wrote, "Educate yourself on the course dementia takes. It is beyond a full time job once the night waking, incontinence, shadowing the caregiver, loss of constructive pastimes, and so many other things set in. Backbreaking, exhausting work" (June 3, 2020).

Responding to a man who wondered what he should say to friends and family who were pushing him to have a plan for memory care, Lynn wrote, "A caregiver should always have a Plan A, Plan B, and Plan C. Go ahead and call some facilities, get pricing and tour them if possible. Find a facility that offers respite care. If you get sick, need surgery, or decide you need a vacation or break for your own personal care, you will have a place you trust to temporarily care for your wife. If she suddenly progresses and you can no longer care for her you will be prepared for placement" (December 26, 2020).

Although many writers may have struggled over the decision to place relatives in institutions, their advice to others displayed little ambivalence. A recurrent statement was that caregivers who ask if their spouses are ready for institutionalization usually know the time has come. They should look for the highest level of care possible. Assisted living facilities are useful, but only up to a certain point. Keeping someone with advanced dementia in independent living was, in one man's words, "like trying to rearrange the deck chairs on the Titanic" (January 17, 2020). After a woman complained that an assisted living facility had transferred her mother to the memory care unit, Jacqueline replied, "Most all of us dream of our LO living for a few years in assisted living. The harsh reality is, by the time we place because of care needed, the AL ship has either sailed or is very, very short lived. The discussion boards are full of members who found this out. It's shocking—a splash of cold water to our face. It's upsetting" (November 19, 2019). The writers also noted that after institutionalization, many people wonder if they made the right decision. They should know that they undoubtedly did. Family members can transfer patients to other facilities if the care at the present one is unacceptable. Under no circumstances, however, should they bring elders home.

Third, although grief around nursing home placement is common, it can be endured and eventually will fade. "I still miss him so much but it does get easier," wrote Rita seven months after her husband left home (June 2, 2016). Guilt, however, should not be allowed to take its natural course. Over and over caregivers were told to fight against that emotion. A daughter counseled others, "I think guilt—over many things—is one of the most destructive forces in this whole experience. Any time you can avoid or alleviate that feeling is a good thing" (May 18, 2020). After one woman wrote that she felt guilty after placing her partner of thirty-two years in a facility, a man replied, "You should not feel guilty. I know it's tough on you and certainly tough on your partner, but I can attest being a 24/7 caregiver is very challenging and stressful" (March 1, 2018). We recall Sherry, who wrote that she felt guilty visiting her husband in a facility although he had been abusive and their pastor and five children had urged her to send him there. The responses to her post read, "Your children and pastor are wise and care about you. You have nothing to be guilty over"; "Oh my goodness. No, don't feel guilty. The disease is taking over his mind"; "Guilt? I think most people feel some type of guilt when they have done their best but it wasn't good enough to eradicate the disease. But when we feel guilt for something that is beyond our control, it is not realistic, no matter how badly we feel. You have done your job and more. No reason to feel guilt"; "You did the right thing, even though you feel guilty. Alzheimers doesn't care who it grabs or what it does to spouses" (April 23, 2018).

Fourth, caregivers should greet all assertions by facilities with skepticism. If a nursing home guarantees that a private-pay patient can convert to Medicaid after a year, the caregiver should demand a written statement to that effect. Administrators of assisted living facilities who promise that everyone can "age in place" should be held accountable. They also should be forced to disclose the rates for all levels of care before patients enroll. Family members should be wary of all marketers and especially of A Place for Mom, a for-profit senior care referral service with branches in major cities throughout the country.[2] Because few sources of information exist for people searching for facilities, many forum participants had consulted the service. Most had serious complaints. Robin wrote that when her husband was about to be discharged from a geriatric psych ward, she "tried place for mom—that was an awful experience—the guy said well, it doesn't matter what the place is like, you have to get him somewhere. Really? I am going to pay $600 a month for him to be in substandard housing with a roommate and there is one shower for 12 people??? I don't think so" (July 23, 2014). Kevin "just had to rant a little" about "this miserable company. They were essentially a marketing company for their contracted care facilities" (January 30, 2020). Raymond, who gave up his contracting business to care for his wife, agreed: "This company deliberately misled me, lied to me, and used aggressive (if not predatory) sales tactics. In fact, just seconds after entering my phone number on their website, they were calling me. Red flags galore. And they are hard to shake. Maybe there are others who have gotten some benefit from them, but I wished I had never contacted them" (January 20, 2020). When one woman wrote that she found representatives of A Place for Mom "very kind, sensitive, and helpful," another warned, "When using these referral agencies, you will be killed with kindness. That is part of their job and they do it well. Lovely empathy, kindly swift responses, spelling out information quite quickly and staying in close contact. This is part of their business model and how they format their business. And believe me, it is all about 'business.' They really need you" (June 3, 2014).

Some writers generalized about the profit motive throughout the long-term care system. Paula explained what happened when a for-profit company took over the independent homecare agency she had been using for her husband: "The Agency being bought was a small agency and very good to their nursing staff (benefits, compensation etc.). The agency which purchased them was driven by many layers of bureaucracy which ultimately has to be paid off the back of the nurses (thus continuously decreasing benefits and compensation). Nurses were very dedicated to us but very unhappy with their employer." Because many staff left, Paula switched to a nonprofit agency (August 6, 2017).[3]

Profit-making facilities received many more complaints. "I am not a revolutionary," Anthony assured other forum members. "I just think our sick and elderly deserve better especially when they cannot speak for themselves. The Assisted Living reality in the USA is horrible. I am in a caregiving group and the horror stories make me shake in fear. You may tour a facility that has gorgeous public rooms with lovely landscaping and a wood paneled library with gleaming chandeliers. But you have to remind yourself that every one of these facilities is a FOR PROFIT corporation" (September 2, 2014). Linda identified herself as the woman whose husband was "badly neglected" in overnight care. After a 2013 PBS *Frontline* program exposed the many serious safety violations of the largest US assisted living operator, she urged other participants to check their local stations for the show: "It's an eye opener. In essence there are many people being put in assisted living facilities who should be in skilled nursing homes, but the profit motive is strong to fill those beds, no matter what the individual needs. There are some sad stories on this program. . . . Please watch the program" (September 27, 2013).[4] A post two weeks later read, "The system operates on finance and profit and where that is the driver, the actual service is often compromised to meet the bottom line outcome" (October 12, 2013). Other caregivers focused on nursing homes. In response to the woman who complained that the only two available nursing homes for her husband were basically "kennels for old people," George wrote, "I agree that I would not put my dog in a nursing home if they are the same as the ones around here. These seem to be just a place to warehouse the really sick people until they die. Most are owned by large for profit corporations so the more they can pack in and the less care they can provide, the more profit there is. Look for non-profit facilities" (May 3, 2018). A woman whose husband died after a fall in a nursing home decided that "a synonym for a for-profit home is an understaffed one" (Simone, July 17, 2018).

Finally, and most importantly, caregivers must fight for what they need. To be sure, we saw in the previous chapter that some writers met disappointment with resignation. When respite services let them down, caregivers made comments such as the following: "I guess that is the way it is"; "Such is the life of a dementia caregiver"; "Now it's back to 24/7"; "The moral of this story is that we are all on our own and can only depend on ourselves." In response to the last comment, a woman wrote, "I agree. When we think we are getting help something goes wrong" (December 17, 2013). But many others urged family members to act more aggressively. The wife of a man with hearing loss and Parkinson's as well as Alzheimer's explained, "Those of us taking care of a loved one who has dementia have our hands full. We need all the help we can get. So we're pretty vulnerable. Agencies and workers can take advantage of our vulnerability. The solution is to understand the system and make sure that doesn't happen" (January 12, 2015).

As a first step, caregivers must know their rights. Jane had refused to allow a nursing home to discharge her husband without any place to go. "Don't let them bully you," she instructed others. George wrote in response, "Good for you. Standing your ground" (February 10, 2018). Marcus posted the Tennessee law about involuntary transfers and discharges by nursing homes and noted that most other states had enacted similar legislation (February 10, 2018). A woman received similar advice after writing that the director of her husband's assisted living facility said he no longer could stay. She knew that "legally they have to give us 30 days notice." Dennis had two additional suggestions: "First of all immediately file an appeal to the involuntary discharge notice with the facility. That will buy you more time to look around if nothing else. Secondly CALL YOUR LONG TERM CARE OMBUDSMAN in your state and file a complaint. Surely they knew he had dementia when they took him in and they can't just decide they don't want him. They often use the claim that he is a danger to himself or others when in fact if he had close supervision that wouldn't be a problem. They may need more staffing to do a good job" (December 13, 2015). Replying to Janice, the woman who wrote in desperation because she could not get anyone from the Veterans Administration to return her calls, Beverly described her own "hard battle" to get her husband into the state VA facility: "I called several government officials but our luck changed for the better after I contacted Senator McCain and his office referred me to our Senator Lieberman. Go to the media if you have to. That would have been my next step. And good luck. I used to think I was a tactful polite person, that all changed when I engaged in the fight to get my Vietnam vet sweetie the care he deserved. Good luck and tell them 'no' is not in your vocabulary" (June 24, 2015). Gloria also urged Janice to pursue every option: "Have you exhausted everything and everybody at your VA Medical Center? Have you talked to the Patient Advocate, the Chief, Social Work Service, the Director of the Medical Center, the Chief of Staff? If you've done all this and gotten nowhere, you can still contact the VA central office. . . . Hang in there, don't give up. Be persistent, you know the squeaky wheel gets the grease!" (June 23, 2015).

In addition, caregivers should apply for Medicaid, regardless of their financial situation. In a qualitative study of Los Angeles caregivers, sociologist Sandra R. Levitsky found that most believed that Medicaid, rather than Medicare, provided the model for expanded government funding of long-term care. The reason, Levitsky argued, was that that program was aligned with their deeply held beliefs about family responsibility. Recipients could not qualify for Medicaid until they had fulfilled that responsibility by spending down to the rigid Medicaid eligibility standard.[5] But the caregivers who submitted posts in this study appear to have believed that they had discharged their family obligation by providing unpaid care. They urged others to apply for Medicaid early in the disease trajectory to avoid spending money they could have saved on care.

A constant refrain was that caregivers should hire a certified elder care attorney (CELA) who could exploit the loopholes in the application process. In response to a husband who noted that his wife needed institutional care but was not eligible for Medicaid, Roger wrote, "If you won't take our advice and speak with a good CELA, you'll never know, but it could well be the worst financial mistake of your life. Several 'high net worth' husbands in my support group were able to qualify their wives" (April 28, 2020). When another man complained that his caseworker had "botched the asset evaluation" for his wife, the reply focused on the government's parsimony: "States depend on people trying to 'do it yourself' so the state can save money when the application is screwed up. . . . It is not a do it yourself job. You are asking for a lot of money from the state while at the same time you can preserve assets for yourself. THE STATE HATES THAT and if they can beat you down you won't get it" (April 4, 2020). Although there were many legal ways to "game" the Medicaid application process, one woman did not protest when she learned that her lawyer had engaged in unlawful activity. On June 7, 2014, she wrote,

> Peter is now in a long term facility. He has been away from home 5 months, in the facility the last 3. My attorney applied for Medicaid on March 19th and it has taken this long. I have been so stressed about it all this time because I knew I could not pay the $7000 private pay where he is and it is such a wonderful place and they love him and he is happy in his new world. I really down deep didn't think he would qualify because of the requirements that everyone always talks about and our assets, we are not poor but certainly not rich. I can honestly say that a lot of the rules you hear about are not true. . . . It was well worth the Elder Care Attorney fee. I was told by a regular lawyer that some of the things were illegal, but they were signed off by a Superior Court Judge and approved by Medicaid, so thankful for MY attorney.

A few people did reject the suggestion that they apply for Medicaid. Some writers refused to allow the government to scrutinize their financial affairs, hoped to leave money for their children, or recoiled from what they viewed as the humiliation of having their spouses declared financially destitute. Moreover, Medicaid restricted elders to the least desirable facilities, most of which had long waiting lists. Ethical considerations, however, were conspicuously absent in the posts. Critics have long condemned the practice of middle-class seniors spending down to Medicaid eligibility levels to be able to use government funds to pay for long-term care.[6] Viewing Medicaid as an entitlement rather than a welfare program for the poor, the caregivers in this study made no mention of those concerns.

* * *

As issues of care and caring enter the political discourse, some observers look to family caregivers as a force for change.[7] The forums provide contradictory evidence about whether or not family members are likely to engage in collective action. The names of the major advocacy groups for caregivers (Caregiver Action Network, Family Caregiver Alliance, National Alliance for Caregiving, Well Spouse Association) rarely appeared on the posts. The many expressions of guilt we read suggest that caregivers believe that they, rather than the government, should assume primary responsibility for sick and disabled spouses. Holding themselves responsible when elders fail to obtain the care they need, many caregivers do not insist that the government broaden access to supportive services or try to improve their quality.

But guilt does not stem solely from self-blame. Contrasting shame and guilt, psychologists argue that guilt is "other-directed" and associated strongly with empathy.[8] To some extent, then, guilt flows from the same confluence of factors that encourages family caregiving. We have seen that many caregivers were exquisitely attuned to their spouses' feelings. After Michelle's husband left home, she kept hearing him call her name. She prayed "he is calm and able to sleep tonight." When Frances's husband said he missed her, "We both had tears in our eyes, and it took all my strength not to break down and cry." The word "heart" frequently appeared. Vicki feared that transferring her husband to a nursing home would "rip his heart out" (May 10, 2019). Sonia hoped she could "steel my heart" when the time came to place her husband. Jo was "heartbroken" visiting her husband in a facility (March 14, 2018). Sheila said that making the final decision to move her husband to residential care was "breaking my heart" (September 13, 2016).

Psychologists note that guilt "tends to be strongest with intimate partners."[9] Marriage, of course, is one of the most intimate relationships, and the marriages discussed in the forum were very long. We saw that Timothy alluded to his "wife of 56 years"; Sherry wrote about her "hus-

band of 59 years of marriage." One of the few writers to refer to a partner rather than a spouse stressed that they had been together thirty-two
years. Other writers noted the length of their marriages in the introduc-
tions they wrote. When writers described themselves as having betrayed
their spouses by resorting to institutionalization, they may have meant
that they had reneged on the promise to rely exclusively on home care.
But they also may have meant that they had violated their wedding vows
("in sickness and in health") and the trust that had been built into their
relationships over several decades. Alexandra interpreted her responsibilities as a wife very broadly. Recognizing that the time had come to
place her husband, she asked, "How do you deal with the guilt of what
will feel like abandonment to him? He will be scared and sad. I stay
awake every night now worrying about this. I am the one who is supposed to make everything as OK as possible for him, and it feels like I'm
letting him down" (February 14, 2020). (By contrast, a woman caring for
her ex-husband who lacked other sources of help wrote that she viewed
herself as his "administrator." She hoped to put together a team to care
for him but was planning to leave for five months.)

In addition, many forum participants believed family responsibility
should be strictly bounded. Explaining why she had stopped phoning to
check on the aides from an agency caring for her husband while she was
at work, Gloria insisted that she should not always be the one in charge:
"As my stress level goes up, my tolerance goes down and I start to think,
'They are adults and I'm not their direct employer. Is it my responsibility to have to call and check up on them when they don't do what they
said they were gonna do?' Maybe that's a selfish attitude but that's where
I've been brought to with all the passing the buck that has gone on with
not much of anybody taking responsibility for anything except us and
it being us that has to deal with the fall out of being without the help"
(December 12, 2012). When writers complained of overwhelming guilt
after enrolling spouses in respite services or institutions, others insisted
that those caregivers already had discharged their obligations and could
not be expected to do more.

The anger and cynicism that ran through the posts also suggest that many caregivers did not accept the present situation. True, the advice rendered in the forum resonated strongly with messages caregivers heard elsewhere. A multitude of books and articles implore family members to care for themselves and use whatever supportive services are available. The tone of the posts, however, was markedly different. The writers made it clear that their expectations had met a harsh reality. They were enraged when services had failed to treat elders with respect and kindness or even satisfy their basic needs. Several pointed to the dominance of profit-making motives to explain why the elder care system was not geared toward serving their needs and those of their spouses. Although members directed their anger at specific providers rather than the long-term care system as a whole, they were well aware of the need for change. Many other support groups on health issues have converted their sense of community into political action.[10] The following chapter demonstrates that after the 2020 pandemic descended, caregivers were more likely to follow that example.

"No One Is Coming out of This Unscathed"

The Nursing Home Tragedy in the Pandemic

"Disasters have the power to reveal who we are, what we value, what we're willing—and unwilling—to protect," writes sociologist Eric Klinenberg. "They can shame us, unite outrage, inspire protest, and make transformation seem necessary, if not inevitable."[1] Devastating the long-term care system and posing special hazards to elderly people with chronic health problems, the COVID-19 pandemic in 2020 exacerbated virtually all the difficulties of family caregiving. At the same time, the crisis demonstrated the urgent need for social change by exposing the calamitous conditions of nursing homes, the lack of respect for the work of care, and the indifference of federal and state officials to human suffering. Several groups, including many family caregivers, were spurred to action.

On March 8, 2020, Tom Friedan, former director of the US Centers for Disease Control and Prevention (CDC), declared long-term care institutions "ground zero for Covid-19."[2] Two weeks later the nation learned that thirty of the forty-six deaths in Washington had occurred at the Life Care Center in Kirkland, Washington. One-fourth of the residents had died and dozens of others were in the hospital.[3] It was soon clear that the Kirkland facility was not an aberration. By June 26, the virus had killed fifty-four thousand nursing home residents and workers, representing 43 percent of all US fatalities.[4] Many of the deaths were of people with dementia, not only because dementia sufferers constitute nearly half of nursing home residents but also because they were less likely to survive the disease.[5]

The tragedy unfolding in nursing homes was, in the words of two researchers, a "perfect storm."[6] They housed an elderly population with multiple health problems in close quarters. Moreover, increasing control by profit-making entities left facilities unprepared and unable to resist the virus. Most had severely inadequate staffing levels and infection-control procedures. A 2014 study found that 80 percent of non- food-borne outbreaks of norovirus occurred at long-term care institutions.[7] A US General Accountability Office study released on May 20, 2020, reported that 82 percent of nursing homes had been cited for deficiencies in infection control and that more than half of facilities cases had "persistent problems."[8] Other studies demonstrated that nursing homes with histories of low staffing levels and poor quality ratings had the highest number of COVID infections.[9]

Privileged Americans traditionally have viewed outsiders and poor people, especially members of marginalized groups, as disease carriers.[10] One of the clearest recent examples was Trump's insistence on blaming the pandemic on the "China virus." Other responses to the pandemic also followed that pattern. Among the charges leveled at nursing home aides was that they disregarded safety protocols, traveled on public transportation, brought the virus from their communities, and worked at multiple facilities, thus spreading disease from one to another. Various commentators pointed out, however, that many administrators refused to provide adequate personal protective equipment, low wages and part-time jobs forced staff to seek employment at different institutions, few could afford to travel by car, the lack of paid sick days compelled them to work when ill, and they transferred disease not only to their workplaces but also to communities with overcrowded homes and high rates of morbidity and mortality.[11]

State governments did little to remedy the situation. Despite the mounting death toll, they sent whatever protective gear and testing equipment they could garner first to hospitals, leaving nursing homes to scrounge for supplies.[12] Soon after the pandemic began, New York governor Andrew Cuomo ordered nursing homes to accept patients discharged from hospitals even if they had been treated for COVID-19; the facilities were not allowed to test the patients to determine if they were still contagious or had been newly infected.[13] In June the Associated Press estimated that hospitals had sent as many as forty-five hundred infected patients to New York nursing homes.[14] New Jersey and California instituted similar policies.[15] (It is likely that at least some nursing homes were happy to comply. As acute-care patients recently discharged from the hospital, the transferred patients were eligible for Medicare, which paid at a much higher rate than Medicaid, the primary funding source for long-term care. Elder care lawyers, social workers, and former nursing home directors charged that facilities occasionally used the transfers as an excuse to evict old and very disabled residents, who require the most expensive care, to such unsafe places as dilapidated motels and even homeless shelters.)[16] In addition, several states granted nursing home owners protections from lawsuits for negligence related to COVID-19. By October 28, more than half of the states had passed some form of immunity laws.[17]

Although the federal government sent hundreds of millions of dollars of stimulus payments to nursing homes, it failed to ensure that the money went to improving patient care rather than to corporate owners' pocketbooks.[18] Similarly, Seema Verma, the administrator of the federal government's Center for Medicare and Medicaid (CMS), vowed to strengthen nursing home inspections, but 80 percent of the facilities were cleared of infection-control violations. Few of the others received significant penalties.[19]

The most widely publicized CMS action occurred early in the pandemic. On March 13, 2020, it restricted all visitation by family members except to deliver "compassionate care" for residents near death. Although the CMS has no jurisdiction over assisted living facilities, most voluntarily followed those guidelines.[20] A few medical experts initially viewed the directive as a sensible measure, but opposition quickly mounted. Suddenly everyone seemed to discover the critical role families play in long-term care institutions. A geriatrician who served as the medical director of a long-term care facility wrote in the *Journal of the American Medical Directors Association*, "Family is not synonymous with visitor. . . . The daughter who feeds her bedbound mother lunch or husband who combs and braids his wife's hair every morning, despite her anoxic injury that prevents her spoken word, are not visitors in our buildings. . . . Maintaining connections between residents and their loved ones has safety, socio-emotional, and ethical components."[21] A guest editorial in the *Washington Post* by a professor of medicine, a professor of healthcare policy, and a professor of law underlined that argument:

> Many family members are not company as much as essential caregivers and care monitors. Their involvement is vital, especially at facilities with shortages in staffing. Caring visitors make sure that their loved ones eat, can communicate with the staff, and receive daily hygiene and dignified engagement. Family members are often the first to see changes in a resident's condition or other issues. Unsurprisingly, quality of care has been found to be poor for residents without regular visitors.
>
> The sudden disruption in residents' contact with loved ones has caused notable declines in residents' cognition and function, depression, as well as anguish for family members.[22]

The media publicized stories of residents and family members harmed by the ban. Caregivers and advocates protested in various ways. California Advocates for Nursing Home Reform urged individuals to post photographs, articles, and videos on Facebook and Instagram, using the hashtag #VisitationSavesLives. Robyn Grant, the director of public policy and advocacy for the National Consumer Voice of Quality Long-Term Care, reported that many nursing home residents were losing the will to live and that Minnesota doctors were listing "social isolation" as a cause on death certificates of nursing home residents.[23] The headline of an article in the *AARP Newsletter* asked, "Is Extended Isolation Killing Older Adults in Long-Term Care?"[24] The answer clearly was yes. The article summarized a study conducted and published by the *Washington Post* in September that found that isolation had the most serious effect on people with Alzheimer's disease and other dementias. Since March, 134,200 people had died from dementia. That figure was much higher than expected, leading to the conclusion that 13,200 excess deaths had occurred. The article concluded, "People with dementia are dying not just from the virus but from the very strategy of isolation that's supposed to protect them. In recent months, doctors have reported increased falls, pulmonary infections, depression, and sudden frailty in patients who had been stable for years."[25] Individuals organized rallies, wrote letters to pressure state officials to reverse the ban, attended legislative hearings on the issue, and posted protest signs on nursing homes.[26]

In addition, family members organized new Facebook groups. By far the largest was Caregivers for Compromise—Because Isolation Kills Too. The goal was to restore visitation rights in a "safe and reasonable way" by providing rapid COVID testing for staff members and visitors and designating as an "essential caregiver" a family member who was screened and tested and previously had regularly visited a resident. The group's founder was Mary Daniels, a fifty-seven-year-old patient advocate in Jacksonville, Florida, whose salesman husband, Steven, had been diagnosed with early-onset Alzheimer's disease at the age of fifty-nine in 2013. After he entered a nursing home, she went every evening, to feed him his dinner, help him change into pajamas, and lie next to him in bed watching television. When the facility shut its doors, she applied first for a paid position and then for a volunteer one. At the end of June, the nursing home finally hired her as a dishwasher two days a week. After each shift, she and Steven were able to resume their evening ritual. Her story soon captured the attention of the national media. Capitalizing on her newfound fame, she established the Facebook group. It had 6,000 members within two weeks and 13,549 on October 28, 2020.[27]

Daniels posted regular reports chronicling her Florida campaign, which she hoped would inspire members in other states to follow her lead. Appointed to Governor Ron DeSantis's Task Force to Explore the Safe and Limited Re-opening of Long-Term Care Facilities, she lobbied successfully for the essential caregiver designation. The Facebook page also included information about how to submit complaints to various public officials and members' stories about the impact of the visitation ban on relatives' lives. After seeing her mother for the first time in months, one member wrote, "She is a shell of her former self, picking at her skin, not talking. I cried all the way home. Thank God for this group. You are the only ones that understand." Others posted before and after photographs of their relatives to demonstrate how much they had declined as a result of the lockdown.

Reopening occurred slowly and unevenly. A CMS directive on May 18 permitted family visitation in nursing homes that had had no new cases in the previous twenty-eight days, as well as adequate staff, protective gear, and testing. The CMS, however, took no steps to help facilities meet those standards, and few were able to do so. Moreover, states adopted different regulations.[28] A study on July 7 found that twenty-six states and the District of Columbia had allowed nursing homes to reopen. The visits had to be scheduled in advance, supervised by a staff member, and conducted outside; only one or two visitors were allowed at a time.[29]

A new CMS directive on September 17 easing the restrictions was a welcome relief to families and residents. Indoor as well as outdoor visits could now occur in facilities that had not had new outbreaks in fourteen days and that followed certain safety guidelines.[30] Limitations on visitation, however, persisted for many months. Some facilities that relaxed their restrictions in the summer reimposed them in the fall when the number of cases and deaths began to climb. It seemed doubtful that the situation would soon improve. "Nothing Much Has Changed: COVID-19 Nursing Home Cases and Deaths Follow Fall Surges," read the title of a November 2020 article in the *Journal of the American Geriatrics Society*. The authors noted that both the Centers for Disease Control and CMS had issued guidelines incorporating widely accepted "best practices": testing staff and residents regularly, isolating COVID-positive residents, ensuring that staff used personal protective equipment, and instituting better sanitation control. In the six states studied, however, many facilities lacked the resources needed to comply, and the number of cases had soared.[31] The CMS finally relaxed virtually all regulations in March 2021, by which time a high proportion of nursing home residents had received vaccinations and the incidence of COVID-19 had significantly declined.[32]

The View from Caregiver Support Groups

The Alzheimer's Association's online support groups help us understand caregivers' experiences in greater depth. Because this chapter covers a much shorter time period than the three previous ones, it relies on the Caregivers Forum as well as the Spouse or Partner Caregiver Forum and the LGBT Community and Allies Forum in order to obtain a sizeable sample. The Caregivers Forum is larger than the other two. By December 31, 2020, it had a total of 242,194 posts on 33,037 topics. Abbreviations used by the association and recommended for forum participants include DX (diagnosis), MC (memory care), DW (dear wife), and DH (dear husband). I again use pseudonyms instead of screen names to protect anonymity.

Participants who read the message boards regularly had a front-row seat on the calamity in long-term care institutions.[33] Marcus, an emeritus professor of law, posted daily briefings about the mounting death toll. Since joining the forum for spouses and partners in February 2014, Marcus had become a familiar figure on it. By March 2020, he had posted nearly two thousand messages. Although a few members recoiled from his left-of-center views, many had consulted him about various issues over the years, and his information was generally considered authoritative. Along with a few other writers, he also provided links to newspaper articles about such issues as the struggle of hospice nurses to gain access to nursing homes, the discharge of positive COVID patients from hospitals to nursing homes, and lobbying by nursing homes to gain immunity from lawsuits related to the disease. As caregivers learned more, their anger grew. Alerting other participants to a *New York Times* article about the evictions of nursing home residents to make room for more profitable patients, Bruce wrote, "This is a TRAGEDY!!! If you abandoned a dog or a cat you could go to prison in many states, someone should be prosecuted. Another example of the failure of the system for elders with dementia" (June 12, 2020).

In addition, support-group members posted personal accounts. "In light of the tragedy at the Kirkland facility," Paula wrote on March 8 of the many deaths that occurred there, "I'm wondering—for those of you with loved ones in ALF [assisted living facility] and MC [memory care]—what preparations or guidance you've been getting from those facilities? My mother's facility suggests that if family members are sick they not visit, but in the meantime, it seems to be business as usual with the staff and it just doesn't feel like enough" (March 8, 2020). The recommendations the CMS issued five days later did little to dispel anxieties. "Yesterday I received the dreaded message from DW's care unit," wrote Cindy on March 20, 2020.

> Four Coronavirus DX on March 18 (I didn't know until the 19th). The outbreak is on the main floor, of a 3 story 200 bed facility. DW is in a secure area on the 3rd floor. This is an award receiving facility. Absolutely top notch. Last week it seemed as if they had twice as many cleaning staff on. In spite of this the virus found a way in. . . . Is she strong enough to fight this off??? Will I ever see her again?? So many unanswered questions. You folks that Pray, I could use some help. . . . Just when I thought the tears were all gone. Sorry can't type any longer.

In the middle of April, Virginia accused her father's institution of disregarding safety regulations: "I just learned that my Dad's facility has their first COVID case and that the patient was recently admitted after being discharged from the hospital (it was unknown that he had COVID at time of transfer). In addition to the facility taking supposedly 'Non-COVID' hospital transfers, they also were not quarantining these new admission patients. The new admissions, including the asymptomatic positive case, was allowed to mingle amongst residents, and the staff was not using extra PPE when interacting with these patients. There's nothing I can do about it now, but I'm feeling a bit PO'd" (April 15, 2020). Two weeks later, Randy expressed his fear and frustration: "Tonight I got a call from my wife's AD facility. One of their staff felt unwell yesterday, was immediately sent home and to the doctor, and tested positively for Covid 19. Although staff are all wearing PPE and practicing every precaution practical, these facilities are petrie dishes for diseases like Covid 19 virus and this has to be bad news." He concluded that his wife was "now in deadly danger." He had "never felt so helpless" (April 29, 2020).

The relatives of some support-group members were affected directly. Bonnie had joined the forum in 2014, when she was forty-seven and her husband fifty-one. On April 25 she announced that he "has had a fever off and on since Wednesday. They did labs, urinalysis, and Covid testing. I called last night at 9:00 pm to see how he was doing, and the night nurse told me that the test had just come back positive. I don't even know what to say." Martha's mother was one of seven residents in her memory care unit to test positive for COVID-19 in August. "While I knew it was inevitable, it was still a shock," Martha wrote (August 16, 2020).

Neither woman revealed whether or not her relative recovered. Other writers, however, reported that the condition of survivors had seriously deteriorated. Harold wrote in September, "A new behavior with my 91-year-old mother recovering from a June diagnosis of Covid-19 is that she thinks my sister and I are trying to poison her in giving her medications to her" (September 3, 2020). The virus had an even more devastating effect on Leonore's husband. He had been "doing fairly well at Silverado Beverly Place," an upscale dementia facility in Los Angeles. But then he "picked up COVID from another resident." After two and a half months, first in a hospital and then in a rehabilitation facility, "he was nowhere near his pre-COVID baseline." He "couldn't walk, feed himself, talk or do any of the stuff he loved to do before the COVID hit him" (August 29, 2020). Although we cannot know how much of the husband's deterioration stemmed from his long confinement in the hospital and rehabilitation unit and how much from the disease itself, he clearly suffered an irreparable loss. (In December, relatives of three residents and a nurse who died in Silverado Beverly Place sued the owners, alleging that they had endangered residents and staff by admitting a New York man with the virus.)[34]

The prohibition on visits created other anxieties. "I am devastated!!!!!" wrote Cindy on March 16. "I know it's for the best but the MC facility that my DH is in lockdown for three weeks. I am so afraid that he will no longer know me when this is over." Gail had visited her husband every day since she had placed him in a memory care unit three weeks earlier. She, too, felt "devastated" when she heard about the lockdown. She feared she would never see her husband again and wondered how he would fare without her. "I know they are trying to protect their patients and that he will be taken care of, so why do I feel like this?" she asked (March 24, 2020). Others were not so certain that the level of care would remain the same. A March 28 post offered little reassurance. Russell, a retired pilot, had taken advantage of the exemption for compassionate caregivers. After spending three days in his wife's memory care facility while she was dying, he wrote,

I was able to observe the other residents and the current routine and it was not pretty. Changing the routine of dementia folks is not a good thing. No visits from family and loved ones, no outside entertainments and programs allowed in, no ordinary hustle and bustle of an active facility. Some residents appeared lost and confused, some residents who [usually] were active were just sitting around, some residents who ordinarily were fairly peaceful were acting up and being more agitated and aggressive. The staff and activity directors were trying hard but were overwhelmed at times with the needs of the residents. Never really thought about it but visits and time spent by the family members and friends takes a little pressure off the staff. (March 28, 2020)

On April 15, he wrote again: "Since my Janice passed away three weeks ago, three others have passed away in the memory care facility. Although

Covid 19 is not in the facility, I blame that cursed virus. The change in routine, no visitors and whatever normalcy they had has been uprooted and that can be the catalyst that sends many with dementia down into a vicious spiral. No one is coming out of this unscathed."

Subsequent posts supported his impressions. Joe wrote, "Having a loved one in MC is bad enough under the best of conditions but under these conditions it is 100 times worse [when] you can't visit them and have no idea what's going on" (April 25, 2020). In June three women asserted that, bereft of meaningful human contact, their mothers had lost their fragile hold on reality. After one daughter noted that her mother believed that the staff came into her room at night to take the toys she had for her cat, another posted, "My mom has gotten a lot more paranoid in lockdown too. Today, for instance she was convinced there are 'bad guys' coming into her facility trying to kill her and that she needs to go find her daughter, who's also in danger. She also told my older sister that a truck drove into her facility and that's why she was having a bad day" (June 17, 2020). The third wrote, "Mother is very delusional . . . [She] believes a murder squad kidnap her every evening and she is able to escape and return to her apartment by 3 a.m. Mom can give elaborate details every day, what the murder squad members wear, what she wears, the house she is in, furniture, rooms, and how she wears camouflage and sneakers so she can escape. Today in 62 min on the phone Mom was maniac, talked about this all non stop" (June 13, 2020). As we will see in the following chapter, delirium was extremely widespread among dementia sufferers hospitalized during the pandemic.

Some support-group members argued that because they had been uniquely attentive to their relatives' needs, they deserved exemption from the restrictions. Sally alternated between "rage and tears" when she heard that her mother's facility permitted only essential workers to enter. "I am essential to my mom's care," she exclaimed.

I am the one who makes sure that she has toothpaste, clothes that are clean, that there are no poopy depends in her dresser drawer, that she has soap in her bathroom dispenser, that she is bathing, that she does not smell, that she has her glasses. Is that not essential? Who is supposed to advocate and look out for her??? I have had to [do that] for the past two years while she has lived there and now, all of the sudden, I have to totally and completely trust that the facility is doing what they are supposed to. (June 5, 2020)

Marcia had filled her mother's pill box on the weekend and checked that she took the correct pills every day (May 3, 2020). Susannah had sat by her husband at his dinner meal for an hour to ensure that he drank enough water; no staff member could take the time (March 29, 2020). Rather than focusing on the special services she had rendered, Anita stressed the importance of sustaining an intimate bond. Having learned that "in-person connection" was the only way to deal with her mother's challenging behavior, she wrote, "It's heartbreaking not to be there for her the way we thought we would be able to be" (April 18, 2020).

Opposition to the nursing home rules was not unanimous. Especially in the early weeks of the pandemic, a few writers argued that visitation restrictions were essential. When Samantha wrote that her inability to visit her husband was "severely impacting" her mental health as well as his, Marcus asked, "Have you been tested? How do you know you are not an asymptomatic carrier? How many other people want to break quarantine and do you mind if your Loved one dies? Has nobody told you that this is a DEADLY easily transmitted Disease?" (March 24, 2020). Because Susannah continued to insist that she had to find a way to visit, Marcus wrote again, this time even more emphatically: "*Are you good with your husband dying from someone breaking quarantine?* One person can infect everyone in the facility and perhaps half of them die" (March 29, 2020). Marcus soon stopped expressing that opinion, and as the months went on, it appeared less frequently in the forum.

Nursing homes tried to enable caregivers to remain in contact with relatives in various ways. Staff members phoned caregivers regularly to update them on their relatives' condition, helped residents use Facetime, and positioned them at windows so that family members could wave, blow kisses, and hold up signs.[35] "My mom can't really participate," wrote Jane about Facetime, "but a staff person facilitates the call and it's peace of mind to just see her, plus I get a nice chat with the staff" (May 23, 2020). Others were less positive. Some complained that Facetime was useless to residents who could not understand computers. Alice pointed out that her husband "doesn't speak and he doesn't hear"; she had communicated primarily by physical contact (March 18, 2020). Window visits also disappointed. One woman noted that her husband's window opened only onto a courtyard she could not enter. A man wrote that so many people crowded around the windows in his wife's facility that the staff suspended those visits. And many reported that residents were angry that family members did not enter the building, come close, hold their hands, and hug them.

Nursing home regulations created difficulties not only for caregivers whose relatives were currently enrolled but also for those who were considering placement. Family members who had not previously toured possible facilities no longer could do so. And deciding whether or not to move a relative to an institution provoked even more anguish than before. Kimberly had owned a small company with her husband but was now his full-time caregiver. "My mind's a swirl!" she wrote in June. To some extent her dilemma was familiar. Her husband's name had been on the waiting list of the most desirable memory care unit in her town for eighteen months, and she had just received word it had an opening. Although she was not sure he was ready to move, she knew that if she passed up that opportunity, another probably would not arise any time soon. But, she continued, "now add on COVID." Although the facility had no cases, it had been locked down for more than three months. No visits were permitted, and the residents had to stay in their rooms. Kimberly asked other members of the group for their thoughts and advice (June 10, 2020).

Some caregivers decided to keep relatives home.[36] Others quickly discovered that a pandemic represented the worst possible time to enroll someone with dementia in an institution. Connie had been able to convince her mother to agree to move to an assisted living facility in March only by praising "all of the activities and trips and friends she would meet. Mom is a very social person. She was so excited." But just as Connie was signing the last of the paperwork, the facility suspended all family visits and group activities. As a result, "there have been no activities, no trips, no new friends. I cannot convince her that this is not normal and it will change." Like many others, Connie held herself accountable for circumstances over which she had no control: "The guilt of moving my mother to this place and leaving her alone, even through no fault of my own will haunt me for the rest of my life" (June 9, 2020). When Peggy first received word of a bed for her father in a memory care unit in March, she rejected it. "After all," she explained, "how could I drop Dad and drive, not even being allowed to visit him. How cruel! I said, I would never do that, who would do that to their parent?" Instead, she brought her father to live with her. When he became incontinent two months later, she reconsidered: "Now I am that cruel person. My Dad is going to memory care tomorrow. I have to drop and drive. His room is all ready there, with everything new. Because of Covid he could have nothing on the walls, nothing that couldn't be washed or sanitized. I bought everything new, and I hope he loves everything, but I won't know" (May 18, 2020).

Two women complained that they had been prevented from helping their parents move from their apartments in assisted living facilities to rooms in memory care units. "They told me not to say anything to him," wrote Cathy. "This is just breaking my heart. I can't be with him or help him. I won't even be able to see what his new room will look like or what he can take with him. The home will have to pack up all his belongings because they won't let me in. I woke last night and cried for two hours" (June 16, 2020). The oldest of seven children, Lisa had primary responsibility for their ninety-one-year-old mother. She wrote, "We were called on Monday and told she was being moved Tuesday while she was at lunch. . . . They moved her basics, bed, dresser, chair, tv, clothes. So many things did not go. It was two months before the apartment was emptied. That's when we realized the things that didn't go. Made me sad. Her prayer books and special gifts, things that would bring comfort" (August 24, 2020). In his classic book, *Dementia Reconsidered: The Person Comes First*, psychologist Tom Kitwood noted that the word "comfort" "carries meanings of tenderness, closeness, the soothing of pain and sorrow, the calming of anxiety, the feeling of security which comes from being close to another. . . . In dementia the need for comfort is likely to be especially great when a person is dealing with a sense of loss, whether that arises from bereavement, the failing of abilities, or the ending of a long-established way of life."[37] Lisa's mother must have longed for "things that would bring comfort" when she was suddenly moved to a new room without her daughter around.

Like the move to a memory care unit, the decision about institutional placement was not always a caregiver's to make. On April 8, Ellie wrote that she was "stuck between systems due to Covid!" Her mother had just spent two weeks in a rehabilitation institution after a fall but that facility planned to discharge her soon; at that point, Medicare funding would end. The cost for private-pay patients was four to five hundred dollars a day. The mother's primary doctor had determined that she had advanced dementia and could not safely return home. Ellie's house, an acre away, had three flights of stairs the mother could not navigate. The assisted living facility Ellie had chosen would not accept her mother until the quarantine ended. Two weeks later, Ellie reported that her mother was "miserable at rehab," where she was "stuck in one little room, even for therapies" (April 22, 2020). By the time she finally entered the assisted living facility early in July, Ellie had spent approximately twenty thousand dollars on her care (July 4, 2020).

Forum participants responded to the visitation restrictions in different ways. Judith chose an unusual strategy, moving into an assisted living facility with her mother. "It's not as bad as it sounds," she assured other caregivers. "It's a gorgeous 2 BR apartment with a big balcony that overlooks the pool and mini-golf course. I will have my own bedroom and bathroom." And the plan made sense: "With Covid, this is the only way I can continue to help her on a daily basis, otherwise I must leave things for her at the front desk and they will deliver it" (October 6, 2020). More commonly, caregivers found new ways to stay in touch, sending flowers, cards, food, and photographs. One woman had her portrait printed on her mother's pillowcase so she could see it last thing at night and first thing in the morning. Others joined protests, writing letters and signing petitions to federal and state officials and attending local hearings on visitation rules. Alerting other participants to the newly formed group Caregivers for Compromise on July 19, one daughter wrote, "If you are concerned about your LO in a facility don't just read this. DO SOMETHING to fight to get access. If you don't at least try, that's on you" (July 19, 2020). Eight days later Beverly notified the forum that the New York State Senate and Assembly would soon hold joint hearings on nursing homes and COVID, "including the latest restrictive visiting policy." Imploring other New York residents to provide written testimony, she wrote, "Please use this opportunity to make your voices heard" (July 27, 2020).

A few participants obtained extra services for their relatives in the lockdown by enrolling them in hospice sooner than otherwise might have been the case. Although hospices initially focused exclusively on patients with cancer, they increasingly serve people with other terminal conditions, including dementia. Sylvia had lived with her mother for three years before placing her in a nursing home in 2019. Now she was "just not ready" when the facility suggested the mother might benefit from hospice care. In response, Craig acknowledged that "the 'H' word is a shocker, however having someone from Hospice will not cause your mother to decline. They can be an enormous help to you and your mother—an extra pair of hands, an extra set of eyes, someone you can have real contact with" (August 4, 2020). Joan agreed: "Hospice doesn't mean you are stopping care, comfort, or hope. . . . My mother has been on hospice for TWO YEARS. . . . It's amazing how helpful they can be and how close of an eye they keep on their patients. PLUS, they help the family. Social worker. Chaplain, nurse, all just a call away to help you find out what you want to know and assist you in any way possible. I have weekly phone sessions with my team. It's quite helpful, especially with covid visitation restrictions" (August 4, 2020). (Only the rare hospice allowed patients to remain for two years.)

A few other writers brought relatives home. The wife of a man who had been a CPA, Theresa commented on May 23 that his facility had requested that she hire a sitter because he was falling and losing weight. Unable to afford a full-time companion, she asked if she could stay with him a few hours in the evening. "I am having a hard time understanding why the sitter, a complete stranger, is allowed to be with him—and why I, living a very quiet and careful life, CAN'T! He has been in MC since mid January. I believe now I was very naïve to think they could care for him as his disease progressed and of course, no one counted on the effects that Covid would bring. At what cost are we keeping so many people from their loved ones? My heart is broken tonight" (May 23, 2020). Six days later she wrote again. Because the facility had denied her request, she removed him. "Only God knows how many days he has left but I am so thankful those days are going to be spent at home," she wrote. "He is unable to speak and is so incredibly thin and weak, but he has smiled so much" (May 29, 2020). Another woman was less certain that she had made the right decision. She moved her mother from an assisted living facility on March 13 for what she assumed would be a brief stay in her home. "I didn't have anything organized or her prepared for someone else to step in," she confessed on May 22. "At the time, I did not know what would unfold, or the magnitude of what we would be facing. It was a quick decision based on a gut feeling. I've now been caring for her around the clock by myself for two months while trying to work from home fulltime (and then some). I have been doing what it takes to get through the days, but I am exhausted and this is not sustainable. She continues to decline."

Many other caregivers asked for advice about whether they should take relatives out of facilities. Support-group members were as hostile to such proposals as they had been before the pandemic arrived. Thus, despite the rising nursing home death toll, the responses were overwhelmingly negative. One woman, for example, warned Ruth that bringing her eighty-seven-year-old mother to live with her "may cost you your marriage. If you have children living with you, it will cost them your attention. All of your focus will be on your mother. You will not be able to attend school events or go to any sports practices eventually. Your mother will resent any attention you pay to your children or your spouse" (May 18, 2020). Another woman wrote, "Please be aware you can't take care of her alone. You will need respite help, volunteers or paid. You will need time to get away and recharge. I did this with both my parents; it is not easy" (May 22, 2020). A third woman cautioned Ruth to "go in with eyes wide open. Be ready to have to give up your weekends, being spontaneous, meals that don't include someone with a totally different diet, friends over, being able to take a solo walk, all sorts of things you may not feel are important, but when you just can't [do them], it sucks" (May 23, 2020).

The gradual resumption of visits generated mixed emotions. Bob looked forward to the pleasure of his mother's company, despite its limitations. "My state of Minnesota recently changed their recommendations for care facilities," he wrote on June 22, 2020. "I will be able to sit with my mother outdoors and watch the birds and basically have the same visits as before Covid 19. She doesn't make much conversation these days, but likes to smile at me and gesture at things she sees." Others feared that their relatives had crossed a critical divide and that seeing them might cause more pain than enjoyment. "I am so happy I can finally see my Mom next week," Julia wrote three days later. "It's been a long three months and am very excited. However, as most of you know, the Alzheimer's disease is always progressing so I am very nervous that she will not remember who I am" (June 25, 2020). In November Jack wrote that he would be able to see his father for the first time since he had entered a nursing home three months earlier: "I'm very anxious about this visit, because he has declined significantly and I doubt he'll recognize me. Any suggestions about how to prepare for this visit and deal with the aftermath?" (November 20, 2020). Reflecting on the question ("Does she recognize you?") heard over and over as her mother's dementia progressed, the anthropologist Janelle S. Taylor writes, "She may not 'recognize' me in a narrowly cognitive sense, but my Mom does 'recognize' me as someone who is there with her, someone familiar perhaps, and she does not need to have all the details sorted out in order 'to care' for me." Taylor continues, "I am not so convinced that the inability to remember names necessarily means that a person with dementia cannot 'recognize' or 'care' about other people. . . . But very often, it does mean that other people stop 'recognizing' and 'caring' about *them*."[38] The most serious issue was that people who no longer could recall intimates' names were viewed as less valuable and gradually experienced social erasure. Although we cannot know to what extent, if any, the caregivers quoted above would accept Taylor's interpretation, it is clear that they dreaded discovering that the visitation ban had caused devastating loss.

Many writers protested when states that rescinded the total ban imposed new regulations. "In Illinois we are now allowed 15 minute visits outside but no closer than 6," Ray wrote. "No contact allowed. It's almost easier to just do a window visit due to the barrier that exists to help keep the proper distance and these visits can be longer than 15 minutes" (June 22, 2020). The prohibition on physical contact must have been especially upsetting. According to Francis McGlone, a professor of neuroscience, people often underestimate the importance of touch, even when it is absent: "We might begin to realize that something is missing, but we won't always know that it's touch." Nevertheless, "when we talk about the problem of loneliness, we often ignore the obvious: what lonely people aren't getting is touch."[39] Kitwood adds that "many people with dementia, with their particularly strong social needs, are only able to relax when others are near them, or in actual bodily contact."[40] Jennifer explained her mother's response when she realized her daughter could not touch her: "Just before mom came outside, I asked the staff member monitoring the visiting area if I could hug her. She said she could not allow that. When mom came out, she came over to hug me and I had to tell her she couldn't. I have never, in my life, seen her so defeated and deflated" (June 9, 2020).

Even after the September 17 CMS directive lifting most of the restrictions, obstacles remained. On October 12, 2020, Debbie wrote that she had not seen or visited her mother in seven months. Although visitation was permitted in facilities that had not had an outbreak in fourteen days, her mother's nursing home had not yet reached that goal: "My mom is blind, hearing impaired, and [has] significant dementia. Her place offers FaceTime, phone calls or drive by 'visits,' none of which are suitable for her. And they won't provide any accommodation or alternative for her. I think she's forgotten how to use a phone, and I'm pretty sure she doesn't know it's me calling. She's declined so much in seven months." Debbie was "convinced I'll never see her again until it's time for the funeral home. I alternate between rage and despair. Tonight it's despair."

And soon the fall surge led to more restrictions. In the middle of November Heather wrote that she had been unable to visit her mother "even outside for the month now, and it's been so hard. We do Facetime and talk regularly, but it has sucked tremendously" (November 16, 2020). Three days later Cindy wrote that she had visited her mother "every single time" she could since June, when the lockdown of her mother's facility ended. But now it was about to be reimposed. Cindy realized she would not "see her any time soon, including Thanksgiving and, very likely, Christmas. I am heartbroken for her." Others feared that despite the compassionate care designation, they would not be notified in time, and their relatives would live out their final days alone.

When one woman's father received a COVID-19 diagnosis in December, she realized that the restrictions she had obeyed for months had all been in vain: "His whole unit has it, I've been told. They have been so restrictive since March, and we have both sacrificed so much not being able to be together for visits and outings. So much valuable time wasted for nothing, and he still got COVID. I'm a little bitter about that" (December 9, 2020).

Conclusion

"All of those longstanding issues [in nursing homes] like staffing," a Human Rights Watch researcher stated in April 2021, "they really blew up during the pandemic."[41] Those issues affected caregivers as well as residents and staff. Reports of the mounting death toll terrified family members, and soon some learned that their relatives could be counted among the victims. The visitation regulations exacerbated worries, encouraging several family members to engage in collective action, often for the first time. Although caregivers rejoiced when the CMS gradually relaxed the restrictions, some states imposed new ones. Seeing their relatives after many months, family members discovered that their conditions had seriously deteriorated.

The anger caregivers directed at the restrictions on nursing home visits might have been expected. Many people overcome their reluctance to placing relatives in institutions only by demanding the right to monitor the quality of care and attend to personal needs. Moreover, family members have long protested policies that seek to limit their presence and inhibit their involvement in institutions. Husbands campaigned for many years for the right to remain with their wives, first in labor rooms and then in delivery rooms. By the 1980s, most of those units permitted men to enter.[42] More recently, family pressure has encouraged a growing number of hospitals to remove the most restrictive visitation regulations in intensive care units, and some emergency rooms allow family presence at resuscitation attempts.[43]

The opening of those units was especially critical because families traditionally have insisted that they be present when death is near. "A general norm in American culture is that no one should die alone," observed sociologists Barney G. Glaser and Anselm L. Strauss. "Preferably, death should be attended by a close relative."[44] Throughout the nineteenth century, family members were expected to listen to final words and discern the state of the soul and the prospect of everlasting life. Hospitals posted "danger lists," alerting the relatives of patients on the list and permitting those family members to remain beyond normal visit hours. There was no guarantee, however, that the list contained the names of all patients near death. Moreover, hospitals employed various strategies to bar family members who were poor or members of marginalized racial and ethnic communities.[45]

Although religious concerns are somewhat less prevalent today, the moment of death remains important. Sandra M. Gilbert, a poet and professor of English, filed a wrongful death suit after her sixty-year-old husband died in 1991 following routine surgery for prostate cancer. In a letter she imagined sending his surgeon, she complained that she and her daughters had not been allowed to be "there with him, there when he was forced through the enormous wall between what we know and what we don't know, there to try to comfort him as he was dragged away from us." She asked, "Was there a moment when he realized what was happening, a moment of transition and recognition? Was he frightened? Was he resigned? Did he ask for me? Did he remember me? Did he remember *himself*?" The final moment was "a majestic one in every life," and family members needed to be there.[46] When Kay Redfield Jamison, a professor of psychiatry, was prevented from remaining with her husband who was dying in a hospital in 2002, she realized she experienced "the primitive distress of an animal being taken from its dying mate."[47] The CMS designation of "compassionate caregivers" might be considered an updated version of nineteenth-century danger lists. As we have seen, however, many caregivers feared that their relatives would die without family around them.

9

"This Being Homebound Is So Hard"

*Confronting Hospital Regulations, Sheltering in Place, and
Interacting with Workers*

The impact of the 2020 pandemic on dementia caregiving extended far
beyond nursing homes. The catastrophe also forced family members to
leave severely impaired relatives alone in the hospital, closed opportunities for respite, and sharpened the divide between waged and unwaged
caregivers.

Acute-care facilities are treacherous places for elderly people with dementia even under normal circumstances. A major danger is delirium,
a sudden decline in cognition manifested by either lethargy or agitation, which extends the length of stay, hinders treatment, and increases
the likelihood of death.[1] Journalist Nicci Gerrard recalled that when her
elderly father with dementia was isolated in a hospital for days, his leg
ulcers healed, but, "away from the home he loved, stripped of familiar routines and surrounded by strangers and machines, he swiftly lost
his bearings and his fragile hold upon the self."[2] Essayist Floyd Skloot's
mother also showed signs of dementia when she entered a hospital. Unable to communicate with her when she became agitated, the doctors
administered Haldol, a powerful antipsychotic drug contraindicated
for elderly women. When Skloot finally saw her, "she was in cognitive
chaos. Clearly, she had tumbled over whatever edge she'd been tread-
ing for the last few years."[3] Because similar incidents commonly occur,
the National Institute on Aging advises dementia caregivers never to
leave relatives alone in the emergency room and after admission to remain with them at all times (even during medical procedures) to communicate with doctors and nurses and provide comfort, personal care,

and orientation.⁴ When the pandemic struck, however, hospitals, like nursing homes, excluded family members. The various forums help us understand how dementia caregivers responded.

One participant, a retired pharmacist, summoned the paramedics after his wife fell but refused to allow them to take her to the emergency room "as she would be alone, she can't talk or verbalize well and I was told I would not be allowed to go with her" (August 22, 2020). Those who had no choice described the pain of leaving relatives with serious cognitive deficits at the hospital door and then receiving reports of agitation and confusion. When Amy and her mother took her eighty-seven-year-old father with midstage dementia to an emergency room for a heart problem, they asked to accompany him "because we knew he wouldn't know what was going on or what to say to the doctors and nurses and despite our very strenuous requests, they refused." The mother and daughter also were barred from the intensive care unit, where the father spent several days, becoming "more and more depressed, disoriented, and agitated" (August 3, 2020). Saskia responded to Amy, "I feel your pain; I have Power of Attorney and Power of Medical Attorney and had a similar experience last week!" Her mother, too, had midstage dementia and had entered the hospital through an emergency room. Saskia and her sister had followed the ambulance, but even after explaining that their mother had dementia, sometimes sounded "normal," and would deny taking any medications, they were denied access to the emergency room. Because the hospital was full, the mother was diverted to another facility an hour away. Although that hospital also restricted visits, it sent regular updates. The sisters were not surprised to learn that their mother "became too much for them to handle. She was scared and agitated. They assigned a 24 hour sitter to stay with her; previous to the sitter she had pulled out her IV and blood was splattered all over the room." Because the sitter could not comfort the mother, the hospital "finally decided that a member might be able to keep her calm. So they bent the rule and offered that one of us could come and stay with her—however, once in whomever came could not leave, we were there for the duration"

(August 3, 2020). Saskia accepted the offer. "When I first arrived," she wrote, her mother "cried so hard and hung on to me because she was so scared and alone. I felt like crap for having put her there—still knowing that I had done what I needed to do for her" (August 6, 2020).

Martha, by contrast, was able to stay with her mother in the emergency department but then was prevented from accompanying her to her room. "My mom can't even recall how to push a button for a nurse," Martha wrote. "I know you all know how I feel. I am her comfort zone, caregiver, and protector. It feels like I am leaving a young child to fend for herself." Martha's one hope was that, if her mother became "belligerent" and had a "meltdown," that hospital, too, would relax its rules (August 14, 2020). Lisa lived in a three-bedroom mobile home twenty miles outside Memphis with her husband, son, and grandson; she also had responsibility for her husband's ninety-one-year-old aunt. Rather than becoming uncontrollable, the aunt stopped eating after spending a week in the hospital without visitors. When the hospital phoned to ask for permission to insert a feeding tube, Lisa acted quickly: "We had her in her wheelchair the next morning, and after getting her home, she ate every bit of her breakfast" (July 1, 2020).

Struggling to Provide Care at Home

Several forum participants suddenly realized that they had no contingency plans in case they themselves became seriously ill. Jerome's wife had just been diagnosed with dementia when the pandemic struck: "It took me a couple of weeks to twig to the possibility that I could have to be hospitalized with COVID-19, which would leave her on her own. I checked with her doctor and was told that she would be unable to live on her own if something happened to me. I should note that we never had any children and have no family in the area to which we moved just under 3 years ago." Jerome asked, "How are others who are caregiving at home area providing for the care of their loved one in the face of the COVID-19 pandemic? Are there any options other than a memory care unit or relying on family, which won't work for us?" (March 26, 2020). Annie, a former bank worker, noted that her husband's blindness "adds an extra level of consideration." Although her son assured her that he would step in if she fell ill, "he's 500 miles away. And my daughter has a preschooler and is still working from home. And moving [the husband] would be twice as disorienting between mind and sight. So I worry and fret" (April 10, 2020). Margaret was afraid she already had been infected. "My DH has Alzheimer's and I have been sick with fever, body aches, chills and sore throat for 5 Days," she wrote on July 6. "My MD ordered covid test. I am the only caregiver. Hoping test is negative, but if not I'm concerned. How will I take care of him? He needs assist with meals, medications and wanders out of the yard. He will be tested also and none of our adult children will be able to help for fear of catching covid." She asked other support group members to "pray the test is negative."

The pandemic also pushed care back on the home. Like children's day care centers and schools, adult day services closed either voluntarily or under compulsion. Fearful of allowing strangers in their home, many family members canceled aides. Although forum participants had often complained about the inadequacy of those services, most now realized they had been invaluable. In the middle of April, a woman wrote that since her husband's adult day program closed, "it's just him and I, 24/7. How are others dealing with quarantine? I am going crazy" (April 12, 2020). Two weeks later, Betsy wrote, "Pre Covid-19 DH went to a day program 14 hrs/week. It's been 7 ½ weeks since he attended. 14 hrs/week didn't seem like much at the time, but boy, it sure does now" (May 1, 2020). Another wife missed the aide who had watched her husband "one day a week for three glorious hours so that I could get out to socialize, shop, etc. It made a big difference for my emotional well being and he had a different face to look at too!" (August 21, 2020). James had suspended the aide who had cared for his wife two afternoons a week. "Now I am on my own again," he wrote, "with no respite in sight" (March 17, 2020). Willie worried about what the loss of respite meant to his parents:

"Before the pandemic, my father who is 85 years with early stage dementia began to get used to having home care twice a week 4 hours at a time. It also relieved my mom who was the primary caregiver. When the pandemic happened, my siblings and I decided it was too much risk to have people inside the house so we stopped. Since then my father's condition is much worse—more mood swings, hallucinations, etc. putting more strain on my mom." He wondered whether they should resume home care (June 13, 2020). Family members had no control over day care centers, and many remained closed for months. As time went on, however, several families asked aides to return or hired new ones. On September 12, Judy wrote that she left her husband with a worker for two hours of "'me' time." She had not "been out like that for many, many, many, many months."

Several factors amplified the challenges of sheltering in place. Responsibility for relatives' health now included not only managing medications and incontinence but also detecting signs of COVID and then providing appropriate care to people who could not articulate their symptoms. Caregivers thus had to watch for subtle indications of the virus such as increased agitation or behavior changes. Laura was acutely aware of her lack of medical training while caring for her father, who had tested positive. "Thankfully," she wrote, "he's not had any of the scarier symptoms so far. I'm hoping he's mostly asymptomatic. However, his inability to communicate pain or discomfort concerns me. We're in contact with his primary care via telehealth, and I have a pulse oximeter to keep a close eye on his blood oxygen. I'm basically administering to all of his health care needs via instructions over webinar, and let me tell you—I'm no nurse. . . . Between working and caring for him and my spouse with COVID, I worry that I'm going to give myself a nervous breakdown worrying over everything" (July 14, 2020).

Many elderly relatives also had trouble understanding the public health advice and failed to adhere to it. Jessica described her husband as "very upset, combative, and uncooperative." He "refuses to Social Distance when we go for a walk, he says it's only necessary when you're in public and doesn't see that we are in public!" She beseeched the other support group members to help her (April 7, 2020). Margie explained why going out once a week to relieve her husband's boredom and get groceries had become "a life-threatening adventure":

> He can't (I know!) remember what not to touch, why we don't shake hands, slap backs, take our face-covering off to talk to strangers, let folks walk up in our space without moving quickly out of their way, stand right in front of, or behind, a young worker with no mask and apparently no worries. It is worse than taking a highly strung toddler into a toy store, because DH gets his feelings hurt no matter how gently and quietly I try to steer us around doorknobs and handles, touch screens, other families out shopping like us, and even small groups of chattering neighbors congregating in the cereal aisle. It is really scary given a lot of COVID-19 cases and even lives lost in our area. (May 6, 2020)

A husband complained that his wife "refuses to wear a mask, which is mandated in public indoor places here. This makes it impossible to get her hair cut or her blood sample drawn. Any ideas?" (November 13, 2020). (Respondents urged him to forget the haircut, if not the blood test.)

Dementia caregiving was a lonely experience even in the best of times. Friends disappeared, social outings ceased, affected relatives gradually became silent or unintelligible. A rare visit from friends left one woman even lonelier than before:

> A couple who are very dear friends drove seventy five miles to come see us. It was a lovely day! She and I got out a little bit and even went to a store. The guys went bird watching and had a great time also. DH said later how happy he was that his friend came to see him. I felt the same way. Later that evening, however, a deep sadness came over me and I suddenly felt very lonely. This has happened before when someone comes and then leaves. I want to call after them and ask them to take me with

them! I'm lonely. It feels so good to have a real conversation with someone and then to go back to not having that is almost painful. (August 27,
2020)

The pandemic intensified the problem. "I'm glad I'm an introvert,"
Elizabeth wrote, "but even I am missing normal contacts at this point.
My partner and I have never been big socializers, but at this point we're
down to one couple and one eccentric friend that we see on a regular
basis. My partner forgets every day why we can't see them—I have to
explain the pandemic restrictions over and over. Seems like no matter what, this ends up being a lonely road" (August 28, 2020). Virginia
explained why "this being homebound is so hard." She and her husband
"walk 1–2 times a day for ½ hr. weather permitting. We can't visit kids
as all 3 have high risk jobs. I never knew how much my grandchildren's
hugs helped till they were gone with no end in store. I read/internet,
however my DH can't read anymore and doesn't like me doing it" (May
29, 2020). A husband missed all the activities that previously gave him
a break from caregiving: "support group meetings, water aerobics,
lunches with friends, visits to the library, and family visits." He was calling friends, "visiting on this board, working in the yard, and dusting off
some old exercise equipment. Otherwise, we're just riding it out. Gets
pretty lonely, though" (April 10, 2020). Jacqueline attributed the progression of her husband's disease to the quarantine: "We are five years into
Alzheimers, and just these past few months his short term memory is
becoming worse," she wrote on May 25. "Our isolation due to Covid 19
is part of the reason, I believe."

Working remotely from home presented still other difficulties. Rita,
a special education teacher, complained about her husband, diagnosed
with dementia four years earlier at the age of fifty:

DH just doesn't get the work from home aspect of my job right now. He
thinks that because I'm home I shouldn't be required to work. It's frustrating. And challenging. Closing in on impossible.

He interrupts me an average of every 3 minutes. (I tracked it, I'm a data person.) Each interruption requires at least an answer from me, and I find it difficult to change from thinking about what I'm working on to answer his question. (Do you see that bird on the lawn? What kind of bird is it?)

And he brings me things. Things he finds, while he's going through whatever closet/drawer/room/box he's found to go through. And then asks what we should do with whatever he's found. 99% of the time I'd like it put back. But he doesn't want it put back where it came from. We should use it/keep it out so we can see it/get rid of it/sell it. And he'd really like it if I did that right now. . . .

Not looking for advice. Just needed to get it out. I'd scream in the shower, but he usually follows me into the bathroom. (April 23, 2020)

Like children, elderly relatives occasionally appeared on Zoom business calls but were not quite so endearing. Mike tried to do most of his work early in the morning before his wife, a former nurse practitioner, woke up. One morning, however, she "wandered into my office room in her pajamas" during a presentation with the European vice presidents of his company (April 23, 2020). June worried more about her father, who lived with her, than about herself. "The worst thing," she wrote, was being unable to keep him company. "I just feel terrible leaving him to sit on the couch watching tv for hours. Sometimes he wants to talk and I have to brush him off because I have a meeting. It is distressing to me to not be able to focus on his needs" (April 25, 2020). Helen, who worked virtually as a customer service representative, experienced financial hardship. "My hours have been drastically cut," she explained, "my choice only because hubby walks into my den all the time. I usually put 'Working' on the door, but it does not matter, he comes in anyway." Her "monetary earnings [had] suffered greatly" and she was "just living frugally here to get by" (April 24, 2020). And Sarah reminded others that working from home was a luxury not everyone could enjoy: "I cannot [stay at home]. I am a housekeeper at a hotel. If I don't work, I don't get paid. I also don't want to get fired. So yes, I'm getting exposed to whatever anyone has, everyday. Doing the handwashing, sanitizing, staying six-feet away from everyone. And yes, I have a loved one with dementia who gets exposed to me, everyday" (April 1, 2020).

Assuming that the pandemic would be brief, some caregivers made arrangements they no longer could sustain as the crisis lingered for months. Two brothers, ages twenty-four and twenty-eight, had moved into the house of their father with dementia, soon after the pandemic began. One wrote, "We had been working from home which was okay at first. We felt that this would give us a chance to take care of our dad and figure things out." But now it was June 11. Their father had been unable to get an appointment with a geriatric psychiatrist to confirm the diagnosis, and his behavior had become uncontrollable. The sons needed to return to their own homes and workplaces, but their father could not be left alone (June 11, 2020). Jenny wrote a week later. After her father died early in the pandemic, she and her husband had moved to her parents' farm to care for her eighty-three-year-old mother with Alzheimer's disease. "We have been here for about 3 months," she wrote, "and I am needing to return to my town and work. We can't stay on the farm any longer and neither can mom." Neither of June's sisters' homes could accommodate the mother, and all three sisters disagreed about whether she should go into a memory care unit. June asked the other members for advice: "Those of you who have moved your LO from living with you to living in MC—How was it? What are the pitfalls? Do some flourish and some not? Will I be killing my mother if I move her?" (June 18, 2020).

While confining some caregivers and recipients together, the pandemic separated others. The daughter of an artist asked in early July,

How are people dealing with the long distance caregiving for a LO with Alzheimer's when everything is shut down in town? I have only been able to visit her twice for short times since the pandemic started. The resources I used to rely on to help aren't sending people out to help because of Covid. I have a home health aide one day a week who practices social distancing and masking, but the rest of the time my mom is alone. She can't figure out how to use Alexa so that we can video call, or any of the other video calling programs. HELP! (July 8, 2020)

Even brief visits were impossible for a daughter on the east coast: "My mother lives in California. It's breaking my heart to be so far away from her and not be able to visit. Calling doesn't make sense anymore, as she needs to see me to know who I am. I've been sending videos and letters in the mail" (August 4, 2020). Fear of infecting older relatives also kept families apart. Irene wished she could help her mother care for her father, who had become more belligerent in the preceding few months. "I am losing my mind when I call her and can hear him yelling in the background," Irene wrote on April 24. "She can't get him to do anything and he is having accidents all over the house now. I haven't seen my mom since the end of January in person bc of the virus. I have three young kids and I don't want to risk giving my mom the virus because she is in the 70s. I call and Facetime a lot but can see how hard it's been on her."

Interactions with Direct Care Workers

The pandemic both revealed and reinforced the interdependence of family caregivers and direct care workers. The pressures on nursing home staff quickly mounted when family visits ended. Unable to monitor their relatives' well-being, families had to rely even more than before on nursing assistants to deliver good care, foster communication between residents and kin, and provide regular updates. Without home health aides, family members had no relief from the burdens of care. The inadequate supply of PPE for both nursing home assistants and homecare aides endangered not only those workers but also family caregivers and the people they tended. Workers and families had to trust each other to follow public health advice.

Some support-group members expressed gratitude for the attentive care bestowed on their relatives in very difficult circumstances. We recall that Theresa brought her husband home from a nursing home after learning she would not be allowed to enter the facility. "The MC staff was so kind as they brought him out," she wrote, "and they have called often to check on him. Their jobs are unbelievably demanding through the epidemic" (May 29, 2020). Although worried about the toll the restrictions inflicted on her mother in an assisted living facility, Rose stressed that she "found all of the staff to be amazingly kind and understanding" (August 24, 2020). Replying to a woman whose mother was faring poorly in a nursing home under lockdown, June offered this solace:

> The only thing that gave me a little consolation when my Dad was in a SNF [skilled nursing facility] and then hospitalized this year and I could not see him or even speak to him was that there were some kind and loving nurses on the other end of the phone when I'd call. I regularly had to visualize that he was surrounded by loving and capable hands that would bring him comfort and maybe some smiles. I hope you have been able to connect with some regular staff by phone and that you have a sense that 1 or 2 may be especially kind and treating your Mom like family. (December 8, 2020)

If some forum participants appreciated the tender care relatives received, however, most appeared oblivious to the special hardships the workers experienced in the pandemic. A survey conducted by the National Domestic Workers Alliance in March and April 2020 reported that 72 percent of domestic workers were unemployed, 94 percent stated that the COVID-related cancellations had been by their clients rather than themselves, and 70 percent did not know whether they would be rehired after the pandemic. In addition, 77 percent of the workers were primary breadwinners, and more than half worried about paying for food and rent.[5] In-depth interviews with thirty-three unionized home-care workers in New York City found that most worried about the health of their patients, many of whom had several chronic conditions and were thus at high risk of contracting COVID. As a result, the workers took special precautions in patients' homes. One stated, "I clean like there's no tomorrow. I wipe down every surface—the table—the chair. I walk with the little bleach wipes." Workers also went to grocery stores and pharmacies for their patients, often placing their own health in peril. "He needs to stay inside the house," a worker said, "so he tells me, 'I need you to go there, go here.' I really don't want to, but I can't say no. I'm the aide; I'm supposed to do this." Working in many different houses and traveling on public transportation exacerbated the dangers. Nevertheless, home health agencies varied in the extent to which they offered personal protective equipment and information about COVID. "I don't think we should have to go out and buy masks," one worker stated. "I spent $20.00 to get a box of masks . . . I walk all over just to buy a small can of Lysol for $7.00."[6]

Other studies called attention to the problems nursing home assistants experienced as their workload mushroomed. The pandemic left a smaller staff responsible for a sicker and more distraught population with no help from families. Shantonia Jackson, a nursing assistant in a nursing home in Cicero, Illinois, told a *Guardian* reporter that she worked sixteen-hour days, seven days a week, caring for seventy residents at one time.[7] A survey released in June by the Service Employees International Union (SEIU), the largest union of nursing home staff, reported that nearly 80 percent believed they placed their lives at risk when they went to work.[8] Another study quoted a Filipino migrant worker: "Where I work, it is a skilled nursing facility. It is supposed to be a 5-star facility but what happens is we were not given proper protective gear . . . as soon as it was acknowledged that there is such a virus which is very dangerous." Although she had recently decided to take time off to care for herself, she was still working when the staff "learned that there were already residents in our facilities that had tested positive, and I began fearing for my safety—especially as I am at the age where I am vulnerable and also I have preexisting conditions."[9] Both nursing home assistants and home health aides also worried about transmitting the virus to their communities, which already had borne the brunt of the pandemic and were at heightened risk of infection and mortality. Jackson reported that she quarantined herself from her family in the same house, interacting with them only through video calls.[10]

The issues direct care workers faced had virtually no place in the forums' posts. Most writers viewed homecare aides and nursing home assistants as threats rather than as people who had a moral claim on extra protection. Those who discussed whether or not to rehire homecare aides focused solely on the repercussions for themselves and their relatives. A few argued that direct care workers were especially likely to spread disease because they failed to adhere to public health advice. Insisting on her right to visit her mother in a nursing home, one woman asked,

> How can these facilities be forced to allow family inside? Not, how do I cope? I am done coping. I have not seen my mother for 7 weeks. That is the longest time in my life I have gone without seeing her. She will die alone, lonely as many others will simply because of some unknown rule granted to some unknown entity. All in the name of protecting someone. I am 10 times more isolated and protective than the caregivers. They come and go daily, see family or whatever they do on off time. I see no one. I always used masks, taken care of myself. (Holly, May 10, 2020)

We can explain such attitudes in various ways. Overwhelmed by their own troubles, family members were unable to acknowledge any obligation for the health of others. Direct care workers were the visible face of regulations imposed by administrators and federal and state officials. It was a nursing home assistant, we saw, who prevented one woman from hugging her mother the first time they met after several months. Low-level hospital staff were the ones who barred families from emergency rooms. Caregivers thus may often have held direct care workers responsible for rules over which they had no control. And race and class divided this group of family members and direct care workers. I have noted that the little information we have about the forum participants suggests that many were white and middle-class. A very high proportion of direct care workers were African American, Asian, or Latinx, and many had recently immigrated. As a result, they were especially likely to be viewed as disease carriers.[11]

One of the few writers who repeatedly pointed to the plight of nursing home staff was a woman who called herself "Abuela," perhaps indicating her Latinx identity. Responding to the woman above who stated that she was more protective than nursing home staff and therefore should be allowed to visit, Abuela reminded her, "Those caregivers you say are free to go home each day are going home knowing that they may be bringing the virus home to their families everyday and having to decontaminate each day so as not to infect their loved ones. And if they get infected, they had to isolate at home and not get paid and then there is less help at your mom's nursing home" (May 10, 2020). When another woman asked how often she could phone staff to inquire about her father, who had recently entered a nursing home, Abuela cautioned, "Right now these staff are pretty stressed out and calling them is another issue because of Covid 19. Everyone is calling all day long" (May 23, 2020). Replying to a woman who wrote that she had decided not to place her relative in a memory care facility after learning that a worker had infected several residents, Abuela pointed out, "This is going to happen even in the best of facilities. If the staff are not compensated when they have to quarantine and many have no resources to find a place to quarantine—then this will be an issue. They cannot afford to lose their pay or get fired for not coming to work" (August 15, 2020). Such comments are notable primarily for their rarity in the message boards.

Conclusion

Two quantitative studies demonstrated that the pandemic had a deleterious impact on family caregivers. Comparing large samples of caregivers to noncaregivers, both reported that the caregivers reported significantly higher rates of both mental and physical health problems.[12] The Alzheimer's Association's message boards help us understand those findings. "As if this disease wasn't already hard enough," one woman wrote to the Caregivers Forum two months into the pandemic. Family members of people with Alzheimer's now had to face "some really awful circumstances" (May 18, 2020). The disaster intensified the loneliness and isolation of both caregivers and recipients, trapped some at home together, and separated others for months. Like Katrina and other catastrophes, the COVID pandemic demonstrated which groups the nation was willing to protect. As the death toll in nursing homes mounted, it became clear that old people, especially those with dementia and other chronic health problems, were deemed expendable.

The various Alzheimer's Association caregiver forums challenged that value system. Over and over the participants argued that their relatives' lives mattered and that relationships with them were precious and must be sustained. Sadness and longing suffused the posts we read in the previous chapter. Forbidden to visit their relatives, writers described themselves as heartbroken, in despair, and, most commonly, devastated. Some brought relatives home although they had vowed never to resume full-time caregiving. For one woman it was enough that her husband had begun to smile after leaving a facility, even as death approached. This chapter demonstrated that family members were acutely aware of the terror experienced by people with serious cognitive impairments alone in the hospital. Unsurprised to learn that their relatives had become uncontrollable, caregivers begged to stay with them.

But the forum participants failed to recognize the plight of direct care workers. Ai-Jen Poo, the director of the National Domestic Workers Alliance, writes that "meaningful societal transformation" depends on workers and employers finding "common ground—being able to see and take into account the other's experience."[13] Overburdened themselves, however, the caregivers we have studied were unable to cross the divides of class and race to join forces with direct care workers. Ignoring the sacrifices homecare aides and nursing home assistants made to provide essential assistance to vulnerable populations, the caregivers missed an opportunity to extol the importance of all caring labor. As a result, they undermined their ability to fight for the policy changes that could help them.

Conclusion

How the Pandemic Exposed and Exacerbated the Crisis in Care

Two perspectives on people with dementia vie for dominance. One is that the sufferers impose intolerable burdens, inflicting a terrible toll on their caregivers. In a society that glorifies self-sufficiency and independence, anyone who depends on others can be viewed as burdensome. In addition, hundreds of studies document the stresses family members experience. The participants in the Alzheimer's Association caregivers' forums routinely noted the emotional, physical, and financial costs of care. Delighted with the few hours of relief she received from her husband's first morning in an adult day program, one woman wrote, "Hope that others can take advantage of this service or something similar to take a much needed break from the endless tasks and caregiving job that we fall heir to." Several writers emphasized their exhaustion to explain why they sought institutional placement. A woman whose husband was rejected by every facility in the area worried that she no longer had the energy to keep him home.

But many caregivers also focused on the deep bonds connecting them to the recipients. I have quoted the British psychologist Tom Kitwood's definition of personhood: "a standing or status that is bestowed upon one human being by others, in the context of relationship and social being." Forum participants often wrote in relational terms. Because the writers felt intimately tied to the sufferers, their lives had special meaning. When the pandemic revealed the low value society placed on nursing home residents with dementia, the caregivers called attention to their worth and humanity. And when nursing homes and hospitals ruptured relationships between residents and writers, they responded with fury.

Just as many forum participants felt torn between those two positions, competing perspectives on the government's response to family caregiving divide policy analysts into two opposing groups. According to one, the primary goal is to contain costs by ensuring that family members remain the backbone of the long-term care system. Ironically, some advocacy groups have helped to bolster that position. Seeking to demonstrate that caregivers deserve greater recognition and respect, they have calculated the monetary value of family contributions. In 2019, the AARP Public Policy Institute reported that the forty-one million caregivers in the United States provided approximately thirty-four billion hours of care to disabled adults. Assigning a value of $13.81 per hour, the association estimated that the total value of caregiving was $470 billion, more than all out-of-pocket spending on health care and three times as much as all Medicaid spending on long-term care.[1] Such a massive sum strengthens the argument that the United States cannot afford to pay for the care of the rapidly expanding frail elderly population and that the responsibility must continue to rest with kin.

Other policy analysts argue that the country faces an elder care crisis that requires public solutions rather than private ones. Although I have criticized the contention that caregiving today is more challenging than ever before, this book clearly demonstrates that something is very wrong with our elder care system. It rests on the exploitation of workers, mostly women and people of color, who are paid too little to make ends meet. The cries of desperation we read on the Alzheimer Association's message boards remind us that the present situation also is unsustainable for family caregivers. To be sure, many of the problems they encounter are not amenable to government intervention. Although Arthur M. Kleinman was able to afford all the help he wanted, he described the period he cared for his wife as a "long dark decade"; the final years "felt like the next circle of hell." Forum participants wrote in excruciating detail about the anguish of witnessing the decline of intimates' mental powers.

Government action is needed, however, to address the issues of service cost, access, and quality that leave many caregivers without adequate support. Although few forum participants mentioned how they paid for home- and community-based services, several noted that they had too much income to qualify for Medicaid but too little to afford nursing home fees. Many also wrote about the difficulty of gaining access to either institutional or noninstitutional services for people with advanced dementia who engage in challenging behaviors. Caregivers who were most in need of assistance were thus often least likely to obtain it.

Although numerous researchers have examined the extent to which family caregivers have access to respite services, caregivers' assessments of the quality of those services have received little attention.[2] Several support-group members were stunned to discover that the workers to whom they entrusted their relatives knew little about caring for people with dementia. The most serious complaints focused on instances of negligence. The staff of the day care center attended by one woman's husband failed to notice when he left on his own; he arrived home after walking several miles in cold weather without a jacket. When another woman picked her husband up from overnight respite care, she found him in the same clothes he had worn when she left him several days earlier. He had not been shaved or bathed, and his diaper was filled with feces. A third woman wondered why the staff members of an overnight respite service were unaware that her husband had become seriously ill under their care.

Many writers blamed the for-profit entities that control nursing homes for the dismal quality of care they provide. One man explained why nursing homes are "places to warehouse the really sick people until they die: Most are owned by large corporations so the more they can pack in and the less care they can provide, the more profit there is." He urged other support-group members to "look for non-profit facilities." A woman whose husband died after repeated falls in a nursing home declared that "a synonym for a for-profit home is an understaffed one."

The poor quality of nursing homes had disastrous consequences when the COVID-19 pandemic struck. Forum participants became frantic as they read about the rising death toll or received notifications about cases in the facilities where their relatives resided. Visitation restrictions imposed other hardships. When nursing home visits resumed, relatives remained unreachable. Caregivers longing to hug those they had not seen in months were instructed to stand several feet away. The first visits after the lockdown ended also revealed how much residents had deteriorated in the absence of families. Caregivers did not have to wait to learn the consequence of the prohibition on hospital visits. Within days of leaving dementia sufferers at the hospital door, several family members received reports of delirium.

The pandemic also focused attention on the broader issues of care. As widespread sickness and suffering highlighted our common fragility and interdependence, the nation learned what happened when a president focused only on himself and his political fortunes and failed to display any compassion for the widespread suffering around him. Trump refused to say the names of the thousands of people who died under his watch (apart from those of a few close allies) and disputed their number. Rebuffing the aides who urged him to take advantage of his own bout with the virus to display empathy, he used it instead as an occasion to portray himself as a strong man who could vanquish any disease. After failing to protect us from the pandemic, he remained indifferent to the mismanagement of the vaccine rollout.[3]

Simultaneously, however, growing numbers of Americans became aware of the many caregivers they never before had associated with that role. The national press continually reminded us that farmworkers, grocery store clerks, cleaners, ambulance and delivery drivers, and meat processors, although never cheered from balconies and windows, were essential to sustaining our lives. The failure to grant them respect, decent employment conditions, and living wages suddenly seemed especially indefensible. A long feature article titled "Voices from the Front Lines of America's Food Supply" appeared in the New York Times on January 5, 2021. Antonia Rios Hernandez, a former farmworker in Immokalee, Florida, described a typical day: "We would be picking, for example, cucumbers in the morning and tomatoes in the afternoon and they're both very heavy work. My fingers would hurt by the end of the day. It hurts your back and makes your lungs ache to work that hard. I would sometimes come home and would just cry." Because she knew her work was "so important," she thought she would receive extra pay. But "all we got from the government was the one Covid check."[4]

Two days later the *Washington Post* followed with "Voices from the Aisles," an equally lengthy article which began, "Grocery stores have helped keep Americans afloat as the coronavirus pandemic has enveloped the country, ensuring families stay fed and supplied while hunkering down in their homes." The author recounted stories of Houston-area grocery clerks who risked their own health as well as that of their families to help feed the country. Combative customers, fighting with others for the last item on the shelf and refusing to wear masks, amplified the daily dangers. The workers' sacrifices received scant rewards: "Some grocery chains that provided . . . hazard pay at the beginning of the pandemic quietly allowed wage bumps to expire, even as sales remain robust and coronavirus infection rates soar."[5] Soon afterwards, a *Politico* article noted the numerous challenges farm and food-processing workers encountered in gaining access to vaccines.[6]

The pandemic also illuminated the consequence of sending care work back to the home. This book examined the plight of dementia caregivers deprived of respite services. Family members who had complained about the inadequacy of those services now realized how indispensable they had been. As one woman commented after the closure of a day care center her husband had attended part-time, "14 hrs/week didn't seem like much at the time, but boy, it sure does now." The wife of another man whose adult day program ended wrote that she was "going crazy." The media focused on the problems parents faced after day care centers and schools shut their doors. The burdens fell overwhelmingly on women.[7] A *New York Times* poll found that although 45 percent of men thought that they spent more time home schooling their children under twelve than their wives, just 3 percent of their wives agreed. Eighty percent of the women stated that they spent more time on that chore than their spouses.[8] Unsurprisingly, mothers were far more likely than husbands to cut back on work or withdraw entirely from the labor force, thus undermining a major feminist goal.[9] The dilemma was especially stark for single mothers and those in precarious, low-paid jobs. A *New York Times* article cited the case of Cindy Urena, a thirty-nine-year-old home health aide in Queens who had to decide whether to stop visiting a client with serious epilepsy or leave her seven-year-old daughter home alone after her public school closed. Even when working, Urena relied on food stamps to supplement her wages. After quitting, she had no income at all.[10]

The calamity also exposed the nation's disregard for different social groups. The rising nursing home death toll and lack of efforts to control it served as sharp reminders that old and sick people and the workers who care for them are widely considered disposable. Racial health disparities demonstrated the nation's callousness toward people of color. If some commentators pointed to the disproportionate impact of the virus on Blacks, Latinos, and Native Americans as evidence of their innate vulnerability, many more focused on social and economic factors.[11] Individuals in communities hardest hit by the pandemic frequently live in overcrowded, multigenerational households in environmentally unsafe neighborhoods, work in dangerous jobs, rely on public transportation, experience high rates of chronic health problems, and have little access to good medical care.[12] A video by Susan Moore, a fifty-two-year-old African American physician hospitalized with COVID-19 in Indianapolis, circulated widely. After a doctor denied her request for adequate pain relief, she said she felt "crushed," adding, "I put forth and I maintain if I was white, I wouldn't have to go through that."[13] As California's attorney general, Xavier Becerra (later head of the Department of Health and Human Services), told an interviewer, "COVID unmasked how serious many of these issues [of health inequities] are. The camouflage that may have hidden some of these disparities has been ripped away."[14]

The pandemic dramatically revealed the problems of relying on the market to care for vulnerable populations. Studies support the contention of several forum participants that nursing homes owned and operated as businesses tend to provide inferior care.[15] The for-profit enterprises that control nearly three-fourths of US nursing homes had neither the staffing levels nor the infection-control procedures that might have helped the facilities confront the virus's onslaught.[16] Although Americans have long looked to Europe and Canada for examples of state-supported long-term care, they have less reason to do so now. Despite Sweden's reputation as a generous social welfare state, profit-making businesses own and operate many of the country's nursing homes. As in the United States, they save money by relying on part-time and temporary workers.[17] Britain began handing over nursing homes to private corporations under Prime Minister Thatcher, and today they own a higher proportion of the market than in the United States (86 percent versus 70 percent). By the end of May 2020 outbreaks had occurred in two-thirds of the 328 British facilities owned by the largest chain; four employees and 934 residents had died.[18] In Ontario, Canada, for-profit nursing homes had a higher incidence of COVID-19 morbidity and mortality than municipal, nonprofit ones.[19]

But if the pandemic revealed long-standing problems, it also directed new attention to the issue of care. In July 2020, presidential nominee Joe Biden announced a $775 billion "Caregiver Workforce Plan" to provide increased support for family and paid caregivers of both children and elderly people.[20] After his inauguration, commentators pointed repeatedly to his "empathy" and "compassion," a welcome change from the tone of the previous administration. Other words we heard frequently were "solidarity" and "community." And soon a number of groups and individuals, both nationally and internationally, prepared statements explaining why care should have a more prominent place on the policy agenda. "If COVID-19 has taught us nothing else, it is that we need a new approach to caring for each other in this country," declared the Canadian academics and advocates who drafted the "Care Economy Statement."[21] The UK Women's Budget Group, a nonprofit organization, issued "A Care-Led Recovery from Covid-19: Investing in High Quality Care to Stimulate and Rebalance the Economy."[22] Another British group published *The Care Manifesto*, demanding a vast expansion of the number of publicly supported, low-carbon jobs that sustain both human life and the planet.[23] More than two hundred individuals signed the "Statement to the Biden-Harris Administration," drafted by the Carework Network, an international organization of academics, advocates, and policy makers, offering recommendations for expanding the government's role in caregiving.[24] In addition, several prominent US philanthropic organizations announced the formation of the Care for All with Respect and Equity (CARE) Fund, investing $50 million in projects that seek to improve the conditions of both paid and unpaid caregivers.[25]

The major development was the release of President Biden's "American Jobs Plan" in March 2021. Noting that the pandemic had "unmasked the fragility of our caregiving infrastructure," the plan called for $400 billion over the next eight years for long-term care, along with massive investments in roads, bridges, airports, the transit system, and the water supply.[26] "For too long," Biden stated, "caregivers who are disproportionately women, and women of color and immigrants, have been unseen, underpaid, and undervalued."[27] Some critics argued that the proposal fell short of offering the radical reform America needs. The plan assumed that funding for home- and community-based services would continue to come from Medicaid, the welfare program for the poor, rather than a social insurance program, and that the profit-making organizations that have reduced access and devastated quality of care would remain in control of those services.[28] Many more critics came from the right, objecting to the high price tag of Biden's plan and ridiculing the notion that caregiving could be considered part of the nation's infrastructure. As a *Slate* business reporter tweeted, "We don't have to pretend that every good thing is 'infrastructure.'"[29]

In response, advocates focused on public support for caregiving as a way to increase labor-force participation and bolster the economy. "Here's the thing—think about it," Vice-President Kamala Harris implored a North Carolina audience in April 2021. "Care—childcare, home care—keeps us working. . . . Just ask any parent who has been home with their kids for the last year. Ask anybody who has been caring for their mother or father for the last year. Care should be readily available and affordable to working people."[30] A *New York Times* headline read, "The Debate over What 'Infrastructure' Is Is Ridiculous: Both Snarled Traffic and a Morning without a Home Health Aide Can Make You Late for Work."[31] That argument privileges some groups of caregivers over others. This book has focused on the plight of spousal caregivers of dementia sufferers. Although their caregiving responsibilities tend to be especially onerous, many are elderly and no longer work outside the home. Concentrating on the labor force ignores their needs. We should emphasize the intrinsic as well as the instrumental value of care. Because vulnerability and dependence are inescapable features of all human life, caregiving is an essential activity that deserves greater recognition and support.

The Build Back Better Bill passed in the House slashed the money for HCBS from $400 to $150. It then died in the Senate. Nevertheless, the inclusion of caregiving in the American Jobs Plan had enormous significance. It represented an acknowledgment by a major political party of our ultimate interdependence, a recognition that caregiving is a social responsibility, not simply an individual one, and a commitment to creating a more caring world in which neither family members nor direct care workers will continue to be left entirely on their own.

ACKNOWLEDGMENTS

Because I have been thinking about the issue of care for more than thirty years, I cannot name all the people to whom I am indebted. I am very grateful to Mary Felstiner, who allowed me to use her beautiful poem, and to those who read parts or all of the manuscript, including Rick Abel, Carla Bittel, Charlotte Borst, Janet Farrell Brodie, Sharla Fett, Janet Golden, Robert Gottlieb, Dorien Grunbaum, Margaret Nelson, Jennifer A. Reich, Vivian Rothstein, Alice Wexler, and two anonymous reviewers. At NYU Press, Ilene Kalish provided welcome support and terrific editorial comments. Alexia Traganas skillfully shepherded the manuscript through the production process. I also wish to acknowledge the Alzheimer's Association, which operates the online support groups for caregivers on which I relied.

NOTES

INTRODUCTION

1 See Deborah L. O'Connor, "Self-Identifying as a Caregiver: Exploring the Positioning Process," *Journal of Aging Studies*, 21 (2007): 165–74.

2 See, e.g., *A Labour of Love: Women, Work, and Caring*, ed. Janet Finch and Dulcie Groves (Boston: Routledge and Kegan Paul, 1983); Kari Waerness, "The Rationality of Caring," *Economic and Industrial Democracy*, 5, no. 2 (1985): 185–211.

3 See, e.g., Eva Feder Kittay, *Love's Labor: Essays on Women, Equality, and Dependency* (New York: Routledge, 1999).

4 See, e.g., Nancy Folbre, *The Invisible Heart: Economics and Family Values* (New York: New Press, 2001).

5 See, e.g., Nancy Fraser, "Contradictions of Capital and Care," *New Left Review*, July–August 2016.

6 See, e.g., Stacey Oliker, "Sociology and Studies of Gender, Caregiving, and Inequality," *Sociology Compass*, 5, no. 11 (2011): 968–83.

7 *Care in Practice: On Tinkering in Clinics, Homes, and Farms*, ed. Annemarie Mol, Ingunn Moser, and Jeannette Pols (New Brunswick, NJ: Transaction Publishers, 2010).

8 Evelyn Nakano Glenn, *Forced to Care: Coercion and Caregiving* (Cambridge, MA: Harvard University Press, 2010), 4–5.

9 Ai-Jen Poo with Ariane Conrad, *The Age of Dignity: Preparing for the Elder Boom in a Changing America* (New York: Free Press, 2015).

10 Robyn I. Stone, "The Direct Care Worker: The Third Rail of Home Care Policy," *Annual Reviews in Public Health*, 25 (2004) 521–37.

11 *Global Dimensions of Gender and Carework*, ed. Mary K. Zommerman, Jacquelyn S. Litt, and Christine E. Bose (Stanford, CA: Stanford University Press, 2006).

12 Leah Zallman, Karen E. Finnegan, David U. Himmelstein, Sharon Touw, and Steffie Woolhandler, "Care for America's Elderly and Disabled People Relies on Immigrant Labor," *Health Affairs*, 38, no. 6 (2019): 919–26.

13 See E. C. Apesoa-Varano, Y. Tang-Feldman, S. C. Reinhard, R. Choula, and H. M. Young, "Multi-Cultural Caregiving and Caregiver Interventions: A Look Back and a Call for Future Action," *Generations*, 39, no. 4 (Winter 2015–2016): 39–48; Peggye Dilworth-Anderson, Heehyul Moon, and Maria P. Arranda, "Dementia Caregiving Research: Expanding and Reframing the Lens of Diversity, Inclusivity, and Intersectionality," *Gerontologist*, 60, no. 5 (2020): 797–805.

14 Amanda Singleton, "The Future of Caregiving Support," AARP, March 4, 2020, www.aarp.org.

15 Nancy Krieger, "Measures of Racism, Sexism, Heterosexism, and Gender Binarism for Health Equity Research: From Structural Injustice to Embodied Harm—an Ecosocial Analysis," *Annual Reviews of Public Health*, 41 (2020): 37–62; Valentine M. Villa, Steven P. Wallace, Sofya Bagdasaryan, and Maria P. Aranda, "Hispanic Baby Boomers: Health Inequities Likely to Persist in Old Age," *Gerontologist*, 552, no. 2 (2012): 166–76.

16 Chanee D. Fabius, Jennifer L. Wolff, and Judith D. Kasper, "Race Differences in Characteristics and Experiences of Black and White Caregivers of Older Americans," *Gerontologist*, 60, no. 10 (2020); see also Judith J. McCann, et al., "Comparison of Informal Caregiving by Black and White Older Adults in a Community Population," *Journal of the American Geriatrics Society*, 48 (2000): 1612–17.

17 Steven A. Cohen, Natalie J. Sabik, Sarah K. Cook, Ariana B. Azzoli, and Carolyn A. Mendez-Luck, "Differences within Differences: Gender Inequalities in Caregiving Intensity Vary by Race and Ethnicity in Informal Caregivers," *Journal of Cross-Cultural Gerontology*, 34 (2019): 245–63.

18 Steven P. Wallace, Nadereh Pourat, Linda Delp, and Kathryn G. Kietzman, "Long-Term Services and Supports for the Elderly Population," in *Changing the U.S. Health Care System: Key Issues in Health Services Policy and Management*, 4th edition, ed. Gerald F. Kominsky (San Francisco: Jossey-Bass, 2013).

19 Atul Gupta, Sabrina T. Howell, Constantine Yannelis, and Abhinav Gupta, "Does Private Equity Investment in Healthcare Benefit Patients? Evidence from Nursing Homes," National Bureau of Economic Research working paper 28474, February 2021, https://doi.org/10.3386/w28474.

20 Jennifer L. Wolff, John Mulcahy, Jin Huang, David L. Roth, Kenneth Covinsky, and Judith D. Kasper, "Family Caregivers of Older Adults, 1999–2015: Trends in Characteristics, Circumstances, and Role-Related Appraisal," *Gerontologist*, 58, no. 6 (2018): 1021–32.

21 See David G. Stevenson and David C. Grabowski, "Sizing Up the Market for Assisted Living," *Health Affairs*, 29, no. 1 (2009).

22 See Rosanna Hertz and Margaret K. Nelson, *Random Families: Genetic Strangers, Sperm Donor Siblings, and the Creation of New Kin* (New York: Oxford University Press, 2018).

23 Elaine M. Brody, "'Women in the Middle' and Family Help to Older People," *Gerontologist*, 21, no. 5 (1981): 471–80.

24 Elana D. Buch, "Anthropology of Aging and Care," *Annual Review of Anthropology*, 44 (2015): 286.

25 "What Is Dementia?" Alzheimer's Association, 2021, www.alz.org.

26 Alzheimer's Association, "2019 Alzheimer's Disease Facts and Figures," *Alzheimer's and Dementia*, 15 (2019): 321.

27 National Center for Health Statistics, "Alzheimer Disease," Centers for Disease Control and Prevention, October 14, 2021, www.cdc.gov.

28 Judith D. Kasper, Vicki A. Freedman, Brenda C. Spillman, and Jennifer L. Wolff, "The Disproportionate Impact of Dementia on Family and Unpaid Caregiving to Older Adults," *Health Affairs*, 34, no. 10 (October 2015): 1642.

29 Linda McK. Stewart, *25 Months: A Memoir* (New York: Other Press, 2004), 176.

30 Kasper, Freedman, Spillman, and Wolff, "The Disproportionate Impact of Dementia," 1642–49.

31 Tom Kitwood, *Dementia Reconsidered: The Person Comes First* (New York: Open University Press, 1997), 8.

32 Institute for Women's Policy Research, "Women and the Care Crisis: Valuing In-Home Care in Policy and Practice," April 2013, www.iwpr.org; Ruth Rosen, "The Care Crisis," *Nation*, February 27, 2007; see Fraser, "Contradictions of Capital and Care."

CHAPTER 1. REFORMULATING STRESS AND BURDEN

1 Hans Selye, "A Syndrome Produced by Diverse Nocuous Agents," *Nature*, July 34, 1936, 32.

2 Anne Harrington, *The Cure Within: A History of Mind-Body Medicine* (New York: Norton, 2008), 155–57.

3 Meyer Friedman and Ray Rosenman, *Type A Behavior and Your Heart* (New York: Random House, 1974).

4 See Peggy A. Thoits, "Stress and Health: Major Findings and Policy Implications," *Journal of Health and Social Behavior* (2010): S41–S53.

5 Elizabeth Siegel Watkins, "Stress and the American Vernacular: Popular Perceptions of Disease Causality," in *Stress, Shock, and Adaptation in the Twentieth Century*, ed. David Cantor and Edmund Ramsden (Rochester, NY: University of Rochester Press, 2014), 65; see also Allan Young, "The Discourse on Stress and the Reproduction of Conventional Knowledge," *Social Science and Medicine*, 14B (1980): 133–46.

6 "STRESS! Seeking Cures for Modern Anxieties," *Time*, June 6, 1983.

7 Graham Greene, *A Burnt-Out Case* (New York: Viking, 1960).

8 Herbert J. Freudenberger, "Staff Burn-Out," *Journal of Social Issues*, 30 (1974): 161; Douglas Martin, "Herbert Freudenberger, 73, Coiner of 'Burnout' Is Dead," *New York Times*, December 5, 1999.

9 Herbert J. Freudenberger, "Burnout: Past, Present, and Future Concerns," *Loss, Grief, and Care*, 3, nos. 1–2 (1989): 1–10.

10 Institute of Medicine, *Report on Stress and Human Health* (Washington, DC: National Academies Press, 1981), 2.

11 See *The Overselling of Population Ageing: Apocalyptic Demography, Intergenerational Challenges, and Social Policy*, ed. Ellen Gee and Gloria Gutman. (New York: Oxford University Press, 2000); A. Robertson, "The Politics of

Alzheimer's Disease: A Case Study in Apocalyptic Demography," *International Journal of Health Services*, 20, no. 3 (1990): 429–42.

12 J. S. Siegel and C. M. Taeuber, "Demographic Perspectives on the Long-Lived Society," *Daedalus*, 115 (1986): 77–118.

13 Jesse F. Ballenger, *Self, Senility, and Alzheimer's Disease in Modern America: A History* (Baltimore, MD: Johns Hopkins University Press, 2006).

14 Robert Katzman, "The Prevalence and Malignancy of Alzheimer Disease," *Archives of Neurology*, 33 (April 1976): 217–18; H. Roger Segelken, "Robert Katzman, Alzheimer's Activist, Dies at 82," *New York Times*, September 23, 2008.

15 Lewis Thomas, "The Problem of Dementia." First published in the early 1980s in *Discover*, a popular science magazine, the essay was reprinted in Lewis Thomas, *Late Night Thoughts on Listening to Mahler's Ninth Symphony* (New York: Penguin, 1995), 117–18.

16 United States. Congress. Senate. Committee on Labor and Human Resources. Subcommittee on Aging, *Impact of Alzheimer's Disease on the Nation's Elderly* (Ann Arbor: University of Michigan Library, 1980), p. 2.

17 Quoted in Ballenger, *Self, Senility*, 136.

18 Eleanor Cooney, "Death in Slow Motion: A Descent into Alzheimer's," *Harper's*, October 2001.

19 Donna Cohen and Carl Eisdorfer, *The Loss of Self: A Family Resource for the Care of Alzheimer's Disease and Related Disorders* (New York: Norton, 1986).

20 Thomas, "The Problem of Dementia," 118.

21 United States. Congress. Senate. Committee on Labor and Human Resources. Subcommittee on Aging, *Impact of Alzheimer's Disease*, 3–4.

22 Leonard Cohen, *No Aging in India: Alzheimer's, the Bad Family, and Other Modern Things* (Berkeley: University of California Press, 1998), 54.

23 Steven H. Zarit, Nancy K. Orr, and Judy M. Zarit, *The Hidden Victims of Alzheimer's Disease: Families under Stress* (New York: NYU Press, 1985), 87.

24 Leonard I. Pearlin, Joseph T. Mullin, Shirley J. Semple, and Marilyn M. Skaff, "Caregiving and the Stress Process: An Overview of Concepts and Their Measures," *Gerontologist*, 30 (1990): 584.

25 Lynn Etters, Debbie Goodall, and Barbara E. Harrison, "Caregiver Burden among Dementia Patient Caregivers: A Review of the Literature," *Journal of the American Academy of Nurse Practitioners*, 20 (2008): 423.

26 Carol S. Aneshensel, Leonard I. Pearlin, Joseph T. Mullan, Steven H. Zarit, and Carol J. Whitlatch, *Profiles in Caregiving: The Unexpected Career* (San Diego: Academic Press, 1995).

27 Scholar.google provided that information.

28 Marina Bastawrous, "Caregiver Burden—A Critical Discussion," *International Journal of Nursing Studies*, 50 (2013): 431–41.

29 Michelle Murphy, "Occupational Health from Below: The Women Office Workers' Movement and the Hazardous Office," in *Emerging Illnesses and Society:*

Negotiating the Public Health Agenda, ed. Randall M. Packard, Peter J. Brown, Ruth L. Berkelman, and Howard Frumkin (Baltimore, MD: Johns Hopkins University Press, 2004), 212–13.

30 Cited in Etters, Goodall, and Harrison, "Caregiver Burden among Dementia Patient Caregivers," 423.

31 National Alliance for Caregivers and AARP Public Policy Institute, *Caregiving in the U.S.*, Executive Summary, AARP, June 2015, 20–21, www.aarp.org.

32 Alissa Sauer, "The Reasons Why Alzheimer's and Dementia Caregivers Are So Stressed," alzheimers.net, January 18, 2019, www.alzheimers.net.

33 See K. J. Gilhooly, et al., "A Meta-Review of Stress, Coping, and Interventions in Dementia and Dementia Caregiving," *BMC Geriatric*, 16 (2016); Francine C. Ducharme, "'Learning to Become a Family Caregiver': Efficacy of an Intervention Program for Caregivers Following Diagnosis of Dementia in a Relative," *Gerontologist*, 51, no. 4 (2011): 484–94; Laura Cousino Klein, et al., "Anticipating an Easier Day: Effects of Adult Day Services on Daily Cortisol and Stress," *Gerontologist*, 56, no. 2 (2016): 303–12.

34 American Medical Association, *Caring for the Caregiver: A Guide for Physicians*, 2018, 2, www.ama-assn.org.

35 On the preponderance of quantitative studies, see Ifah Arbel, Kathleen S. Bingham, and Deirdre R. Dawson, "A Scoping Review of Literature on Sex and Gender Differences among Dementia Spousal Caregivers," *Gerontologist*, 59, no. 6 (November 16, 2019): e811.

36 Theodore M. Porter, *Trust in Numbers: The Pursuit of Objectivity in Science and Public Life* (Princeton, NJ: Princeton University Press, 1995), ix.

37 Aneschensel, et al., *Profiles*, 42.

38 Lynn Friss Feinberg, "Recognizing the Work of Family and Informal Caregivers: The Case for Caregiver Assessment," in *Family Caregivers on the Job: Moving beyond ADLs and IADLs*, ed. Carol Levine (New York: United Hospital Fund, 2004), 72.

39 Aneshensel, et al., *Profiles*, 156.

40 Arthur Kleinman, *The Soul of Care: The Moral Education of a Husband and a Doctor* (New York: Viking, 2019), 138, 155, 169.

41 Christine Stirling, Sharon Andrews, Toby Croft, James Vickers, Paul Turner, and Andrew Robinson, "Measuring Dementia Carers' Unmet Need for Services: An Exploratory Mixed Method Study," *BMC Health Services Research*, 10 (2010).

42 Rachel Hadas, *Strange Relation: A Memoir of Marriage, Dementia, and Poetry* (Philadelphia: Paul Dry Press, 2011).

43 American Medical Association, "Caregiver Self-Assessment Questionnaire," HealthinAging.org, 2021, www.healthinaging.org; G. Epstein-Lubow, et al., "Evidence for the Validity of the American Medical Association's Caregiver Self-Assessment Questionnaire as a Screening Measure for Depression," *Journal of the American Geriatrics Society*, 58, no. 2 (2010): 387–88.

44 Hadas, *Strange Relation*, 41.

45 Hadas, *Strange Relation*, 57.

46 Hadas, *Strange Relation*, 61.

47 "Kingston Caregiver Stress Scale (KCSS)," Providence Care, accessed November 9, 2021, https://providencecare.ca; Tatiana Sadak, et al., "Psychometric Evaluation of Kingston Caregiver Stress Scale," *Clinical Gerontology*, 40, no. 4 (2017): 268–80.

48 Hadas, *Strange Relation*, 22.

49 Hadas, *Strange Relation*, 22.

50 Eula Biss, "The Pain Scale," *Harper's*, June 2005, 30.

51 Yin Liu, David M. Almeida, Michael J. Rovine, and Steven H. Zarit, "Care Transitions and Adult Day Services Moderate the Longitudinal Links between Stress Biomarkers and Family Caregivers' Functional Health," *Gerontology*, 63, no. 6 (2017): 538–49; see Jennifer R. Piazza, David M. Almeida, Natalia O. Dmitrieva, and Laura C. Klein, "Frontiers in the Use of Biomarkers of Health in Research on Stress and Aging," *Journal of Gerontology: Psychological Sciences*, 65B, no. 5 (2010): 512–24.

52 Nancy Fraser, *Unruly Practices: Power, Discourse, and Gender in Contemporary Social Theory* (Minneapolis: University of Minnesota Press, 1989).

53 See Pamela Doty and Brenda Spillman, "Help for Family Caregivers Available from Government Programs and Policies," in *Family Caregiving in the New Normal*, ed Joseph E. Gaugler and Robert L. Kane (Boston: Elsevier, 2015), 174; Brenda C. Spillman and Sharon K. Long, "Does High Caregiver Stress Predict Nursing Home Entry?" *Inquiry*, 46 (Summer 2009): 140–61.

54 Sung-chull Hong and Constance L. Coogle, "Spousal Caregiving for Partners with Dementia: A Deductive Literature Review Testing Calasanti's Gendered View of Care Work," *Journal of Applied Gerontology*, 35, no. 7 (2016): 759–87; Jennifer L. Yee and Richard Schulz, "Gender Differences in Psychiatric Morbidity among Family Caregivers: A Review and Analysis," *Gerontologist*, 40, no. 2 (2000): 147–64; Eleanor Palo Stoller and Casey Schroeder Miklowski, "Spouses Caring for Spouses: Untangling the Influences of Relationship and Gender," in *Caregiving Contexts: Cultural, Familial, and Societal Implications*, ed. Maximiliane E. Szinovacz and Adam Davey (New York: Springer, 2008), 115–32.

55 See Hélène Corbonneau, "Development of a Conceptual Framework of Positive Aspects of Caregiving in Dementia," *Dementia*, 9, no. 3 (2010): 327–53.

56 See, e.g., Steven A. Cohen, Natalie J. Sabik, Sarah K. Cook, Ariana B. Azzoli, and Carolyn A. Mendez-Luck, "Differences within Differences: Gender Inequalities in Caregiving Intensity Vary by Race and Ethnicity in Informal Caregivers," *Journal of Cross-Cultural Gerontology*, 34 (2019): 245–63; Chanee D. Fabius, Jennifer L. Wolff, and Judith D. Kasper, "Race Differences in Characteristics and Experiences of Black and White Caregivers of Older Americans," *Gerontologist*, 60, no. 10 (2020); Judith J. McCann, et al., "Comparison of Informal Caregiving by Black and White Older Adults in a

Community Population," *Journal of the American Geriatrics Society*, 48 (2000): 1612–17.

57 For more information about that research, see chapters 5–7.

58 Virginia Stem Owens, *Caring for Mother: A Daughter's Long Goodbye* (Louisville, KY: Westminster John Knox Press, 2007), 92–93.

59 This support group is discussed in chapter 5.

60 June Price Tangney, Jeff Stuewig, and Debra J. Mashek, "Moral Emotions and Moral Behavior," *Annual Review of Psychology*, 58 (2007): 346.

61 Sandra R. Levitsky, *Caring for Our Own: Why There Is No Political Demand for New American Social Welfare Rights* (New York: Oxford University Press, 2014), 105; American Medical Association, *Caring for the Caregiver*, 1.

62 Wendy Nelson Espeland and Michael Sauder, *Engines of Anxiety: Academic Rankings, Reputation, and Accountability* (New York: Russell Sage Foundation, 2016), 22.

63 Nicci Gerrard, *The Last Ocean: A Journey through Memory and Forgetting* (New York: Penguin, 2019), 85.

64 American Medical Association, *Caring for the Caregiver*, 1.

65 Kathryn G. Keitzman, "A Portrait of Older Californians with Disabilities Who Rely on Public Services to Remain Independent," *Home Health Care Services Quarterly*, 31, no. 4 (2012).

66 Zoe Blake Samson, Monica Parker, Clinton Dye, and Kenneth Hepburn, "Experiences and Learning Needs of African American Family Dementia Caregivers," *American Journal of Alzheimer's Disease and Other Dementias*, 31, no. 6 (2016): 494.

67 See, e.g., C.-Y. Chiao, H.-S. Wu, and C.-Y. Hsiao, "Caregiver Burden for Informal Caregivers of Patients with Dementia: A Systemic Review," *International Nursing Review*, 62, no. 3 (2015): 340–50.

68 Mark Jackson, *The Age of Stress: Science and the Search for Stability* (New York: Oxford University Press, 2013), 2–3.

69 "What Is Stress?" American Institute of Stress, accessed June 20, 2019, www.stress.org.

70 Peter J. Whitehouse, with Daniel George, *The Myth of Alzheimer's: What You Aren't Being Told about Today's Most Dreaded Diagnosis* (New York: St. Martin's Griffin, 2008).

71 Evelyn Nakano Glenn, *Forced to Care: Coercion and Caregiving* (Cambridge, MA: Harvard University Press, 2010).

72 Quoted in Ballenger, *Self, Senility*, 113.

73 See Aaron T. Seaman, "The Consequence of 'Doing Nothing': Family Caregiving for Alzheimer's Disease as Non-Action in the U.S.," *Social Science and Medicine*, 197 (2018): 63.

74 See, e.g., Justine McGovern, "Couple Meaning-Making and Dementia: Challenge to the Deficit Model," *Journal of Gerontological Social Work*, 54, no. 7 (2011): 678–90.

CHAPTER 2. CHALLENGING THE MEDICAL MODEL OF DEMENTIA

1 On authoritative knowledge, see Lorraine Code, *What Can She Know? Feminist Theory and the Construction of Knowledge* (Ithaca, NY: Cornell University Press, 1991).

2 Emily Abel, *Hearts of Wisdom: American Women Caring for Kin, 1850–1940* (Cambridge, MA: Harvard University Press, 2000).

3 Barbara Sicherman, *Alice Hamilton: A Life in Letters* (Cambridge, MA: Harvard University Press, 1984), 119; Robyn Muncy, *Creating a Female Dominion in American Reform, 1909–1935* (New York: Oxford University Press, 1991), 114–15.

4 Emily Abel and Nancy Reifel, "Interactions between Public Health Nurses and Clients on American Indian Reservations during the 1930s," *Social History of Medicine*, 9 (1996): 89–108.

5 Tom Kitwood, *Dementia Reconsidered: The Person Comes First* (New York: Open University Press, 1970), 8.

6 See, e.g., Jill Manthorpe and Kritika Samsi, "Person-Centered Dementia Care: Current Perspectives," *Clinical Interventions in Aging*, 11 (2016) 1733–40; Karen Love and Jackie Pinkowitz, "Person-Centered Care for People with Dementia: A Theoretical and Conceptual Framework," *Generations* (Fall 2013): 23–29; Peter Reed, Jennifer Carson, and Zebbedia Gibb, "Transcending the Tragedy Discourse of Dementia: An Ethical Imperative for Promoting Selfhood, Meaningful Relationships, and Well-Being," *AMA Journal of Ethics*, 19, no. 7 (July 2017): 693–703; Sun Kyung Kim and Myonghwa Park, "Effectiveness of Person-Centered Care on People with Dementia: A Systemic Review and Meta-Analysis," *Clinical Interventions in Aging*, 12 (2017): 381–97; Mary Jane Koren, "Person-Centered Care for Nursing Homes Residents: The Culture Change Movement," *Health Affairs*, 29, no. 2 (2010); David C. Grabowski, et al., "Culture Change and Nursing Home Quality of Care," *Gerontologist*, 54, no. S1 (2014): S35–S45; Elaine O. Siegel, et al., "Supporting and Promoting Personhood in Long Term Care Settings: Contextual Factors," *International Journal of Older People Nursing*, 7 (2012): 295–302.

7 See Ruth Bartlett and Deborah O'Connor, "From Personhood to Citizenship: Broadening the Lens for Dementia Practice and Research," *Journal of Aging Studies*, 21 (2007): 107–18; *Care in Practice: On Tinkering in Clinics, Homes, and Farms*, ed. Annemarie Mol, Ingunn Moser, and Jeannette Pols (New Brunswick, NJ: Transaction Publishers, 2010); Michael Gabriel Fetterolf, "Personhood-Based Dementia Care: Using the Familial Caregiver as a Bridging Model for Professional Caregivers," *Anthropology and Aging*, 36, no. 1 (2015): 82–100. Kitwood, *Dementia Reconsidered*; Athena McLean, *The Person in Dementia: A Study of Nursing Home Care in the US* (Peterborough, Ontario: Broadview Press, 2007); Janice L. Palmer, "Preserving Personhood of Individuals with Advanced Dementia: Lessons from Family Caregivers," *Geriatric Nursing*, 34 (2013): 224–29; Steven R. Sabat, "Voices of Alzheimer's Disease Sufferers: A Call for Treatment Based on Personhood," *Journal of Clinical Ethics*, 9, no. 1 (Spring 1998): 35–48; Steven R. Sabat and Rom

Harré, "The Construction and Deconstruction of Self in Alzheimer's Disease," *Ageing and Society*, 12 (1992): 443–61; Jeff A. Small, Kathey Geldart, Gloria Gutman, and Mary Ann Clarke Scott, "The Discourse of Self in Dementia," *Ageing and Society*, 18 (1998): 291–316.

8 Most research seeking to answer that question describes couples in which one partner has dementia. See, e.g., Elise Hernandez, Beth Spender, Berit Ingersoll-Dayton, Alexandra Faber, and Allison Ewert, "'We Are a Team': Couple Identity and Memory Loss," *Dementia*, 18, no. 3 (2019): 1166–80

9 Emily K. Abel, *Who Cares for the Elderly? Public Policy and the Experiences of Adult Daughters* (Philadelphia: Temple University Press, 1991). I also discussed the interviews in Emily K. Abel and Carole Browner, "Selective Compliance with Biomedical Authority and the Uses of Experiential Knowledge," in *Pragmatic Women and Body Politics*, ed. Margaret Lock and Patricia A. Kaufert (Cambridge: Cambridge University Press, 1998), 310–26. For more information about the methodology, see Abel, *Who Cares for the Elderly?*

10 Emily K. Abel, *Living in Death's Shadow: Family Experiences of Terminal Care and Irreplaceable Loss* (Baltimore, MD: Johns Hopkins University Press, 2017).

11 Sue Miller, *The Story of My Father: A Memoir* (New York: Random House, 2003), 29, 31, 32.

12 Nancy L. Mace and Peter V. Rabins, *The 36-Hour Day: A Family Guide to Caring for People Who Have Alzheimer's Diseases, Other Dementias, and Memory Loss* (Baltimore, MD: Johns Hopkins University Press, 2017).

13 John Daniel, *Looking After: A Son's Memoir* (Washington, DC: Counterpoint, 1996), 85.

14 Aaron Alterra, *The Caregiver: A Life with Alzheimer's* (Ithaca, NY: Cornell University Press, 1999), 191–92. Alterra probably used a consumer version of the *Merck Manual of Diagnosis and Therapy*, a widely used medical textbook.

15 Dan W. Grupe and Jack B. Nitschke, "Uncertainty and Anticipation in Anxiety: An Integrated Neurobiological and Psychological Perspective," *Nature Reviews Neuroscience*, 14 (2013): 488–501.

16 Miller, *The Story of My Father*, 29, 31, 32.

17 Alterra, *Caregiver*.

18 Floyd Skloot, *In the Shadow of Memory* (Lincoln: University of Nebraska Press, 2003), 220.

19 Skloot, *In the Shadow of Memory*, 241.

20 Judith Levine, *Do You Remember Me? A Father, a Daughter, and a Search for the Self* (New York: Free Press, 2004), 149.

21 Owens, *Caring for My Mother*, 43.

22 Eleanor Cooney, *My Mother's Descent into Alzheimer's: Death in Slow Motion* (New York: HarperCollins, 2003), 31.

23 Madeleine L'Engle, *The Summer of the Great-Grandmother* (New York: Farrar, Straus, and Giroux, 1974), 4.

24 John Thorndike, *The Last of His Mind: A Year in the Shadow of Alzheimer's* (Athens, OH: Swallow Press, 2009), 11.

25 Sam Fazio, Douglas Pace, Janice Flinner, and Beth Kallmyer, "The Fundamentals of Person-Centered Care for Individuals with Dementia," *Gerontologist*, 58, no. S1 (2018): S18.

26 See McLean, *The Person in Dementia*, 48, 54, 181; Sabat, "Voices of Alzheimer's Disease Sufferers."

27 Fazio, et al., "Fundamentals," S18.

28 Ingunn Moser, "'Perhaps Tears Should Not Be Counted but Wiped Away': On Quality and Improvement," in *Care in Practice*, ed. Mol, Moser, and Pols, 277–300.

29 Justine McGovern, "Couple Meaning-Making and Dementia: Challenges to the Deficit Model," *Journal of Gerontological Social Work*, 54, no. 7 (2011): 678–90.

30 JoAnn Perry and Deborah O'Connor, "Preserving Personhood: (Re)Membering the Spouse with Dementia," *Family Relations*, 51 (2002): 60.

31 L'Engle, *Summer*, 37.

32 Reeve Lindbergh, *No More Words: A Journal of My Mother, Anne Morrow Lindbergh* (New York: Simon and Schuster, 2001), 84.

33 Lauren Kessler, *Finding Life in the Land of Alzheimer's: One Daughter's Hopeful Story* (New York: Penguin Books, 2007), 67.

34 Elinor Fuchs, *Making an Exit: A Mother-Daughter Drama with Machine Tools, Alzheimer's, and Laughter* (New York: Henry Holt, 2005), 95.

35 Fuchs, *Making an Exit*, 114.

36 Thorndike, *Last of His Mind*, 161.

37 Lindbergh, *No More Words*, 120.

38 Janelle S. Taylor, "On Recognition, Caring, and Dementia," *Medical Anthropology Quarterly*, 22, no. 4 (2008): 313–35, quotation on 327.

39 Skloot, *In the Shadow of Memory*, 194.

40 Barry Petersen, *Jan's Story: Love Lost to the Long Goodbye of Alzheimer's* (Lake Forest, CA: Behler, 2010), 79.

41 Petersen, *Jan's Story*, 118.

42 Petersen, *Jan's Story*, 131.

43 Levine, *Do You Remember Me?*, 155, 182–83.

44 Alix Kates Shulman, *To Love What Is: A Marriage Transformed* (New York: Farrar, Straus, and Giroux, 2008), 87, 98–99, 104.

45 Mary Gordon, *Circling My Mother* (New York: Pantheon Books, 2007), 4.

46 L'Engle, *Summer*, 102.

47 Lucette Lagnado, *The Arrogant Years: One Girl's Search for Her Lost Youth, from Cairo to Brooklyn* (New York: HarperCollins, 2011), 330.

48 Lynn Casteel Harper, *On Vanishing: Mortality, Dementia, and What It Means to Disappear* (New York: Catapult, 2020), 34–35. Nicci Gerrard, a British journalist,

wrote that "even at the bitter end" her father remained himself. "There was something that endured beyond language and recollection, a trace perhaps, like grooves that life had worn into him the way a river carves into a rock. He still had his sweetness; his past lived on in his smile, his frown, the way he raised his busy silver eyebrows. . . . He might not have recognized us, but we could recognize him." Gerrard could not find a word "for this indelible essence," though once "it would have been 'soul'" (Nicci Gerrard, *The Last Ocean: A Journey through Memory and Forgetting* [New York: Penguin, 2019], 3).

49 Arthur Kleinman, *The Soul of Care: The Moral Education of a Husband and a Doctor* (New York: Viking, 2019).

50 Kleinman, *Soul of Care*, 7.

51 Arthur Kleinman, "Curriculum Vitae," accessed November 9, 2021, anthropology. fas.harvard.edu; Kleinman, *Soul of Care*.

52 Kleinman, *Soul of Care*, 121.

53 Kleinman, *Soul of Care*, 127.

54 Kleinman, *Soul of Care*, 128.

55 Kleinman, *Soul of Care*, 50.

56 Kleinman, *Soul of Care*, 51.

57 Kleinman, *Soul of Care*, 52.

58 Kleinman, *Soul of Care*, 76.

59 Arthur Kleinman, *The Illness Narratives: Suffering, Healing, and the Human Condition* (New York: Basic Books, 1988).

60 Kleinman, *Soul of Care*, 187.

61 Kleinman, *Soul of Care*, 139.

62 Kitwood, *Dementia Reconsidered*, 89.

63 Kleinman, *Soul of Care*, 168.

64 Kleinman, *Soul of Care*, 165.

65 Kleinman, *Soul of Care*, 169.

66 Kleinman, *Soul of Care*, 169.

67 Kleinman, *Soul of Care*, 171.

68 Emilie Wawrziczny, Guillaume Berna, Francine Ducharme, Marie-Jeanne Kergoat, Florence Pasquier, and Pascal Antoine, "Characteristics of the Spouse Caregiving Experience: Comparison between Early- and Late-Onset Dementia," *Aging and Mental Health*, 22, no. 9 (2018): 1213.

69 Paul Jolly, "Medical Education in the United States, 1960–1987," *Health Affairs*, 7, no. Suppl. 2 (1988).

70 See *Working It Out: 23 Women Writers, Artists, Scientists, and Scholars Talk about Their Lives and Work*, ed. Sara Ruddick and Pamela Daniels (New York: Pantheon, 1977).

71 Margaret K. Nelson and I discuss Jasmine Mehta in "Intimate Care for Hire," *American Prospect*, May 21, 2001.

CHAPTER 3. LOOKING TO THE PAST

1 Institute for Women's Policy Research, "Women and the Care Crisis: Valuing In-Home Care in Policy and Practice," April 2013, www.iwpr.org; Ruth Rosen, "The Care Crisis," *Nation*, February 27, 2007; see Nancy Fraser, "Contradictions of Capital and Care," *New Left Review*, July–August 2016.

2 Sandra R. Levitsky, *Caring for Our Own: Why There Is No Political Demand for New American Social Welfare Rights* (New York: Oxford University Press), 50; Nadine Marks, "Caregiving across the Lifespan: National Prevalence and Predictors," *Family Relations*, 45 (January 1996): 27; Susan C. Reinhard and Lynn Friss Feinberg, "The Escalating Complexity of Family Caregiving: Meeting the Challenge," in *Family Caregiving in the New Normal*, ed. Joseph E. Gaugler and Robert L. Kane (Boston: Academic Press, 2015), 291.

3 Jennifer L. Wolff and Barry J. Jacobs, "Chronic Illness Trends and the Challenges to Family Caregivers: Organizational and Health System Barriers," in *Family Caregiving*, ed. Gaugler and Kane, 79–80; World Bank, "Population Ages 65 and Above (% of Total Population)," 2019, https://data.worldbank.org.

4 Ari Houser, Wendy Fox-Grage, and Kathleen Ujvari, *Across the States: Profiles of Long-Term Services and Supports*, AARP, August 27, 2018, 11, www.aarp.org; Robyn I. Stone, "Factors Affecting the Future of Family Caregiving in the United States," in *Family Caregiving*, ed. Gaugler and Kane, 58.

5 Administration for Community Living, U.S. Department of Health and Human Services, *2018 Profile of Older Americans*, April 2018, 1, https://acl.gov.

6 Houser, Fox-Grage, and Ujvari, *Across the States*, 2.

7 Jennifer L. Wolff, et al., "Family Caregivers of Older Adults, 1999–2015: Trends in Characteristics, Circumstances, and Role-Related Appraisal," *Gerontologist*, 58, no. 6 (2018): 1021.

8 Administration for Community Living, *2018 Profile*, 12.

9 U.S. Bureau of Labor Statistics, *Women in the Labor Force: A Databook*, December 2018, www.bls.gov.

10 Courtney Harold Van Houtven, "Informal Care and Economic Stressors," in *Family Caregiving*, ed. Gaugler and Kane, 105–36.

11 Levitsky, *Caring for Our Own*, 39.

12 Carroll Estes, "Aging, Health, and Social Policy: Crisis and Crossroads," *Journal of Aging and Social Policy*, 1, nos. 1–2 (1989): 17–32.

13 Susan C. Reinhard, Carol Levine, and Sarah Samis, *Home Alone: Family Caregivers Providing Complex Chronic Care* (Washington, DC: AARP, 2012).

14 Susan C. Reinhard, Heather M. Young, Carol Levine, Kathleen Kelly, Rita B. Choula, and Jean Accius, *Home Alone Revisited: Family Caregivers Providing Complex Care* (Washington, DC: AARP, 2019); see Sherry N. Mong, *Taking Care of Our Own: When Family Caregivers Do Medical Work* (Ithaca, NY: Cornell University Press, 2020).

15 Harold Braswell, *The Crisis of U.S. Hospice Care: Family and Freedom at the End of Life* (Baltimore, MD: Johns Hopkins University Press, 2019), 77.

16 Mignon Duffy, "Beyond Outsourcing: Paid Care Work in Historical Perspective," in *Caring on the Clock: The Complexities and Contradictions of Paid Care Work*, ed. Mignon Duffy, Amy Armenia, and Clare L. Stacey (New Brunswick, NJ: Rutgers University Press, 2015), 17–18.

17 Emily K. Abel, *Hearts of Wisdom: American Women Caring for Kin, 1850–1940* (Cambridge, MA: Harvard University Press, 2000).

18 "Letters of John and Sarah Everett, 1854–1864," *Kansas Historical Quarterly*, 8, no. 2 (May 1939): 149–66.

19 Quoted in John Mack Faragher, *Women and Men on the Overland Trail* (New Haven, CT: Yale University Press, 1979), 140.

20 Quoted in Faragher, *Women and Men on the Overland Trail*, 138.

21 Quoted in Lee Virginia Chambers-Schiller, *Liberty, a Better Husband: Single Women in America; The Generations of 1780–1840* (New Haven, CT: Yale University Press, 1982), 114.

22 Nannie Stillwell Jackson, *Vinegar Pie and Chicken Bread: A Woman's Diary of Life in the Rural South, 1890–1891*, ed. Margaret Jones Bolsteri (Fayetteville: University of Arkansas Press, 1982), 41, 47, 76, 39.

23 *"A Secret to Be Burried": The Diary of Emily Hawley Gillespie, 1858–1888*, ed. Judy Nolte Lensink (Iowa City: University of Iowa Press, 1989), 17–18.

24 Emily French, *Emily: The Diary of a Hard-Worked Woman*, ed. Janet Lecompte (Lincoln: University of Nebraska Press, 1987), 19.

25 Mary Ann Webber to Dear Ones, October 28, 1861, Parker Family Letters, in the possession of Marianne Parker Brown, Berkeley, California.

26 Agnes Just Reid, *Letters of Long Ago* (Caldwell, ID: Caxton Printers, 1923), 78–79. These letters were written by the daughter, who based them on her mother's experiences.

27 Sheila M. Rothman, *Living in the Shadow of Death: Tuberculosis and the Social Experience of Illness in American History* (New York: Basic Books, 1994), 13.

28 Abel, *Hearts of Wisdom*, 85–118.

29 Quoted in Daniel M. Fox, *Power and Illness: The Failure and Future of American Health Policy* (Berkeley: University of California Press, 1993), 32.

30 Louis I. Dublin, Edwin W. Kopf, and George H. Van Buren, *Cancer Mortality among Insured Wage Earners and Their Families: The Experience of the Metropolitan Life Insurance Company Industrial Department, 1911–1922* (New York: Metropolitan Life Insurance Co., 1925).

31 Quoted in Keith Wailoo, *How Cancer Crossed the Color Line* (New York: Oxford University Press, 2011), 13.

32 George St. J. Perrott, "The Problem of Chronic Disease," *Psychosomatic Medicine*, 7 (January 1, 1945): 22.

33 Quoted in Emily K. Abel, *The Inevitable Hour: A History of Caring for Dying Patients in America* (Baltimore, MD: Johns Hopkins University Press, 2013), 66.

34 Fox, *Power and Illness*, 38.

35 Mary C. Jarrett, *Chronic Illness in New York City* (New York: Columbia University Press, 1933), 1:4.

36 Abel, *Hearts of Wisdom*.

37 Jackson, *Vinegar Pie*, 71.

38 "The Letters of Effie Hanson, 1917–1923: Farm Life in Troubled Times," ed. Frances M. Wold, *North Dakota History*, 48, no. 1 (Winter 1981): 30.

39 Mary Ann Webber to daughter, n.d., Parker Family Letters.

40 "Journal of Marian L. Moore, 1831–1860," in Gerda Lerner, *The Female Experience: An American Documentary* (Indianapolis: Bobbs-Merrill, 1977), 176–77.

41 Malenda M. Edwards to Sabrina Bennett, Bristol, New Hampshire, August 18, 1845, in *Farm to Factory: Women's Letters, 1830–1860*, ed. Thomas Dublin (New York: Columbia University Press, 1981), 85–86.

42 Quoted in Abel, *Hearts of Wisdom*, 45.

43 Samuel Lilienthal to Mary Holywell Everett, New York, September 8, 1876, in Lerner, *Female Experience*, 179.

44 "'Between Hope and Fear': The Life of Lettie Teeple," 1: 1829–1850, ed. John H. Yzenbaard and John Hoffman, *Michigan History*, 58, no. 3 (Fall 1974): 272.

45 Abel, *Hearts of Wisdom*, 11–36.

46 Abel, *Hearts of Wisdom*, 60–66.

47 Morris J. Vogel, *The Invention of the Modern Hospital, Boston, 1870–1930* (Chicago: University of Chicago Press, 1980), 1.

48 "Civil War Wife: The Letters of Harriet Jane Thompson," ed. Glenda Riley, *Annals of Iowa*, 44, no. 4 (Spring 1978): 312–13.

49 *Lamps on the Prairie: A History of Nursing in Kansas*, comp. Writers' Program of the Work Projects Administration in Kansas (New York: Garland, 1984), 49.

50 Abel, *Hearts of Wisdom*, 40–41.

51 Martha Saxton, *Louisa May: A Modern Biography of Louisa May Alcott* (New York: Avon Books, 1978).

52 "Private Journal of Mary Ann Owen Sims," part 1, ed. Clifford Dale Whitman, *Arkansas Historical Quarterly*, 35, no. 4 (Winter 1976): 171.

53 Quoted in Abel, *Hearts of Wisdom*, 14.

54 "A Secret to be Burried," ed. Lensink, March 15, 1888.

55 Quoted in Abel, *Hearts of Wisdom*, 92.

56 Abel, *Hearts of Wisdom*, 68–82.

57 Louisa May Alcott to Ellen Conway, Concord, Massachusetts, May 1, 1878, *The Selected Letters of Louisa May Alcott*, ed. Joel Myerson and Daniel Shealy (Boston: Little, Brown, 1987), 229–30.

58 Elana D. Buch, "Anthropology of Aging and Care," *Annual Review of Anthropology*, 44 (2015): 278.

CHAPTER 4. THE ELDER CARE CRISIS

1 Rebecca Solnit, "The Impossible Has Already Happened: What Coronavirus Can Teach Us about Hope," *Guardian*, April 7, 2020.

2 Melinda Cooper, *Family Values: Between Neoliberalism and the New Social Conservatism* (New York: Zone Books, 2017).

3 See Eva Feder Kittay, *Love's Labor: Essays on Women, Equality, and Dependency* (New York: Routledge, 1999); Joan Tronto, *Caring Democracy: Markets, Equality, and Justice* (New York: NYU Press, 2013); Marian A. Verkerk, "Negotiating Responsibilities," in *What about the Family? Practices of Responsibility in Care*, ed. Marian A. Verkerk, Hilde Lindemann, and Janice McLaughlin (New York: Oxford University Press, 2019), 89–99.

4 F. Colombo, A. Llena-Nozal, J. Mercier, and P. Tjadens, *Help Wanted? Providing and Paying for Long-Term Care* (Paris: OECD Health Policy Studies, OECD Publishing, 2011), www.oecd.org; Jeffrey E. Stokes and Sarah E. Patterson, "Intergenerational Relationships, Family Caregiving Policy, and COVID-19 in the United States," *Journal of Aging and Social Policy*, 32, nos. 4–5 (2020): 416–24, https://doi.org/10.1080/08959420.2020.177031.

5 Cooper, *Family Values*, 101.

6 Feather Ann Davis, "Medicare Hospice Benefit: Early Program Experiences," *Health Care Financing Review*, 9, no. 4 (Summer 1988): 99–100.

7 Andrea Sankar, *Dying at Home: A Family Guide for Caregiving* (Baltimore, MD: Johns Hopkins University Press, 1991).

8 Joy Buck, "Policy and Re-Formation of Hospice: Lessons from the Past for the Future of Palliative Care," *Journal of Hospice and Palliative Nursing*, 13, no. 6 (November–December 2011): S35–S43; *Implementation of the Medicare Hospice Benefit: Hearing before the Subcommittee on Health of the Senate Committee on Finance*, 98th Cong. 2 (1984) (Statement of Senator Robert Dole, Member, Senate Committee on Finance); Harold Braswell, *The Crisis of U.S. Hospice Care: Family and Freedom at the End of Life* (Baltimore, MD: Johns Hopkins University Press, 2019).

9 Sara M. Evans, "E-mails to Family and Friends: Claude and Maxilla—Declining Gently," in *Final Acts: Death, Dying, and the Choices We Make*, ed. Nan Bauer-Maglin and Donna Perry (New Brunswick, NJ: Rutgers University Press, 2009), 88.

10 Kathryn Temple, "Unintended Consequences: Hospice, Hospitals, and the Not-So-Good Death," in *Final Acts*, ed. Bauer-Maglin and Perry, 192; Hillary Johnson, *My Mother Dying* (New York: St. Martin's Press, 999), 177.

11 Quoted in Gina Kolata, "More Americans Are Dying at Home Than in Hospitals," *New York Times*, December 26, 2019.

12 Carroll Estes, "Aging, Health, and Social Policy: Crisis and Crossroads," *Journal of Aging and Social Policy*, 1, nos. 1–2 (1989): 17–32.

13 Susan C. Reinhard, Heather M. Young, Carol Levine, Kathleen Kelly, Rita B. Choula, and Jean Accius, *Home Alone Revisited: Family Caregivers Providing Complex Care* (Washington, DC: AARP, 2019).

14 Emily K. Abel, *Living in Death's Shadow: Family Experiences of Terminal Care and Irreplaceable Loss* (Baltimore, MD: Johns Hopkins University Press, 2017), 107.

15 "Assessing the Out-of-Pocket Affordability of Long-Term Services and Supports," a research brief of the HHS Office of the Assistant Secretary for Planning and Evaluation, Office of Disability, Aging, and Long-Term Policy, Open Minds, May 2019, 6, https://openminds.com.

16 D. L. Rabin and P. Stockton, *Long-Term Care for the Elderly: A Factbook* (New York: Oxford University Press, 1997).

17 James J. Callahan Jr., Lawrence D. Diamond, Janet Z. Giele, and Robert Morris, "Responsibility of Families for Their Severely Disabled Elders," *Health Care Financing Review*, 1, no. 3 (Winter 1980): 29–47.

18 Callahan Jr., Diamond, Giele, and Morris, "Responsibility of Families."

19 Jon B. Christianson, "Channeling Effects on Informal Care, Executive Summary," Office of the Assistant Secretary of Planning and Evaluation, April 30, 1986, https://aspe.hhs.gov.

20 Rosalie A. Kane, "The Noblest Experiment of Them All: Learning from the National Channeling Evaluation," *HSR: Health Services Research*, 23, no. 1 (April 1989): 190.

21 Christianson, "Channeling Effects on Informal Care."

22 Patrick Fox, Robert Newcomer, Cathleen Yordi, and Pamela Arnsberger, "Lessons Learned from the Medicare Alzheimer Disease Demonstration," *Alzheimer Disease and Associated Disorders*, 14, no. 2 (April–May–June 2000): 87–93.

23 N. A. Miller, S. Ramsland, and C. Harrington, "Trends and Issues in the Medicaid 1915(c) Waiver Program," *Health Care Financing Review*, 20, no. 4 (1999): 139–60.

24 David C. Grabowski, "The Cost-Effectiveness of Noninstitutional Long-Term Care Services: Review and Synthesis of the Most Recent Evidence," *Medical Care Research and Review*, 63, no. 1 (February 2006); Ari Houser, Wendy Fox-Grage, and Kathleen Ujvari, "Across the States 2018: Profiles of Long-Term Services and Supports," American Association of Retired Persons, August 27, 2018, 9, www.aarp.org.

25 United States Department of Justice, Civil Rights Division, "Information and Technical Assistance on the Americans with Disabilities Act," accessed November 9, 2021, www.ada.gov.

26 Darcy K. McMaughan Moudouni, Robert L. Ohsfeldt, Thomas R. Miller, and Charles D. Phillips, "The Relationship between Formal and Informal Care among Adult Medicaid Personal Care Services Recipients," *Health Services Research*, 47, no. 4 (2012): 1636.

27 Ellen O'Brien, Wendy Fox-Grage, and Kathleen Ujvari, *Home- and Community-Based Services beyond Medicaid: How State-Funded Programs Help Low-Income*

Adults with Care Needs Live at Home (Washington, DC: AARP Public Policy Institute, 2016), 4.

28 K. G. Kietzman, S. P. Wallace, E. M. Durazo, J. M. Torres, A. Soon Choi, A. E. Benjamin, and C. Mendez-Luck, "A Portrait of Older Californians with Disabilities Who Rely on Public Services to Remain Independent," *Home Health Care Services*, 31, no. 4 (2012): 317.

29 Sandra R. Levitsky, *Caring for Our Own: Why There Is No Political Demand for New American Social Welfare Rights* (New York: Oxford University Press, 2014).

30 R. J. V. Montgomery, "Respite Care: Lessons from a Controlled Design Study," *Health Care Financing Review*, Annual Supplement (1988): 133–38.

31 Emily K. Abel, *Who Cares for the Elderly? Public Policy and the Experiences of Adult Daughters* (Philadelphia: Temple University Press, 1991).

32 Toni Calasanti and Neal King, "Taking 'Women's Work' 'like a Man': Husbands' Experiences of Care Work," *Gerontologist*, 47, no. 4 (2007): 516–27; Sung-chull Hong and Constance L. Coogle, "Spousal Caregiving for Partners with Dementia: *Applied Gerontology*, 35, no. 7 (2014): 759–87.

33 Oregon Department of Human Services, "Homecare Worker Guide," Oregon Home Care Commission, accessed June 7, 2020, www.ohccworkforce.org; Oregon Department of Human Services, "Natural Supports: Putting the Puzzle Together," accessed June 7, 2020, dhs.state.or.us.

34 O'Brien, Fox-Grage, and Ujvari, *Home- and Community-Based Services*, 4.

35 See Ann Bookman and Delia Kimbrel, "Families and Elder Care in the Twenty-first Century," *Future of Children*, 21, no. 2 (Fall 2011): 117–40.

36 Alexander Sammon, "The Collapse of Long-Term Care Insurance," *American Prospect*, October 20, 2020.

37 Houser, Fox-Grage, and Ujvari, "Across the States 2018."

38 Charlene Harrington, Terence Ng, H. Stephen Kaye, and Robert J. Newcomer, "Medicaid Home and Community Based Services: Proposed Policies to Improve Access, Costs, and Quality," *Public Policy and Aging Report*, 19, no. 2 (March 2009): 13–18. In 2017, more than 707,000 people were on waiting lists for Medicaid waivers; most spent more than two years on those lists (Amber Knight, "Unfinished Business: Deinstitutionalization and Medicaid Policy," *Politics, Groups, and Identities* [2020], https://doi.org10.1080/21565503.2020.1854324.

39 Harriet L. Komisar, Judith Feder, and Judith D. Kasper, "Unmet Long-Term Care Needs: An Analysis of Medicare-Medicaid Dual Eligibles," *Inquiry*, 42 (Summer 2005): 171–82.

40 Kathryn G. Keitzman, et al., "A Portrait of Older Californians with Disabilities Who Rely on Public Services to Remain Independent," *Home Health Care Services Quarterly*, 31, no. 4 (2012).

41 Institute for Women's Policy Research and Status of Women in the States, "Spotlight on Older Women," 2013, https://statusofwomendata.org.

42 PHI, *Direct Care Workers in the United States, Key Facts*, 2020, 2, http://phinational.org.

43 PHI, *Direct Care Workers*, 5.

44 PHI, *Direct Care Workers*, 8.

45 Robyn Stone, "Workers at Risk: The Lessons of COVID-19," LTSS Center @UMass Boston, August 10, 2020, www.ltsscenter.org.

46 Abel, *Who Cares for the Elderly?*

47 Elinor Fuchs, *Making an Exit: A Mother-Daughter Drama with Machine Tools, Alzheimer's, and Laughter* (New York: Henry Holt, 2005), 90.

48 Judith E. Heumann, "Consumer-Directed Personal Care Services for Older People in the U.S.," AARP Issue Brief 64, revised and updated by Barbara Coleman, October 2003, https://assets.aarp.org.

49 Keiza Scales, *It's Time to Care: A Detailed Profile of America's Direct Care Workforce*, PHI, January 21, 2020, 7, https://phinational.org.

50 PHI, *Direct Care Workers*, 8.

51 PHI, *Direct Care Workers*, 5.

52 Saba Waheed, Michele Wong, and Megan Whelan, "Profile of Domestic Workers in California," UCLA Labor Center, 2020, 10, www.labor.ucla.edu.

53 Evelyn Nakano Glenn, *Forced to Care: Coercion and Caregiving in America* (Cambridge, MA: Harvard University Press, 2010).

54 Rhacel Salazar Parreñas, *Servants of Globalization: Migration and Domestic Work*, 2nd edition (Stanford, CA: Stanford University Press, 2001).

55 Joanna Dreby, *Divided by Borders* (Berkeley: University of California Press, 2010); Pierrette Hondagneu-Sotelo and Ernestine Avila, "I'm Here, but I'm There," *Gender and Society*, 11 (October 1997): 562; Cecilia Menjivar and Leisy Abrego, "Parents and Their Children across Borders," in *Across Generations: Immigrant Families in America*, ed. Nancy Foner (New York: NYU Press, 2009), 160–89.

56 Nancy Foner, *The Caregiving Dilemma: Work in an American Nursing Home* (Berkeley: University of California Press, 1994), 112. See Cynthia L. Port, Sheryl Zimmerman, Christianna S. Williams, Debra Dobbs, John S. Preisser, and Sharon Wallace Williams, "Families Filling the Gap: Comparing Family Involvement for Assisted Living and Nursing Home Residents with Dementia," *Gerontologist*, 43, special issue 1 (2005): 87–95.

57 Celia Berdes and John M. Eckert, "Race Relations and Caregiving Relationships: A Qualitative Examination of Perspectives from Residents and Nurses' Aides in Three Nursing Homes," *Research on Aging*, 23, no. 1 (January 2001): 109–26. See also Lois Grau and Edward Wellin, "The Organizational Culture of Nursing Homes: Influences of Responses to External Regulatory Controls," *Qualitative Health Research*, 2 (1992): 242–60.

58 Ai-Jen Poo, with Ariane Conrad, *The Age of Dignity: Preparing for the Elder Boom in a Changing America* (New York: New Press, 2015), 74.

59 Ruth Glasser and Jeremy Brecher, "We Are the Roots: The Culture of Home Health Aides," *New England Journal of Public Policy*, 13, no. 1 (1997): 113–34. Quotation on 115.

60 Clare L. Stacey, *The Caring Self: The Work Experiences of Home Care Aides* (Ithaca, NY: Cornell University Press, 2011), 73.

61 Stacey, *Caring Self.*

62 Poo, *Age of Dignity*, 74.

63 Institute of Medicine, *Retooling for an Aging America: Building the Health Care Workforce* (Washington, DC: National Academies Press, 2008); see Lourdes R. Guerrero, Amy Shim, Daphna Gans, Heather Bennett Schickedanz, and Zaldy S. Tan, "Training for In-Home Supportive Services Caregivers in an Underserved Area," *Journal of Health Care for the Poor and Underserved*, 30, no. 2 (May 2019): 739–48.

64 Steven P. Wallace, Nadereh Pourat, Linda Delp, and Kathryn G. Kietzman, "Long-Term Services and Supports for the Elderly Population," in *Changing the U.S. Health Care System: Key Issues in Health Services Policy and Management*, 4th edition, ed. Gerald F. Kominski (San Francisco: Jossey-Bass, 2013), 511.

65 Robyn I. Stone, "Developing a Quality Direct Care Workforce: Searching for Solutions," *Public Policy and Aging Report*, 27, no. 3 (2017): 96–100.

66 Matthew Desmond, "Americans Want to Believe Jobs Are the Solution to Poverty. They're Not," *New York Times Magazine*, September 11, 2018.

67 Kimiko de Freytas-Tamura, "'They Call Me a Criminal': Nursing Home Workers Who May Spread the Virus," *New York Times*, September 10, 2020.

68 Linda Burnham and Nik Theodore, *Home Economics: The Invisible and Unregulated World of Domestic Work* (New York: National Domestic Workers Alliance and Center for Urban Development, University of Illinois at Chicago, and DataCenter, 2011).

69 Michelle Chen, "Home-Care Workers Are Now Protected by Minimum-Wage Laws," *Nation*, July 1, 2016, www.thenation.com.

70 Emily K. Abel and Margaret K. Nelson, "Intimate Care for Hire," *American Prospect*, May 21, 2001.

71 PHI, *Direct Care Workers*, 5.

72 See Janette S. Dill and John Cagle, "Caregiving in a Patient's Place of Residence: Turnover of Direct Care Workers in Home Care and Hospice Agencies," *Journal of Aging and Health*, 22, no. 6 (2010): 713–33; Krista Ruffini, "Worker Earnings, Service Quality, and Firm Profitability: Evidence from Nursing Homes and Minimum Wage Reforms," Washington Center for Equitable Growth, Working paper series, June 2020, https://equitablegrowth.org.

CHAPTER 5. "THAT WAS NO RESPITE FOR ME!"

1 See Steven H. Zarit and Allison M. Reamy, "Future Directions in Family and Professional Caregiving for the Elderly," *Gerontology*, 59 (2013): 152–58.

2 See Jan Colvin, Lillian Chenoweth, Mary Bold, and Cheryl Harding, "Caregivers of Old Adults: Advantages and Disadvantages of Internet-based Social Support," *Family Relations*, 53, no. 1 (2004): 49–57; Emma Scharett et al., "An Investigation of the Information Sought by Caregivers of Alzheimer's Patients on Online Peer Support Groups," *Cyberpsychology, Behavior, and Social Networking*, 20, no. 10 (2016) 640–57.

3 Information from Emily Shubeck, Senior Associate Director, Quality of Care, Alzheimer's Association, August 6, 2020.

4 Information from Shubeck.

5 Edward Alan Miller, Susan M. Allen, and Vincent Mor, "Commentary: Navigating the Labyrinth of Long-Term Care: Shoring up Informal Caregiving in a Home- and Community-Based World," *Journal of Aging and Social Policy*, 21, no. 1 (January–March 2009): 1–16.

6 Information from Shubeck.

7 Ai-Jen Poo, with Ariane Conrad, *The Age of Dignity: Preparing for the Elder Boom in a Changing America* (New York: New Press, 2015), 53.

8 "It's Time for Historical Investments in Caregiving and Early Education," info@ joebiden.com to eabel@ucla.edu, July 21, 2020.

9 Christopher Rowland, "Adult Children Pay the Price of Keeping Aging Parents at Home," *Washington Post*, May 11, 2020.

10 Brenda C. Spillman, Jennifer Wolff, Vicki A. Freedman, and Judith D. Kasper, *Informal Care of Older Americans: An Analysis of the 2011 National Survey of Caregiving* (Washington, DC: Assistant Secretary for Planning and Evaluation, 2014), n.p.

11 Martin Pinquart and Silvia Sörensen, "Spouses, Adult Children, and Children-in-Law as Caregivers of Older Adults: A Meta-Analytic Comparison," *Psychology and Aging*, 26, no. 1 (March 2011): 1–14.

12 Jennifer L. Wolff, John Mulcahy, Jin Huang, David L. Roth, Kenneth Covinsky, and Judith D. Kasper, "Family Caregivers of Older Adults, 1999–2015: Trends in Characteristics, Circumstances, and Role-Related Appraisal," *Gerontologist*, 58, no. 6 (2018): 1027.

13 National Alliance for Caregiving, *Dementia Caregiving in the U. S., Research Report*, February 2017, www.caregiving.org.

14 Courtney Harold Van Houtven, "Informal Care and Economic Stressors," in *Family Caregiving in the New Normal*, ed. Joseph E. Gaugler and Robert L. Kane (Boston: Elsevier, 2015), 109.

15 National Alliance for Caregiving, *Dementia Caregiving*.

16 Ifah Arbel, Kathleen S. Bingham, and Deirdre R. Dawson, "A Scoping Review of Literature on Sex and Gender Differences among Dementia Spousal Caregivers," *Gerontologist*, 59, no. 6 (2019): e802–e815.

17 Lisa Freitag, *Extreme Caregiving: The Moral Work of Raising Children with Special Needs* (New York: Oxford University Press, 2018), 14.

18 Miriam Rose, Linda Noelker, and Jill Kagan, "Improving Policies for Caregiver Respite Services," *Gerontologist*, 55, no. 2 (April 2015): 302–8.

19 Steven H. Zarit, Joeseph E. Gaugler, and Shannon E. Jarrott, "Useful Services for Families: Research Findings and Directions," *International Journal of Geriatric Psychiatry*, 14 (1999): 166.

20 H. Stephen Kaye, Charlene Harrington, and Mitchell P. LaPlante, "Long-Term Care: Who Gets It, Who Provides It, Who Pays, and How Much?" *Health Affairs*, 29, no. 1 (January 2010): 16.

21 Dorie Seavey, "Written Statement before the Subcommittee on Workforce Protections Committee on Education and Labor, U.S. House of Representatives, Hearing on 'H.R. 3582: The Fair Home Health Care Act,'" Education and Labor Committee, October 25, 2007, 6, https://edlabor.house.gov.

22 William Cabin, David U. Himmelstein, Michael L. Siman, and Steffie Woolhandler, "For-Profit Medicare Home Health Agencies' Costs Appear Higher and Quality Appears Lower Compared to Nonprofit Agencies," *Health Affairs*, 33, no. 8 (2014): 1460; L. Harris-Kojetin, M. Sengupta, J. P. Lendon, V. Rome, R. Valverde, and C. Caffrey, *National Center for Health Statistics, Vital Health Statistics*, 3, no. 43 (2019): 9.

23 Robert Cook-Deegan, "Progress against Alzheimer's Disease?" *Issues in Science and Technology*, 35, no. 1 (Fall 2019).

24 Quoted in Keith A. Anderson, et al., "Developing a Set of Uniform Outcome Measures for Adult Day Services," *Journal of Applied Gerontology*, 39, no. 6 (2020): 670–76.

25 Anderson, et al., "Developing a Set of Uniform Outcome Measures."

26 National Adult Day Services Association, "About Adult Day Services," accessed November 10, 2021, www.nadsa.org.

27 Anderson, et al., "Developing a Set of Uniform Outcome Measures."

28 Lauren Harris-Kojetin, et al., "Long-Term Care Providers and Services Users in the United States: Data from the National Study of Long-Term Care Providers, 2013–2014," *Vital Health Statistics* 3, no. 38 (February 2016): 9.

29 Zarit, Gaugler, and Jarrott, "Useful Services," 167.

30 Lynn Friss Feinberg and Sandra L. Newman, "Preliminary Experiences of the States in Implementing the National Family Caregiver Support Program," *Journal of Aging and Social Policy*, 18, nos. 3–4 (2006): 95–113.

31 Debra J. Lipson, "The Policy and Political Environment of Family Caregiving: A Glass Half Full," in *Family Caregiving in the New Normal*, ed. Joseph E. Gaugler and Robert L. Kane (Boston: Elsevier, 2015), 141.

32 For studies on the impact of respite services on caregivers, see Joseph E. Gaugler, Shannon E. Jarrott, Steven H. Zarit, Mary-Ann Parris Stephens, Aloen Townsend, and Rick Greene, "Adult Day Service Use and Reductions in Caregiving Hours: Effects on Stress and Psychological Well-Being for Dementia Caregivers," *International Journal of Geriatric Psychiatry*, 18 (2003): 55–62; Rose, Noelker, and

Kagan, "Improving Policies for Caregiver Respite Services"; Sophie Vandepitte, Nele Van Den Noortgate, Koen Putman, Sofie Verhaeghe, Caroline Verdonck, and Lieven Annemans, "Effectiveness of Respite Care in Supporting Informal Caregivers of Persons with Dementia: A System Review," *International Journal of Geriatric Psychiatry*, 31 (2016): 1277–88; Steven H. Zarit, Lauren R. Bangerter, Yin Liu, and Michael J. Rovine, "Exploring the Benefits of Respite Services to Family Caregivers: Methodological Issues and Current Findings," *Aging and Mental Health*, 21, no. 3 (2017): 224–31; Laura Cousino Klein, et al., "Anticipating an Easier Day: Effects of Adult Day Services on Daily Cortisol and Stress," *Gerontologist*, 56, no. 2 (2016): 303–12; Zarit, Gaugler, and Jarrott, "Useful Services"; Steven H. Zarit, et al., "The Effects of Adult Day Services on Family Caregivers' Daily Stress, Affect, and Health: Outcomes from the Daily Stress and Health (DaSH) Study," *Gerontologist*, 54, no. 5 (2014): 570–79; Steven H. Zarit, et al., "Patterns of Adult Day Use by Family Caregivers: A Comparison of Brief versus Sustained Use," *Family Relations*, 48, no. 4 (1999): 355–61.

33 Family Caregiver Alliance, "Respite Tips," accessed November 10, 2021, www.caregiver.org.

34 Lynn Friss Feinberg, "Recognizing and Supporting Family Caregivers: The Time Has Come," *Public Policy and Aging Report*, 24 (2014): 65–69; Rose, Noelker, and Kagan, "Improving Policies."

35 Alix Kates Shulman, *To Love What Is: A Marriage Transformed* (New York: Farrar, Straus, and Giroux, 2008), 142.

36 Zarit et al., "Patterns of Adult Day Service Use," 165–81. Dementia caregivers' use of respite services, however, doubled between 1999 and 2015, from 13.4 percent to 26.9 percent (Jennifer L. Wolff, John Mulcahy, Jin Huang, David L. Roth, Kenneth Covinsky, and Judith D. Kasper, "Family Caregivers of Older Adults, 1999–2015: Trends in Characteristics, Circumstances, and Role-Related Appraisal," *Gerontologist*, 58, no. 6 [2018]: 1028).

37 See also Neena L. Chappell, R. Colin Reid, and Elizabeth Dow, "Respite Reconsidered: A Typology of Meanings Based on the Caregiver's Point of View," *Journal of Aging Studies*, 15 (2002): 201–16; L. P. Gwyther, "Barriers to Service Use among Alzheimer's Patients and Their Families," *Caring*, 8, no. 8 (August 1989): 12–16; Andrew J. Potter, "Factors Associated with Caregivers' Use of Support Services and Caregivers' Nonuse of Services Sought," *Journal of Aging and Social Policy*, 30, no. 2 (2018): 155–72; "Programs and Supports for Family Caregivers of Older Adults," in *Families Caring for an Aging America*, ed. R. Schulz and J. Eden (Washington, DC: National Academies Press, 2016).

38 Christine Neville, Elizabeth Beattie, Elaine Fielding, and Margaret MacAndrew, "Literature Review: Use of Respite Carers of People with Dementia," *Health and Social Care in the Community*, 23, no. 1 (2015): 51–69

39 For studies of the guilt caregivers experience when using respite services, see Emily Roberts and Kristopher M. Struckmeyer, "The Impact of Respite

Programming on Caregiver Resilience in Dementia Care: A Qualitative
Examination of Family Caregiver Perspectives," *INQUIRY: The Journal of Health
Care Organization, Provision, and Financing*, 55 (2018): 1–11.

40 See Aaron T. Seaman, "The Consequence of 'Doing Nothing': Family Caregiving
for Alzheimer's Disease as Non-Action in the U.S.," *Social Science and Medicine*,
197 (2018): 63–70; Norah Keating, Jacquie Eales, Laura Funk, Janet Fast, Joohong
Min, "Life Course Trajectories of Family Care," *International Journal of Care and
Caring*, 3, no. 2 (2019): 147–63; Sam Fazio, Douglas Pace, Katie Maslow, Sheryl
Zimmerman, and Beth Kallmyer, "Alzheimer's Association Dementia Care
Practice Recommendations," *Gerontologist*, 58, no. S1 (2018): S1–S9.

41 Laura Balbo, "The Servicing Work of Women and the Capitalist State," *Political
Power and Social Theory*, 3 (1982): 26–29.

42 Miller, Allen, and Mor, "Commentary."

43 See Angela Schnelli, Melanie Karrer, Hanna Mayer, and Adelheid Zeller,
"Aggressive Behavior of Persons with Dementia towards Professional Caregivers
in the Home Care Setting: A Scoping Review," *Journal of Clinical Nursing* (2010),
wileyonlinelibrary.com.

44 Dementia Care Central, "Respite Care for Dementia Caregivers," updated August
30, 2020, www.dementiacarecentral.com.

45 See, e.g., Institute of Medicine, *Retooling for an Aging America: Building the Health
Care Workforce* (Washington, DC: National Academies Press, 2008).

CHAPTER 6. "THEY CAN'T POSSIBLY LOVE HIM AS I DO"

1 Fangli Geng, David G. Stevenson, and David C. Grabowski, "Daily Nursing Home
Staffing Levels Highly Variable, Often below CMS Expectations," *Health Affairs*,
38, no. 7 (2019): 1095–1100.

2 Charlene Harrington, Clarilee Hauser, Brian Olney, and Pauline Vaillancourt
Rosenau, "Ownership, Financing, and Management Strategies of the Ten Largest
For-Profit Nursing Home Chains in the United States," *International Journal of
Health Services*, 41, no. 4 (2011): 725–46; Charlene Harrington, Frode F. Jacobsen,
Justin Panos, Allyson Pollock, Shailen Sutaria, and Marta Szebehely,
"Marketization in Long-Term Care: A Cross-Country Comparison of Large
For-Profit Nursing Home Chains," *Health Services Insights*, 10 (2017): 1–23.

3 Atul Gupta, Sabrina T. Howell, Constantine Yannelis, and Abhinav Gupta, "Does
Private Equity Investment Benefit Patients? Evidence from Nursing Homes,"
March 2020, https://papers.ssrn.com, abstract id 3537612; Geng, Stevenson, and
Grabowski, "Daily Nursing Home Staffing"; Charlene Harrington, Steffie
Woolhandler, Joseph Mullan, Helen Carrillo, and David U. Himmelstein, "Does
Investor Ownership of Nursing Homes Compromise the Quality of Care?"
American Journal of Public Health, 91, no. 9 (September 2001): 1452–55.

4 David C. Grabowski, Joseph J. Angelelli, and Vincent Mor, "Medicaid Payment
and Risk-Adjusted Nursing Home Quality Measures," *Health Affairs*, 23, no. 5

(September/October 2004): 243–53; Vincent Mor, Jacqueline Zinn, Joseph Angelelli, Joan M. Teno, and Susan C. Miller, "Driven to Tiers: Socioeconomic and Racial Disparities in the Quality of Nursing Home Care," *Milbank Quarterly*, 82, no. 2 (2004): 227–56; "Testimony of David C. Grabowski before the United States Senate Committee on Finance: Not Forgotten: Protecting Americans from Abuse and Neglect in Nursing Homes," United States Senate Committee on Finance, March 6, 2019, www.finance.senate.gov.

5 Karen Brown Wilson, "Historical Evolution of Assisted Living in the United States, 1979 to the Present," *Gerontologist*, 47, issue suppl. (December 2007): 8–22.

6 Harris-Kojetin, et al., *Long-Term Care Providers*, 9.

7 Mary M. Ball, et al., "Managing Decline in Assisted Living: The Key to Aging in Place," *Journal of Gerontology: Social Sciences*, 598, no. 4 (2004): S202–12; Paula C. Carder, "Promoting Independence: An Analysis of Assisted Living Marketing Materials," *Research on Aging*, 24, no. 1 (2002): 97–123; Rosemary Chapin and Debra Dobbs-Kepper, "Aging in Place in Assisted Living: Philosophy versus Policy," *Gerontologist*, 41, no. 2 (2001): 43–50; Susan G. Kelsey, Sarah B. Laditka, and James N. Laditka, "Dementia and Transitioning from Assisted Living to Memory Care Units: Perspectives of Administrators in Three Facility Types," *Gerontologist*, 50, no. 2 (2010): 192–203.

8 Joseph E. Gaugler, Fang Yu, Heather W. Davila, and Tetyana Shippee, "Alzheimer's Disease and Nursing Homes," *Health Affairs (Millwood)*, 33, no. 4 (April 2014): 650–57.

9 Carol S. Aneshensel, Leonard I. Pearlin, Joseph T. Mullan, Steven H. Zarit, and Carol J. Whitlatch, *Profiles in Caregiving: The Unexpected Career* (San Diego, CA: Academic Press, 1995); Ethel Shanas, "The Family as a Support System in Old Age," *Gerontologist*, 19 (1979): 169–74.

10 On caregivers' responses to institutionalization, see Joseph E. Gaugler, Anne Margriet, and Steven H. Zarit, "Long-Term Adaptation to Institutionalization in Dementia Caregivers," *Gerontologist*, 47, no. 6 (2007): 730–40.

11 See, e.g., Self Advocates Becoming Empowered, "Position on Closing Institutions," April 1995, www.sabeusa.org.

12 Emily K. Abel, *Hearts of Wisdom: American Women Caring for Kin, 1850–1940* (Cambridge, MA: Harvard University Press, 2000), 201–50; Kim E. Nielsen, *A Disability History of the United States* (Boston: Beacon Press, 2012).

13 Paul Starr, *The Social Transformation of American Medicine: The Rise of a Sovereign Profession and the Making of a Vast Industry* (New York: Basic Books, 1982), 365.

14 A. B. Hatfield, "Families as Caregivers: A Historical Perspective," in *Families of the Mentally Ill: Coping and Adaptation* (New York: Guilford Press, 1987), 8.

15 E. Fuller Torrey, *Nowhere to Go: The Tragic Odyssey of the Homeless Mentally Ill* (New York: Harper and Row, 1988); Leslie J. Scallet, "Mental Health and Homelessness: Evidence of Failed Policy?" *Health Affairs* (Winter 1989): 184–88; Daniel Yohanna, "Deinstitutionalization of People with Mental Illness: Causes and Consequences," *AMA Journal of Ethics*, 15, no. 10 (2013): 886–91.

CHAPTER 7. "OH NO, DON'T FEEL GUILTY"

1 B. C. Kleijer et al., "Variability between Nursing Homes in Prevalence of Antipsychotic Use in Patients with Dementia," *International Psychogeriatrics*, 26 (2014): 363–71; "Under-Enforced and Over-Prescribed: The Antipsychotic Drug Epidemic Ravaging America's Nursing Homes," Report of the Committee on Ways and Means Majority, US House of Representatives, June 2020; Human Rights Watch, "They Want Docile: How Nursing Homes in the United States Overmedicate People with Dementia," February 5, 2018, www.hrw.org.

2 Julia Anderson, "Silver Dollars: Entrepreneurs Seize Opportunities Presented by Aging Boomers," *Seattle Business*, June 2014.

3 For background, see William Cabin, David U. Himmelstein, Michael L. Siman, and Steffie Woolhandler, "For-Profit Medicare Home Health Agencies' Costs Appear Higher and Quality Appears Lower Compared to Nonprofit Agencies," *Health Affairs*, 33, no. 8 (2014): 1460–65.

4 "Life and Death in Assisted Living," *Frontline*, PBS, July 30, 2013, www.pbs.org.

5 Sandra R. Levitsky, *Caring for Our Own: Why There Is No Political Demand for New American Social Welfare Rights* (New York: Oxford University Press, 2014).

6 See, e.g., Coalition Concord, "It's Time to Say No to Medicaid for the Middle Class," *Facing Facts Alert*, no. 14 (February 19, 1996); Ron Lieber, "The Ethics of Adjusting Your Assets to Qualify for Medicaid," *New York Times*, July 21, 2017; "Medicaid for Millionaires," *Wall Street Journal*, February 24, 2005; "Pretending to Be Poor," *New York Times*, April 14, 1996.

7 Joanne Lynn, *Sick to Death and Not Going to Take It Anymore! Reforming Health Care in the Last Years of Life* (Berkeley: University of California Press, 2004); Ai-Jen Poo with Ariane Conrad, *The Age of Dignity: Preparing for the Elder Boom in a Changing America* (New York: New Press, 2015).

8 June Price Tangney, "Recent Advances in the Empirical Study of Shame and Guilt," *American Behavioral Scientist*, 38, no. 8 (1995): 1132–45, quotation on 1136.

9 Roy F. Baumeister, Arlene M. Stillwell, and Todd F. Heatherton, "Guilt: An Interpersonal Approach," *Psychological Bulletin*, 115, no. 2 (1994): 243–67, quotation on 246.

10 See Phil Brown, Rachel Morello-Frosch, Stephen Zavestoski, and the Contested Illnesses Research Group, *Contested Illnesses: Citizens, Science, and Health Social Movements* (Berkeley: University of California Press, 2012).

CHAPTER 8. "NO ONE IS COMING OUT OF THIS UNSCATHED"

1 Eric Klinenberg, "Review of Katrina: A History, 1915–2015, by Andy Horowitz," *New York Review of Books*, October 22, 2020, 23.

2 Tom Frieden, "It's Time to Restrict Visits to Nursing Homes," *CNN Health*, March 8, 2020, www.cnn.com.

3   Michael L. Barnett and David C. Grabowski, "Nursing Homes Are Ground Zero for COVID-19 Pandemic," *JAMA Health Forum*, 1, no. 3 (2020), https://jamanet-work.com.

4   "43% of U.S. Coronavirus Deaths Are Linked to Nursing Homes," *New York Times*, June 27, 2020.

5   Francisca Paris, "COVID-19 Takes Health Toll on People with Dementia—Even Those Who Survive," *WBUR*, May 29, 2020, www.wbur.org; see Eric E. Brown, Sanjeev Kumar, Tarek K. Rajji, Bruce G. Pollock, and Benoit H. Mulsant, "Anticipating and Mitigating the Impact of the COVID-19 Pandemic on Alzheimer's Disease and Related Dementias," *American Journal of Geriatric Psychiatry*, 28, no. 7 (2020): 712–20; Babak Tousi, "Dementia Care in the Time of COVID-19 Pandemic," *Journal of Alzheimer's Disease*, 76 (2020): 475–79.

6   Joseph G. Ouslander and David C. Grabowski, "COVID-19 in Nursing Homes: Calming the Perfect Storm," *Journal of the American Geriatrics Society*, 68, no. 10 (October 2020): 2153–62.

7   Barnett and Grabowski, "Nursing Homes Are Ground Zero"; Charlene Harrington, Leslie Ross, Susan Chapman, Elizabeth Halifax, Bruce Spurlock, and Debra Bakerjian, "Nurse Staffing and Coronavirus Infections in California Nursing Homes," *Policy, Politics, and Nursing Practice* (2020): 1–13; Ouslander and Grabowski, "COVID-19 in Nursing Homes" (statistic from Barnett and Grabowski).

8   U.S. Government Accountability Office, "Infection Control Deficiencies Were Widespread and Persistent in Nursing Homes Prior to COVID-19 Pandemic," May 20, 2020, www.gao.gov.

9   C. Harrington, et al., "Nurse Staffing and Coronavirus Infections in California Homes," *Policy, Politics, and Nursing Practice*, 21, no. 3 (2020); H. Temkin-Greener, S. Gao, X. Cai, "Covid-19 Infections and Deaths among Connecticut Nursing Home Residents," *Journal of the American Geriatrics Society*, 68, no. 9 (2020).

10 See, e.g., Emily K. Abel, *Tuberculosis and the Politics of Exclusion* (New Brunswick, NJ: Rutgers University Press, 2007).

11 Rebecca Tan and Rachel Chason, "Too Few Masks, Tests, and Workers: How Covid-19 Spread through Maryland Nursing Homes," *Washington Post*, May 7, 2020; Debbie Cenziper, Alexa Mikhall, Cadence Quaranta, Daniel Konstantino, and Alice Crites, "51 Lost Lives: A Portrait of the Pandemic's Tragic Toll in America's Nursing Homes," *Washington Post*, December 22, 2020; Letter of James E. Clyburn, Chairman of the House of Representatives, to Seema Verma, Centers for Medicare and Medicaid Services, Select Subcommittee on the Coronavirus Crisis, June 16, 2020, https://coronavirus.house.gov; See Lynne Segal, "From Corporate Carewashing to Genuine Care? The Coronavirus Crisis Forces Us to Reconsider the Business of Business," openDemocracyUK, April 6, 2020, www.opendemocracy.net/en.

12 Jennifer Abbasi, "'Abandoned' Nursing Homes Continue to Face Critical Supply and Staff Shortages as COVID-19 Toll Has Mounted," *JAMA*, 324, no. 2 (July 14, 2020): 123; Chris Burrell, "COVID Made Nursing Home Caregiving a Deadly Occupation; Immigrants and Minorities Bear the Brunt," *GBH News* (Boston), August 17, 2020, www.wgbh.org.

13 For many months, Cuomo also hid the number of nursing home deaths from New York's health officials, including the commissioner, Howard Zucker (J. David Goodman, Jesse McKinley, and Danny Hakim, "Cuomo Aides Spent Months Hiding Nursing Home Death Toll," *New York Times*, April 28, 2021).

14 Joaquin Sapien and Joe Sexton, "'Fire through Dry Grass': Andrew Cuomo Saw COVID-19's Threat to Nursing Homes; Then He Risked Adding to It," *ProPublica*, June 16, 2020.

15 Kim Barker and Amy Julia Harris, "'Playing Russian Roulette': Nursing Homes Told to Take the Infected," *New York Times*, April 24, 2020.

16 Charles C. Camosy, "What's behind the Nursing Home Horror," *New York Times*, May 17, 2020; Jessica Silver-Greenberg and Amy Julia Harris, "'They Just Dumped Him like Trash'; Nursing Homes Evict Vulnerable Residents," *New York Times*, June 21, 2020.

17 Ann Neumann, "It Has the Highest Death Rate of Any Nursing Home in the US," *Guardian*, October 28, 2020.

18 Debbie Cenziper, Joel Jacobs, and Shawn Mulcahy, "Nursing Home Companies Accused of Misusing Federal Money Received Hundreds of Millions of Dollars in Pandemic Relief," *Washington Post*, August 4, 2020.

19 Debbie Cenziper, Joel Jacobs, and Shawn Mulcahy, "As Pandemic Raged and Thousands Died, Government Regulators Cleared Most Nursing Homes of Infection-Control Violations," *Washington Post*, October 29, 2020.

20 Edem Hado and Lynn Friss Feinberg, "Amid the COVID-19 Pandemic, Meaningful Communication between Family Caregivers and Residents of Long-Term Care Facilities Is Imperative," *Journal of Aging and Social Policy*, 32, nos. 4–5 (2020).

21 Jeffrey D. Schlaudecker, "Essential Family Caregivers in Long-Term Care during the COVID-19 Pandemic," *JAMDA*, 21 (2020): 1003.

22 Jason Karlawish, David C. Grabowski, and Allison K. Hoffman, "Continued Bans on Nursing Home Visitors Are Unhealthy and Unethical," *Washington Post*, July 13, 2020.

23 Emily Paulin, "Is Extended Isolation Killing Older Adults in Long-Term Care?" AARP, September 3, 2020, www.aarp.org.

24 Paulin, "Is Extended Isolation."

25 William Wan, "Pandemic Isolation Has Killed Thousands of Alzheimer's Patients while Families Watch from Afar," *Washington Post*, September 16, 2020.

26 See, e.g., Barbara Feder Ostrov and Jocelyn Wiener, "In California, Family Members Fight Restricted Access to Loved Ones in Long-term Care," *Desert*

Sun, July 24, 2020; Bill Spender and Debbie Strauss, "More Than 12,000 Texans, Lawmakers Push for Ban on Visitation at Nursing Homes to Be Lifted," *Click2Houston.com*, August 6, 2020, www.click2houston.com; Paula Span, "Nursing Home Families Yearn to Visit Loved Ones Again," *New York Times*, August 14, 2020; Karen DeWitt, "Families of Nursing Home Residents Protest for More Access," WBFO-FM, October 15, 2020, https://news.wbfo.org; Nick Reisman, "Nursing Home Families Seek Essential Designation," *Spectrum News*, September 15, 2020; "Rally Demands Better Conditions for Nursing Home Residents," *My Little Falls* (New York), October 16, 2020, https://mylittlefalls.com.

27 "Florida Has New Plan to Allow Some Visits to Nursing Homes," *Tampa Bay Times*, August 19, 2020; Jessica Glenza, "'Shutdown Is Literally Killing People': Families of Isolated Nursing Home Residents Demand Compromise," *Guardian*, October 12, 2020; Kelli Kennedy, "Can I Get a Job? Wife Tries It All for Nursing Home Reunion," *Washington Post*, July 29, 2020; Abby Walton, "Caregivers for Compromise: Florida Families Looking for Middle Ground between Safety and Seclusion," WCTV, Tallahassee, FL, July 23, 2020; Caregivers for Compromise Facebook page.

28 Amy Taxin, "California Now Allows Nursing Home Visits, but Few Happen," *ABC News*, July 13, 2020.

29 Judith Graham, "States Allow In-Person Nursing Home Visits as Families Charge Residents Die 'Of Broken Hearts,'" *KHN* (Kaiser Health News), July 13, 2020, https://khn.org.

30 "CMS Issues Revised Guidance on Visitation in Nursing Homes," National Consumer Voice for Quality Long-Term Care, September 18, 2020, https://theconsumervoice.org.

31 R. Tamara Konetzka and Rebecca J. Gorges, "Nothing Much Has Changed: COVID-19 Nursing Home Cases and Deaths Follow Fall Surges," *Journal of the American Geriatrics Society*, first published November 12, 2020.

32 CMS, "CMS Updates Nursing Home Guidance with Revised Visitation Recommendations," Centers for Medicare & Medicaid Services, March 10, 2021, www.cms.gov.

33 Here I concentrate on nursing homes because they received far more attention than assisted living facilities did.

34 Harriet Ryan, "Upscale Home for Dementia Patients Sued over Deaths in COVID-19 Outbreak," *Los Angeles Times*, December 15, 2020.

35 See Hado and Feinberg, "Amid the COVID-19 Pandemic."

36 As a result of the pandemic, the occupancy rate of nursing homes substantially declined (Reed Abelson, "Covid Forces Families to Rethink Nursing Home Care," *New York Times*, May 6, 2021).

37 Tom Kitwood, *Dementia Reconsidered: The Person Comes First* (New York: McGraw-Hill, 1997), 81–82.

38 Janelle S. Taylor, "On Recognition, Caring, and Dementia," *Medical Anthropology Quarterly*, 22, no. 4 (2008): 318.
39 Quoted in Eleanor Morgan, "Lost Touch: How a Year without Hugs Affects Our Mental Health," *Guardian*, January 24, 2021. See also Maham Hasan, "What All That Touch Deprivation Is Doing to Us," *New York Times*, October 6, 2020.
40 Kitwood, *Dementia Reconsidered*, 91.
41 Quoted in Michael Sainato, "US Workers Who Risked Their Lives to Care for Elderly Demand Change," *Guardian*, April 19, 2020.
42 Judith Walzer Leavitt, *Make Room for Daddy: The Journey from Waiting Room to Birthing Room* (Chapel Hill: University of North Carolina Press, 2009).
43 Emily K. Abel, *Living in Death's Shadow: Family Experiences of Terminal Care and Irreplaceable Loss* (Baltimore, MD: Johns Hopkins University Press, 2017).
44 Barney G. Glaser and Anselm L. Strauss, *Awareness of Dying* (New Brunswick, NJ: Aldine Transactions, 1968), 146.
45 Emily K. Abel, *The Inevitable Hour: A History of Caring for Dying Patients in America* (Baltimore, MD: Johns Hopkins University Press, 2013).
46 Sandra M. Gilbert, *Wrongful Death: A Memoir* (New York: Norton, 1995), 334–36.
47 Kay Redfield Jamison, *Nothing Was the Same: A Memoir* (New York: Knopf, 2009), 118.

CHAPTER 9. "THIS BEING HOMEBOUND IS SO HARD"
 1 Sharon K. Inlouye, Rudi G. J. Westendorp, and Jane S. Saczynski, "Delirium in Elderly People," *Lancet*, March 8, 2014, 911–22; Sharon K. Inouye, "The Epidemic within the Pandemic: Delirium," *New York Times*, May 10, 2020; Edie Grossfield, "In the Hospital with Dementia: These Patients Need Their Caregivers," *Next Avenue*, April 28, 2020, www.nextavenue.org.
 2 Nicci Gerrard, *The Last Ocean: A Journey through Memory and Forgetting* (New York: Penguin, 2019), 2.
 3 Floyd Skloot, *In the Shadow of Memory* (Lincoln: University of Nebraska Press, 2003), 233.
 4 National Institute on Aging, "Going to the Hospital: Tips for Dementia Caregivers," May 8, 2017, www.nia.nih.gov.
 5 National Domestic Workers Alliance, "Coronavirus' Economic Impact on Domestic Workers," April 8, 2020, www.domesticworkers.org.
 6 Madeline R. Sterling, Emily Tseng, Anthony Poon, Jacklyn Cho, Ariel C. Avgar, Lisa M. Kern, Claire K. Ankuda, and Nicola Deli, "Experiences of Home Health Care Workers in New York City during the Coronavirus Disease 2019 Pandemic: A Qualitative Analysis," *JAMA Internal Medicine*, 180, no. 11 (November 2020): 1453–59.
 7 Quoted in Michael Sainato, "US Workers Who Risked Their Lives to Care for Elderly Demand Change," *Guardian*, April 19, 2021. See also Will Englund, "In a Relentless Pandemic, Nursing-Home Workers Are Worn Down and Stressed

Out," *Washington Post*, December 3, 2020. One study, however, found that because occupancy declined, staffing levels remained fairly constant despite the departure of many staff members (Rachel M. Werner and Norma B. Coe, "Nursing Home Staffing Levels Did Not Change Significantly during COVID-19," *Health Affairs*, 40, no. 5 [May 2021]: 795–801).

8 "National Survey Shows Government, Employers Are Failing to Protect Nursing Home Workers and Residents," Service Employees International Union (SEIU), June 9, 2020, www.seiu.org.

9 Quoted in Kritika Pandey, Rhacel Salazar Parreñas, and Gianne Sheena Sabio, "Essential and Expendable: Migrant Domestic Workers and the COVID-19 Pandemic," *American Behavioral Scientist*, 65, no. 10 (2021).

10 Sainato, "US Workers Who Risked Their Lives."

11 See, e.g., Emily K. Abel, *Tuberculosis and the Politics of Exclusion: A History of Public Health and Migration to Los Angeles* (New Brunswick, NJ: Rutgers University Press, 2007).

12 Scott R. Beach, Richard Schulz, Heidi Donovan, and Ann-Marie Rosland, "Family Caregiving during the COVID-19 Pandemic," *Gerontologist*, 61, no. 5 (2021): 650–60; Sung S. Park, "Caregivers' Mental Health and Somatic Symptoms during COVID-19," *Journals of Gerontology: Social Sciences*, 76, no. 4 (2021): e235–40. See also *Effects of COVID-10 on Family Caregivers: A Community Survey from the University of Pittsburgh* (Pittsburgh, PA: University of Pittsburgh, 2020); Rosalynn Carter Institute for Caregiving, *Caregivers in Crisis: Caregiving in the Time of COVID-19* (Americus, GA: Rosalynn Carter Institute for Caregiving, October 2020).

13 Ai-Jen Poo with Ariane Conrad, *The Age of Dignity: Preparing for the Elder Boom in a Changing America* (New York: New Press, 2015), 116.

CONCLUSION

1 Susan C. Reinhard, Lynn Friss Feinberg, Ari Houser, Rita Choula, and Molly Evans, "Valuing the Invaluable, 2019 Update, Charting a Path Forward," AARP Public Policy Institute, November 14, 2019, www.aarp.org.

2 Steven Zarit and Allison R. Reamy, "Future Directions in Family and Professional Caregiving for the Elderly," *Gerontology*, 59, no. 2 (2013): 156.

3 Yasmeen Abutaleb, Ashley Parket, Josh Dawsey, and Philip Rucker, "The Inside Story of How Trump's Denial, Mismanagement, and Magical Thinking Led to the Pandemic's Dark Winter," *Washington Post*, December 19, 2020; Michael D. Sheear, Maggie Haberman, Noah Weiland, Sharon LaFraniere, and Mark Massetti, "Trump's Focus as the Pandemic Raged: What Would It Mean for Him?" *New York Times*, December 31, 2020.

4 "Voices from the Front Lines of America's Food Supply," *New York Times*, January 5, 2021.

5 "Voices from the Aisles," *Washington Post*, January 7, 2021.

6   Ximena Bustillo and Ryan McCrimmon, "Who Is 'Essential'? Food and Farm
    Workers Left in Limbo in Vaccine Priorities," *Politico*, January 17, 2021.

7   Nicole Bateman and Martha Ross, "Why Has COVID-19 Been Especially Harmful
    for Working Women?," Brookings Institution, October 2020, www.brookings.edu.

8   Claire Cain Miller, "Nearly Half of Men Say They Do Most of the Home
    Schooling: 3 Percent of Women Agree," *New York Times*, May 6, 2020.

9   Moira Donegan, "The Pandemic Threatens to Undo What Generations of
    Feminists Have Fought For," *Guardian*, May 21, 2020.

10 John Leland, "She Had to Choose: Her Epileptic Patient or Her 7-Year-Old
    Daughter," *New York Times*, March 22, 2020.

11 Isaac Chotiner, "How Racism Is Shaping the Corona Virus Pandemic," *New
    Yorker*, May 7, 2020.

12 Elissa M. Abrams and Stanley J. Szefler, "COVID-19 and the Impact of Social
    Determinants," *Lancet*, May 18, 2020; Gina Kolata, "Social Inequities Explain
    Racial Gap in Pandemic, Studies Find," *New York Times*, December 9, 2020; Roni
    Caryn Rabin, "Dr. Marcella Nunez-Smith Takes Aim at Racial Gaps in Health
    Care," *New York Times*, January 8, 2021.

13 John Eligon, "Black Doctor Dies of Covid-19 after Complaining of Racist
    Treatment," *New York Times*, December 23, 2020.

14 Noam N. Levey, "Racial Disparities on Health Agenda," *Los Angeles Times*,
    December 23, 2020.

15 L. A. Ronald, M. J. McGregor, C. Harrington, A. Pollock, and J. Lexchin,
    "Observational Evidence of For-Profit Delivery and Inferior Nursing Home Care:
    When Is There Enough Evidence for Policy Change?" *PLoS Medicine*, 13, no. 4
    (2016): e1001995.

16 See Matthew Goldstein, Jessica Silver-Greenberg, and Robert Gebeloff, "Push for
    Profits Left Nursing Homes Struggling to Provide Care," *New York Times*, May 7,
    2020.

17 Peter S. Goodman and Erik Augustin Palm, "Pandemic Exposes Holes in Sweden's
    Generous Social Welfare State," *Guardian*, October 8, 2020. On the growth of
    for-profit elder care services in the four Nordic countries (Denmark, Norway,
    Sweden, and Finland), see Marta Szebehely and Gabrielle Meagher, "Nordic
    Eldercare: Weak Universalism Becoming Weaker?," *Journal of European Social
    Policy*, 28, no. 3 (2018): 294–308.

18 Benjamin Mueller, "On a Scottish Isle, Nursing Home Deaths Expose a Covid-19
    Scandal," *New York Times*, May 25, 2020.

19 N. M. Stall, A. Jones, K. A. Brown, P. A. Rochon, and A. P. Costa, "For-profit
    Long-Term Care Homes and the Risk of COVID-19 Outbreaks and Resident
    Deaths," *Canadian Medical Association Journal*, 192, no. 33 (2020): E946–55.

20 Robert Holly, "Biden Announces $775B Plan to Boost the Caregiver Economy,
    Support In-Home Care Providers," *Home Health Care News*, July 21, 2020, https://
    homehealthcarenews.com.

21 The Care Economy, "The Care Economy Statement," April 2021, https://thecareeconomy.ca/statement.

22 Jerome De Henau and Susan Himmelweit, "A Care-Led Recovery from Coronavirus," June 2020, a briefing submitted to the UK Women's Budget Group Commission on a Gender-Equal Economy, https://wbg.org.uk.

23 The Care Collective (Andreas Chatzidakis, Jamie Hakim, Jo Littler, Catherine Rottenberg, and Lynne Segal), *The Care Manifesto: The Politics of Interdependence* (New York: Verso, 2020).

24 "Carework Network Statement to the Biden-Harris Administration," Carework Network, accessed January 17, 2022, https://careworknetworkresponds.com; see also Australian Work + Family Policy Roundtable, "Work + Care in a Gender Inclusive Recovery: A Bold Policy Agenda for a New Social Contract," Centre for People, Organisation, and Work, December 16, 2020, https://cpow.org.au; Gregg Gonsalves and Amy Kapczynski, "The New Politics of Care," *Boston Review*, April 27, 2020; Kate Aronoff, Alyssa Battistoni, Daniel Aldana Cohen, and Thea Riofrancos, *A Planet to Win: Why We Need a Green New Deal* (New York: Verso, 2019).

25 "Funders Come Together to Launch $50 Million CARE Fund," Ford Foundation, May 11, 2021, www.fordfoundation.org.

26 "Fact Sheet: The American Jobs Plan," The White House, March 31, 2021, www.whitehouse.gov.

27 Quoted in Ai-jen Poo, "Breaking: Biden's BIG Announcement!" info@email.domesticworkers.org to eabel@ucla.edu, March 15, 2021.

28 See Editorial Board, "Opinion: Long-Term Care Needs a Long-Term Solution," *Washington Post*, April 20, 2021.

29 Quoted in Anne-Marie Slaughter, "Rosie Could Be a Riveter Only Because of a Care Economy: Where Is Ours?" *New York Times*, April 16, 2021.

30 "Remarks by Vice President Harris on the American Jobs Plan," The White House, April 19, 2021, www.whitehouse.gov.

31 "The Debate over What 'Infrastructure' Is Is Ridiculous," *New York Times*, April 26, 2021. See also Amy Armenia, "Care as Infrastructure," Carework Network, May 13, 2021, http://careworknetworkresponds.com; Traci Levy and Elizabeth Palley, "Yes, Care Is Infrastructure," *RealClear Policy*, May 11, 2021, www.realclearpolicy.com.

INDEX

AARP, 50

AARP Newsletter, 132–33

AARP Public Policy Institute, 168

Abuela (online forum participant pseudonym), 164

activities of daily living (ADLs), 50

ADRDA. *See* Alzheimer's Disease and Related Disorders Association

adult children caregivers, 84

"Adult Children Pay the Price of Keeping Aging Parents Home," 84

adult day care, 85–86; access problems with, 91–92; adjustment to, 118; COVID-19 pandemic impacting, 154; difficulties with, 92; discharge from, 94–95; guilt from, 89; inadequate care at, 96; refusal of, 93–94; relief provided by, 88–89, 167; sorrow about, 90

advice literature, 31

African American caregivers, 3, 24

agencies, direct care worker, 74–75

agencies, homecare, 85; for-profit enterprises impacting, 121; inadequate care from, 96–97

The Age of Dignity (Poo), 83

Alcott, Louisa May, 60, 62

Alterra, Aaron, 31, 33

Alz.connected, 8

Alzheimer's Association, 12, 34–35; life partner online forum, 22; online support forums, 81–83, 85, 165, 167. *See also* Alzheimer's online support

group members; life partner caregivers; life partner care recipients

Alzheimer's caregivers, 23, 25; advice givers on, 14; Alzheimer's disease stages observed by, 32; Kleinman, Arthur, as, 42–46; mastery experience of, 17–18; stress-management industry on, 13–14; stress research on, 16

Alzheimer's care recipients: at assisted living facilities, 119; institutionalization decision for, 109; Kleinman, Joan, as, 42–46; memory care facilities for, 105; personhood perspective on, 12–13

Alzheimer's disease, 5, 11; ADRDA on, 12; diagnosis of, 29–30; Medicare Alzheimer's Disease Demonstration on, 69; National Alzheimer's Disease Month, 25; stages, 32

Alzheimer's Disease and Related Disorders Association (ADRDA), 12

Alzheimer's online support group members, 81; on homophobia, 86–87; makeup of, 82; peer support in, 117, 118; questions of, 82–83

American Institute of Stress, 24

"American Jobs Plan," 174, 175

American Medical Association, 16–17, 19

Aneshensel, Carol S., 15

anger, life partner caregivers, 128

apocalyptic demography, 11

Archives of Neurology, 11–12

ars moriendi (art of dying), 51

assisted living facilities: Alzheimer's care recipients at, 119; caregiver institutionalization decision for, 142; for-profit enterprises impacting, 102, 122; inadequate care in, 111; Peterson, Jan, entering, 39

Balbo, Laura, 91
Becerra, Xavier, 172
Biden, Joe, 84, 173
Biden administration, 173, 174–75
biomarkers, 20
Biss, Eula, 20
brain injury, 40–41
Braswell, Harold, 50–51
Britain, nursing homes in, 173
Brody, Elaine M., 4
Build Back Better Bill, 175
Burch, Elana D., 62
"Burden Interview" (Zarit), 15
burden term, 15
burnout, 10–11
A Burnt Out Case (Greene), 10

California Advocates for Nursing Home Reform, 132
Canada, nursing homes in, 173
CARE. See Care for All with Respect and Equity
care, inadequate: at adult day care, 96; in assisted living facilities, 111; of homecare agencies, 96–97; of homecare workers, 96–97; under In-Home Supportive Services, 73; under Medicaid, 72–73; in nursing homes, 101, 102, 103, 111; at overnight respite services, 97–99, 169
Care for All with Respect and Equity (CARE) Fund, 174
caregiver, compassionate, 138, 150
caregiver, essential, 133
caregivers, 167; adult children, 84; advice to, 103; African American, 3, 24; as-

sertiveness of, 122–23; assisted living facility institutionalization decision of, 142; challenges to, 49–50; COVID-19 pandemic regarding, 159–60, 163–66; COVID-19 regarding, 155, 158–59; decline impacting, 32–34; definition of, 23–24; determination of, 68; dignity maintained by, 35; direct care workers regarding, 2–3, 73–74, 160–61; diversity of, 3; family structure influencing, 4; gender distribution of, 1; gratification of, 21; guilt of, 21–23, 119–20; healthcare costs regarding, 65–66, 68–69, 70, 72, 81; hospice labor of, 65–67; institutional care transfer decision of, 119; long distance caregiving of, 159–60; medical care performed by, 67, 155; memory care facilities institutionalization decision, 109, 110, 142–43, 159; monetary value of, 168; nursing home contact with, 132, 140–41; personhood perspective regarding, 7, 34, 47–48; public services regarding, 70–72; rights of, 123–24; stress survey response of, 18; women, 4, 50. See also Alzheimer's caregivers; daughter caregivers; dementia caregivers; direct care workers; life partner caregivers; nineteenth century women caregivers; women caregivers; specific caregivers
caregivers, extreme, 85
caregivers, Latinx, 3
Caregiver Self-Assessment Questionnaire, 19
Caregivers for Compromise Facebook group, 133, 144
Caregivers Forum, 135, 165
caregiver stress, 6; dementia care recipients regarding, 25–26; Kingston Caregiver Stress Scale, 19; policy analysts on, 20–21
"Caregiver Workforce Plan," 173

caregiving. *See specific topics*

care recipient: COVID-19 contraction of, 137, 148; COVID-19 pandemic misunderstanding of, 155–56; decline of, 32–34; dignity of, 35. *See also* Alzheimer's care recipients; dementia care recipients; father care recipient; life partner care recipients; mother care recipient

care system. *See* long-term care system

Carework Network, 174

Caring for My Mother (Owens), 21–22

Carlos, Sheryl, 78

case managers: gray market, 79; public services, 71–72

Catastrophically Disabled Veteran application, 104

CELA. *See* certified elder care attorney

Center for Medicare and Medicaid Services (CMS), 68, 131, 134–35

certified elder care attorney (CELA), 124, 125

Channeling Demonstration, 69

Chapman, Marlene, 76, 77

childbirth, nineteenth century, 53–54

childcare, 53

chronic disease, 49–50; death from, 55; in nineteenth century, 54–56

Circles of Care (Abel and Nelson), 2

CMS. *See* Center for Medicare and Medicaid Services

comfort, for dementia care recipients, 143

Congress, US, 25

Congressional Budget Office, 65

Cooney, Eleanor, 13

Cooper, Melinda, 64

Cooperative Home Care Associates, 77

COVID-19: caregivers regarding, 155, 158–59; care recipient contracting, 137, 148; life partner caregiver contingency plan regarding, 153–54; life partner care recipient contracting, 137

COVID-19 pandemic, 1, 128, 151; adult day care impacted by, 154; caregivers regarding, 159–60, 163–66; care recipient misunderstanding about, 155–56; death from, 129, 133, 165; direct care workers regarding, 163–64, 165–66; essential workers impacted by, 170–71; family members regarding, 163, 165; federal government stimulus payments, 131; health inequities revealed by, 172; home care during, 145–46, 171; homecare workers impacted by, 154–55, 161–62, 163, 172; institutional care impacted by, 8, 116, 136–38, 142–43, 149; institutionalization impacted by, 143; long-term care system impacted by, 129, 132–33, 173–74; National Domestic Workers Alliance on, 161; nursing home aides impacted by, 130, 162–63, 164; nursing homes impacted by, 129–33, 141, 169–70, 172–73; prejudice regarding, 130; respite services impacted by, 171; state government response, 130–31; Trump mismanagement of, 170. *See also* lockdown; visitation; visitation restrictions

Cuomo, Andrew, 130, 205n13

Daniels, John, 31

Daniels, Mary, 133

data templates, 17

daughter caregivers: decline impacting, 34, 37; diagnosis impacting, 29–30; emotion response of, 36; *The 36-Hour Day* impacting, 30–31

death: from chronic disease, 55; from COVID-19 pandemic, 129, 133, 165; family member presence during, 149–50; from isolation, 132–33; in nineteenth century, 50–51, 53, 54, 55

"Death in Slow Motion" (Cooney), 13

"The Debate over What 'Infrastructure' Is Is Ridiculous," 175

decline: of care recipient, 32–34; daughter caregivers impacted by, 34, 37; of mother care recipient, 33, 37

deinstitutionalization: of mental hospitals, 115; of nursing home care, 115, 116

delirium, 139, 151, 170

dementia: diagnosis of, 29; perspectives on, 28, 47, 167. *See also* Alzheimer's disease

DementiaCareCentral, 98

dementia caregivers, 5–6; loneliness of, 19, 156–57; personhood perspective regarding, 28; plan for, 118–19. *See also* Alzheimer's caregivers

dementia care recipients, 5; caregiver stress regarding, 25–26; comfort for, 143; COVID-19 pandemic deaths of, 129, 133; delirium of, 139, 151, 170; in emergency room, 151–52; at hospitals, 151–53; lockdown impacting, 139; personhood perspective on, 6–7; Taylor on, 147; touch importance for, 147–48; training deficiency on, 100. *See also* Alzheimer's care recipients; life partner care recipients

Dementia Reconsidered (Kitwood), 6, 143

Department of Health and Human Services, 69

Desmond, Matthew, 78

diagnosis: of Alzheimer's disease, 29–30; daughter caregivers impacted by, 29–30; of dementia, 29

dignity, 35, 83

direct care workers: agencies, 74–75; caregivers regarding, 2–3, 73–74, 160–61; characteristics of, 75–76; COVID-19 pandemic regarding, 163–64, 165–66; disadvantages of, 77–78, 80; family member conflict with, 76–77; immi-grant, 3, 5; labor force, 74–75; Mehta as, 47–48, 75, 79; personhood perspective regarding, 48; racial divides of, 75–76; Sheilah as, 46, 75; training deficiency of, 100; turnover of, 80. *See also* homecare workers; nursing home aides

direct care workers, undocumented, 76

discharges: from adult day care, 94–95; from institutional care, 105–6, 131, 145–46; legislation on, 123; from memory care facilities, 106, 145; from nursing homes, 135–36

Don Carlo (Verdi), 44

Dublin, Louis I., 55, 56

Duffy, Mignon, 51

economic costs, 72

elderly population, 11, 49, 74

elderly women, 73

embodied harm, 3

emergency room, 151–52

enslaved women, 59

entrapment, 19

essential workers, 170–71

Evans, Sara, 66

Everett, Mary Holywell, 58

Facebook groups, 133–34

families: healthcare costs on, 72; structure, 4

family member caregivers. *See* caregivers

family members: COVID-19 pandemic regarding, 163, 165; during death, 149–50; direct care workers conflict with, 76–77; lockdown exemption of, 139–40; at nursing homes, 131–32; visitation restriction response, 143–45

family responsibility ideology, 64–65; elderly women impacted by, 73; of life partner caregivers, 124, 126 father care recipient: of Gerrard, 188n48; of Levine, 39–40; of Mehta, 47–48, 75, 79; of Miller, 29–30, 32

Fazio, Sam, 34–35

federal government, 131

financial assistance, 86

financial difficulties: of life partner caregivers, 158; of women caregivers, 50

Foner, Nancy, 76

for-profit enterprises: assisted living facilities impacted by, 102, 122; homecare agencies impacted by, 121; institutional care impacted by, 3–4, 121–22; long-term care system impacted by, 128; nursing homes impacted by, 101, 122, 169, 172–73; A Place for Mom as, 120–21

Fox, Daniel M., 55–56

Freitag, Lisa, 85

Freudenberger, Herbert, 10–11

Friedman, Meyer, 10

"From Sitting to Surgery" (Duffy), 51

Frontline program, 122

Fuchs, Eleanor, 37, 75

gender: of caregivers, 1; life partner caregivers differences of, 71

gender socialization: of nineteenth century women caregivers, 46, 62; social conservatives on, 64

Gerrard, Nicci, 23, 151, 188n48

Gilbert, Sandra M., 150

Gillespie, Emily, 58, 61, 62

Gillespie, Sarah, 58, 61, 62

Glaves, Bobbi, 12, 13

Gordon, Mary, 41

government caregiving policy: Biden administration on, 173, 174–75; policy analysts divide on, 168

gratification, 21

gray market, 74–75, 79, 80

Greene, Graham, 10–11

Guardian, 162

guilt: of caregivers, 21–23, 119–20; of life partner caregivers, 22, 89, 112–15, 120, 126, 127

Hadas, Rachel, 19–20

Harper, Lynn Casteel, 41

Harper's, 13

Harris, Kamala, 174–75

Harvard, 42, 45

Hawley, Emily, 53

HCBS. See home- and community-based services

HCFA. See Health Care Financing Administration

healthcare costs, 80; caregivers regarding, 65–66, 68–69, 70, 72, 81; Channeling Demonstration on, 69; on families, 72; Medicaid, 67–68; NS regarding, 72; policy makers perspective on, 81; TEFRA impacting, 65–66

Health Care Financing Administration (HCFA), 68

health inequities, COVID-19 pandemic revealing, 172

health issues: of life partner caregivers, 84, 108, 153; of nineteenth century women caregivers, 62; stress research on, 10

health providers stress questionnaire, 18, 20

Hearts of Wisdom (Abel), 7

herbal care, 61

Hernandez, Antonia Rios, 170–71

Holmes, Thomas H., 9–10

Home Alone report, 50

home- and community-based services (HCBS), 68, 69, 70, 71

home care, during COVID-19 pandemic, 145–46, 171

home care work, 85

homecare workers, 77; COVID-19 pandemic impacting, 154–55, 161–62, 163, 172; inadequate care of, 96–97; life partner care recipients rejecting, 92–93; remuneration of, 78, 79; training deficiency of, 100. *See also* direct care workers

homophobia, 86–87

hospice: caregiver labor during, 65–67; enrollment in, 144–45; limitations of, 66–67; Medicare for, 65–66, 67; TEFRA impacting, 65–66

hospitals: dementia care recipients at, 151–53; nineteenth century, 55, 59

hospitals, mental, 115

household labor, 56–57

Human Rights Watch, 149

IADLs. *See* instrumental activities of daily living

ICU. *See* intensive care unit

The Illness Narratives (Kleinman, Arthur), 43

immigrant direct care workers, 3, 5

infectious diseases, nineteenth century, 53

In-Home Supportive Services, 24; homophobia in, 86–87; inadequate care under, 73

institutional care: COVID-19 pandemic impacting, 8, 116, 136–38, 142–43, 149; deinstitutionalization of, 115, 116; discharge from, 105–6, 131, 145–46; family member involvement with, 149; for-profit enterprises impacting, 3–4, 121–22; skepticism toward, 120–21; transfer, 111, 119, 123. *See also* assisted living facilities; memory care facilities; nursing homes

institutionalization, 103; of Alzheimer's care recipients, 109; assisted living facility decision, 142; COVID-19 pandemic impacting, 143; life partner caregiver decision on, 107–10, 111–12, 114–16; memory care facilities decision for, 109, 110, 142–43, 159; into nursing homes, 106–7, 141; respite services regarding, 100, 108. *See also* deinstitutionalization

instrumental activities of daily living (IADLs), 50

intensive care unit (ICU), 152

"Is Extended Isolation Killing Older Adults in Long-Term Care?," 132–33

Jackson, Mark, 24

Jackson, Nannie Stillwell, 52–53, 56

Jamison, Kay Redfield, 150

Journal of the American Geriatrics Society, 134

Journal of the American Medical Directors Association, 131–32

Kane, Rosalie, 69

Katzman, Robert, 11–12

Kessler, Lauren, 36

kindness, nursing home aides, 161

Kingston Caregiver Stress Scale, 19

Kirkland, Washington, 129

Kitwood, Tom, 6, 28, 167

Kleinman, Arthur, 17–18, 168; advantages of, 45–46; career trajectory of, 42; *The Illness Narratives* by, 43; Kleinman, Joan, care regarding, 42–46; personhood perspective of, 41, 46; *The Soul of Care* by, 41–46

Kleinman, Joan, 42–46

Klinenberg, Eric, 129

Lagnado, Lucette, 41

Latinx caregivers, 3

Lazarus, Richard, 11

Leadbetter, Velma, 57–58

legislation, on involuntary transfers and discharges, 123

L'Engle, Madeleine, 33, 36, 41
Levine, Judith, 39–40
Levitsky, Sandra R., 23, 70–71, 124
LGBT Community and Allies forum, 83, 135
Life Care Center, 129
life partner caregivers, 4, 167; anger, 128; COVID-19 contingency plans of, 153–54; difficulty of, 84, 158, 175; family responsibility ideology of, 124, 126; gender differences of, 71; guilt of, 22, 89, 112–15, 120, 126, 127; health issues of, 84, 108, 153; homophobia against, 86–87; institutional care transfer decision of, 111; institution-alization decision of, 107–10, 111–12, 114–16; Kleinman, Arthur, as, 42–46; lockdown impacting, 157–58; marriage length of, 126–27; on memory care facility pre-admission, 105; nursing homes institutionalization decision of, 106–7, 141; Peterson, Barry R., 38–39; relationship maintenance of, 35–36; self-care for, 117–18; sorrow of, 112, 114; Spouse or Partner Caregiver Forum, 83, 135. See also adult day care; respite services
life partner care recipients, 22, 40–41, 87; adult day care regarding, 93–95, 118; COVID-19 contraction of, 137; escape attempts of, 93, 95–96; homecare workers rejected by, 92–93; institu-tional care discharge, 105–6; Kleinman, Joan, as, 42–46; lockdown impacting, 138–39, 157; marriage length of, 126–27; memory care facility adjustment of, 113–14; pre-admission regarding, 105; remote work misunderstanding of, 157–58; respite service resistance by, 99–100; violence of, 106, 107
life partner online forum, Alzheimer's Association, 22. See also Alzheimer's

online support group members; life partner caregivers
Lindbergh, Reeve, 36
Liu, Yin, 20
Living in Death's Shadow (Abel), 28–29
lockdown: dementia care recipients impacted by, 139; family member exemption from, 139–40; life partner caregiver impacted by, 157–58; life partner care recipients impacted by, 138–39, 157
loneliness, dementia caregivers, 19, 156–57
long-term care system, 8; "American Jobs Plan" on, 174; COVID-19 pandemic impacting, 129, 132–33, 173–74; crisis of, 7, 64, 168; for-profit enterprises impacting, 128
lymphoma, 4–5

Mace, Nancy L., 30–31
marriage length, 126–27
mastery, 17–18
McGlone, Francis, 147
Medicaid: application process to, 104, 124–25; beliefs about, 124; HCBS under, 70, 71; healthcare costs, 67–68; inadequate care under, 72–73; for nursing homes, 67–68, 101–2, 104; wait lists, 195n38. See also Center for Medicare and Medicaid Services
medical care, 50; caregivers performing, 67, 155; of nineteenth century women caregivers, 59–61, 63
medical knowledge, 27
medical perspective, on dementia, 28
medical triumphalism, 25
Medicare, 65–66, 67, 102, 131. See also Center for Medicare and Medicaid Services
Medicare Alzheimer's Disease Demon-stration, 69
medication, 95, 117

Mehta, Jasmine (pseudonym): father care recipient of, 47–48, 75, 79; job expansion of, 79

Meier, Diane, 67

memoir writers, 81–82

memory care facilities: caregiver institutionalization decision to, 109, 110, 142–43, 159; discharge from, 106, 145; life partner care recipient adjustment to, 113–14; pre-admission rejection from, 105; staff, 161

mental hospitals, 115

military studies, 9–10

Miller, Sue, 29–30, 32

Moore, Marian Louise, 57

Moore, Susan, 172

Morgan, Fannie, 52–53

Moser, Ingunn, 35

mother care recipient, 21–22, 31, 36; decline of, 33, 37; Gillespie, Emily, as, 58, 61, 62

Murphy, Michelle, 16

National Adult Day Services Association, 86

National Alzheimer's Disease Month, 25

National Domestic Workers Alliance, 3, 76, 161, 165

National Institute on Aging, 151

National Long Term Care Demonstration, 69

natural supports (NS), 71, 72

Nature, 9

Nelson, Margaret K., 2

neoliberals, 64

neurologists, 45

New York Times, 78; on COVID-19 pandemic homecare worker impact, 172; "The Debate over What 'Infrastructure' Is Is Ridiculous," 175; on nursing home discharges, 135–36; on parent home schooling, 171–72; "Voices from the Front Lines of America's Food Supply," 170–71

nineteenth century: death in, 50–51, 53, 54, 55; hospitals, 55, 59; infectious diseases, 53; nurses in, 60; pharmaceutical care, 61; physicians in, 59–60; teachers, 58

nineteenth century women caregivers, 50–52; childbirth, 53–54; chronic disease caregiving of, 54–56; gender socialization of, 46, 62; health issues of, 62; household labor of, 56–57; medical care regarding, 59–61, 63; profession competing with, 57–58; in slavery, 59

"Nothing Much Has Changed," 134

NS. See natural supports

nurses, 121; in nineteenth century, 60; pre-admission in-home evaluation by, 105

nursing home aides: COVID-19 pandemic impacting, 130, 162–63, 164; kindness of, 161. See also direct care workers

Nursing Home Reform Act (1987), 101

nursing home residents: isolation deaths of, 132–33; visitation restrictions impacting, 134

nursing homes, 35; caregiver contact with, 132, 140–41; Channeling Demonstration regarding, 69; CMS reopening directives for, 134–35; cost of, 103–4; COVID-19 pandemic impacting, 129–33, 141, 169–70, 172–73; discharges from, 135–36; essential caregiver designation for, 133; family members at, 131–32; for-profit enterprises impacting, 101, 122, 169, 172–73; inadequate care in, 101, 102, 103, 111; institutionalization in, 106–7, 141; Kleinman, Joan, entering, 44; Medicaid for, 67–68, 101–2, 104; New York, 76

nursing tasks, 50

OECD. *See* Organization for Economic Cooperation and Development
Olmstead v. L.C., 70
online support forums, Alzheimer's Association, 81–83, 85, 165, 167. *See also* Alzheimer's online support group members; life partner caregivers; life partner care recipients
Organization for Economic Cooperation and Development (OECD), 65
overnight respite services, 85–86, 95–96; encouragement for, 118; inadequate care at, 97–99, 169
Owens, Virginia Stem, 21–22, 33

paid caregivers. *See* direct care workers
paramedics, 152
parent home schooling, 171–72
PBS, 122
Pearlin, Leonard I., 14–15
Pengra, Charlotte Stearns, 52
personal protective equipment (PPE), 162
personhood perspective, 26, 167, 188n48; on Alzheimer's care recipients, 12–13; caregivers regarding, 7, 34, 47–48; dementia caregivers regarding, 28; on dementia care recipients, 6–7; direct care workers regarding, 48; of Kleinman, Arthur, 41, 46; of Levine, 39–40
Peterson, Barry R., 38–39
Peterson, Jan, 38–39
pharmaceutical care, nineteenth century, 61
physicians: medical knowledge of, 27; in nineteenth century, 59–60
A Place for Mom, 84, 120–21
policy analysts: on caregiver stress, 20–21; on government caregiving position, 168
policy makers, 81
Poo, Ai-Jen, 2–3, 76, 83, 165
Power of Attorney, 152

Power of Medical Attorney, 152
PPE. *See* personal protective equipment
pregnancy, 54
Profiles in Caregiving (Aneshensel), 15
public services: caregivers regarding, 70–72; case managers, 71–72

quantitative methods: decontextualization of, 24–25; drawbacks of, 17, 18, 19, 20, 21, 23
Rabins, Peter V., 30–31
racial divides, of direct care workers, 75–76
racism, 172
Rahe, Richard H., 9–10
Reagan, Ronald, 65
Reagan administration, 67
religion, 51
remote work, 157–58
"Resistance Stage," 9
respite services, 8; access problems with, 91–92; benefits of, 87–88; COVID-19 pandemic impacting, 171; financial assistance for, 86; home care work, 85; institutionalization regarding, 100, 108; life partner care recipient resisting, 99–100; limitations of, 91, 169; *Who Cares for the Elderly?* on, 99. *See also* adult day care; overnight respite services
Rosenman, Ray, 10

sandwich generation, 50
Sankar, Andrea, 66
Sawyer, Frances, 52
SEIU. *See* Service Employees International Union
Selye, Hans, 9
Senate Committee on Aging, US, 101
Senate hearing, on Alzheimer's disease, 12
Service Employees International Union (SEIU), 162

Shaw, Johnny, 54–55

Shaw, Martha, 54–55

Sheilah (direct care worker), 46, 75

Shulman, Alix Kates, 40–41, 87

Skloot, Floyd: appreciation of, 38; decline impacting, 33; on delirium, 151

Slate, 174

slave communities, 59

social conservatives, 64

"The Social Readjustment Rating Scale," 9–10

social status, 29

Solnit, Rebecca, 64

sorrow: about adult day care, 90; of life partner caregivers, 112, 114

The Soul of Care (Kleinman, Arthur), 41–46

spousal caregivers. *See* life partner caregivers

spousal care recipient. *See* life partner care recipient

Spouse or Partner Caregiver Forum, 83, 135

Stacey, Clare L., 77

state governments, 130–31

"Statement to the Biden-Harris Administration," 174

Stebbens, Laura, 52

Stewart, Linda McK., 5

stress, 18, 20, 24

stress-management industry, 13–14

stress process care model, 15

stress research: on Alzheimer's caregivers, 16; assessments from, 16–17; gerontology-caregiving literature regarding, 6, 9; on health issues, 10; mastery regarding, 17–18; Pearlin on, 14–15; "The Social Readjustment Rating Scale," 9–10. *See also* quantitative methods

stress surveys, 16, 18

stroke, 5

Sullivan, Vanessa, 78

Sweden, nursing homes in, 173

Task Force to Explore the Safe and Limited Re-opening of Long-Term Care Facilities, 133

Tax, Equity, and Fiscal Responsibility Act (TEFRA), 65–66

Taylor, Janelle S.: appreciation of, 38; on dementia care recipients, 147

teachers, nineteenth century, 58

TEFRA. *See* Tax, Equity, and Fiscal Responsibility Act

The 36-Hour Day (Mace and Rabins), 30–31, 41

Thomas, Lewis, 12

Thorndike, John, 33, 38

Time, 10

touch, for dementia care recipients, 147–48

transnational circulations of care, 5

Trump, Donald, 170

tuberculosis, 54–55

Type A Behavior and Your Heart (Friedman and Rosenman), 10

undocumented direct care workers, 76

United Hospital Foundation, 50

United States (US): Alzheimer's disease Senate hearing, 12; Biden administration, 173, 174–75; Biden regarding, 84, 173; caregiving beliefs in, 23, 65; Congress, 25; Congressional Budget Office, 65; federal government COVID-19 stimulus, 131; government caregiving position, 168, 173, 174–75; hospice care in, 65–66; Reagan administration, 67; Senate Committee on Aging, 101; state government COVID-19 pandemic response, 130–31; Trump COVID-19 pandemic mismanagement, 170

Urena, Cindy, 172

US. *See* United States
US General Accountability Office study, 130

VA. *See* Veterans Administration
Verdi, Giuseppe, 44
Veterans Administration (VA), 95–96, 104, 123–24
violence, of life partner care recipients, 106, 107
visitation: resumption of, 146, 147; rights, 133; by window, 141
visitation restrictions, 131–32; family member response to, 143–45; nursing home residents impacted by, 134; obstacles after, 148; support for, 140
#VisitationSavesLives, 132
"Voices from the Aisles," 171

"Voices from the Front Lines of America's Food Supply," 170–71

Washington Post, 84; on nursing home caregiver presence, 132; "Voices from the Aisles" by, 171
Webber, Mary Ann, 53–54, 57
Who Cares for the Elderly? (Abel), 4, 28, 99
women, elderly, 73
women caregivers, 4, 50. *See also* nineteenth century women caregivers
"'Women in the Middle' and Family Help to Older People" (Brody), 4
woodwork effect, 68

Zarit, Steven H., 15
Zoom business calls, 158

ABOUT THE AUTHOR

EMILY K. ABEL is Professor Emerita at the UCLA Fielding School of Public Health. She is the author of many books, including *Hearts of Wisdom: American Women Caring for Kin, 1850–1940* and *Sick and Tired: An Intimate History of Fatigue.* She received the Viseltear Award for an outstanding book in public health from the Medical Care Section of the American Public Health Association for *The Politics of Exclusion: A History of Public Health and Migration to Los Angeles.*

www.ingramcontent.com/pod-product-compliance
Lightning Source LLC
Chambersburg PA
CBHW020252030426
42336CB00010B/725